MW00698314

```
10 PRINT CHR$(205.5+RND(1)); : GOTO 10
```

**Software Studies**

Matthew Fuller, Lev Manovich, and Noah Wardrip-Fruin, editors

*Expressive Processing: Digital Fictions, Computer Games, and Software Studies*, Noah Wardrip-Fruin, 2009

*Code/Space: Software and Everyday Life*, Rob Kitchin and Martin Dodge, 2011

*Programmed Visions: Software and Memory*, Wendy Hui Kyong Chun, 2011

*Speaking Code: Coding as Aesthetic and Political Expression*, Geoff Cox and Alex McClean, 2012

*10 PRINT CHR$(205.5+RND(1)); : GOTO 10*, Nick Montfort, Patsy Baudoin, John Bell, Ian Bogost, Jeremy Douglass, Mark C. Marino, Michael Mateas, Casey Reas, Mark Sample, and Noah Vawter, 2013

# 10 PRINT CHR$(205.5+RND(1)); : GOTO 10

NICK MONTFORT, PATSY BAUDOIN,
JOHN BELL, IAN BOGOST,
JEREMY DOUGLASS, MARK C. MARINO,
MICHAEL MATEAS, CASEY REAS,
MARK SAMPLE, NOAH VAWTER

THE MIT PRESS
CAMBRIDGE, MASSACHUSETTS
LONDON, ENGLAND

MIT Press books may be purchased at special quantity discounts for business or sales promotional use. For information, email special_sales@mitpress.mit.edu or write to Special Sales Department, The MIT Press, 55 Hayward Street, Cambridge, MA 02142.

This book was designed and typeset by Casey Reas using Avenir by Adrian Frutiger, C64 by Style, and TheSansMono by LucasFonts. Printed and bound in the United States of America.



Library of Congress Cataloging-in-Publication Data

10 PRINT CHR$(205.5+RND(1)); : GOTO 10 / Nick Montfort . . . [et al.].
p. cm.—(Software studies)
Includes bibliographical references and index.
ISBN 978-0-262-01846-3 (hardcover : alk. paper)
1. BASIC (Computer program language)—History. I. Montfort, Nick.
QA76.73.B3A14 2013
005.26'2—dc23

2012015872

10 9 8 7 6 5 4 3 2 1

Ten authors collaborated to write this book. Rather than produce a collection of ten separate articles, we chose a process of communal authorship. Most of the writing was done using a wiki, although this process differed significantly from the most famous wiki-based project, Wikipedia. Our book was not written in public and was not editable by the public. We benefited from comments by reviewers and from discussions with others at conferences and in other contexts; still, the text of the book was developed by the ten of us, working together as one, and we bear the responsibility for what this book expresses.

All royalties from the sale of this book are being donated to PLAYPOWER, a nonprofit organization that supports affordable, effective, fun learning games. PLAYPOWER uses a radically affordable TV-computer based on the 6502 processor (the same chip that was used in the Commodore 64) as a platform for learning games in the developing world.

CONTENTS

# 5
# SERIES FOREWORD

Software is deeply woven into contemporary life—economically, culturally, creatively, politically—in manners both obvious and nearly invisible. Yet while much is written about how software is used, and the activities that it supports and shapes, thinking about software itself has remained largely technical for much of its history. Increasingly, however, artists, scientists, engineers, hackers, designers, and scholars in the humanities and social sciences are finding that for the questions they face, and the things they need to build, an expanded understanding of software is necessary. For such understanding they can call upon a strand of texts in the history of computing and new media, they can take part in the rich implicit culture of software, and they can also take part in the development of an emerging, fundamentally transdisciplinary, computational literacy. These provide the foundation for software studies.

Software studies uses and develops cultural, theoretical, and practice-oriented approaches to make critical, historical, and experimental accounts of (and interventions via) the objects and processes of software. The field engages and contributes to the research of computer scientists, the work of software designers and engineers, and the creations of software artists. It tracks how software is substantially integrated into the processes of contemporary culture and society, reformulating processes, ideas, institutions, and cultural objects around their closeness to algorithmic and formal description and action. Software studies proposes histories of computational cultures and works with the intellectual resources of computing to develop reflexive thinking about its entanglements and possibilities. It does this both in the scholarly modes of the humanities and social sciences and in the software creation and research modes of computer science, the arts, and design.

The Software Studies book series, published by the MIT Press, aims to publish the best new work in a critical and experimental field that is at once culturally and technically literate, reflecting the reality of today's software culture.

# 10

# INTRODUCTION

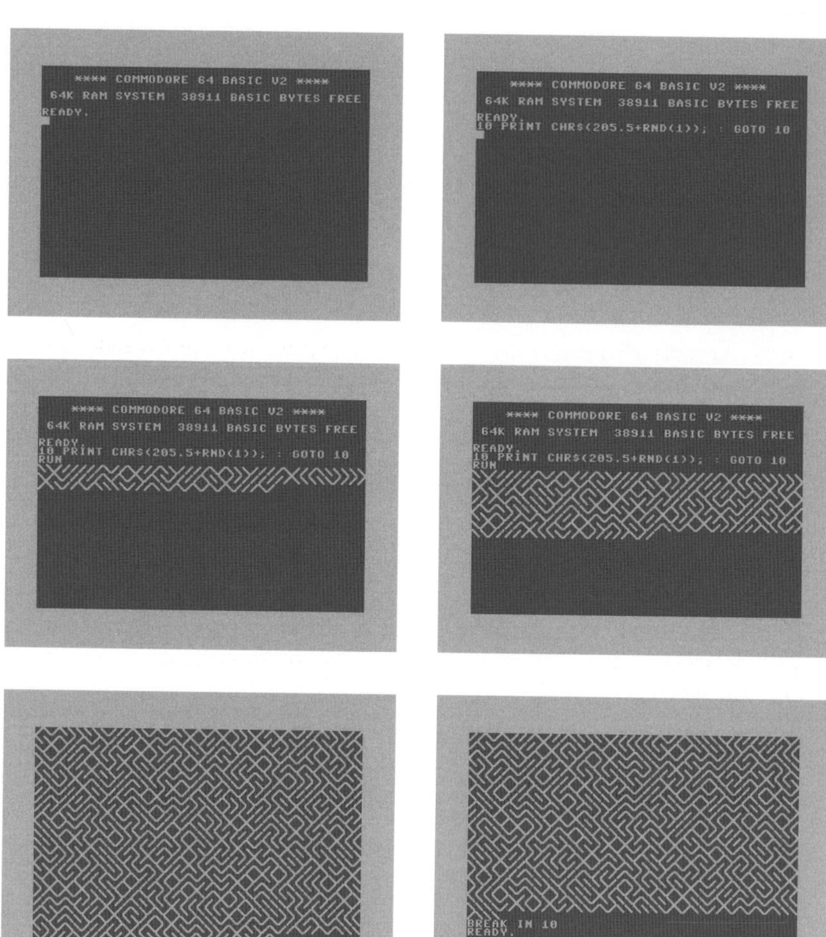


Figure 10.1

From left to right and top to bottom, the `10 PRINT` program is typed into the Commodore 64 and is run. Output scrolls across the screen until it is stopped.

Computer programs process and display critical data, facilitate communication, monitor and report on sensor networks, and shoot down incoming missiles. But computer code is not merely functional. Code is a peculiar kind of text, written, maintained, and modified by programmers to make a machine operate. It is a text nonetheless, with many of the properties of more familiar documents. Code is not purely abstract and mathematical; it has significant social, political, and aesthetic dimensions. The way in which code connects to culture, affecting it and being influenced by it, can be traced by examining the specifics of programs by reading the code itself attentively.

Like a diary from the forgotten past, computer code is embedded with stories of a program's making, its purpose, its assumptions, and more. Every symbol within a program can help to illuminate these stories and open historical and critical lines of inquiry. Traditional wisdom might lead one to believe that learning to read code is a tedious, mathematical chore. Yet in the emerging methodologies of critical code studies, software studies, and platform studies, computer code is approached as a cultural text reflecting the history and social context of its creation. "Code . . . has been inscribed, programmed, written. It is conditioned and concretely historical," new media theorist Rita Raley notes (2006). The source code of contemporary software is a point of entry in these fields into much larger discussions about technology and culture. It is quite possible, however, that the code with the most potential to incite critical interest from programmers, students, and scholars is that from earlier eras.

This book returns to a moment, the early 1980s, by focusing on a single line of code, a BASIC program that reads simply:

```
10 PRINT CHR$(205.5+RND(1)); : GOTO 10
```

One line of code, set to repeat endlessly, which will run until interrupted (figure 10.1).

Programs that function exactly like this one were printed in a variety of sources in the early days of home computing, initially in the 1982 *Commodore 64 User's Guide*, and later online, on the Web. (The published versions of the program are documented at the end of this book, in "Variants of 10 PRINT.") This well-known one-liner from the 1980s was recalled by one of the book's authors decades later, as discussed in "A Personal

Memory of 10 PRINT" in the BASIC chapter. This program is not presented here as valuable because of its extreme popularity or influence. Rather, it serves as an example of an important but neglected type of programming practice and a gateway into a deeper understanding of how computing works in society and what the writing, reading, and execution of computer code mean.

## ONE LINE

This book is unusual in its focus on a single line of code, an extremely concise BASIC program that is simply called `10 PRINT` throughout. Studies of individual, unique works abound in the humanities. Roland Barthes's *S/Z*, Samuel Beckett's *Proust*, Rudolf Arnheim's *Genesis of a Painting: Picasso's Guernica*, Stuart Hall et al.'s *Doing Cultural Studies: The Story of the Sony Walkman*, and Michel Foucault's *Ceci n'est pas une pipe* all exemplify the sort of close readings that deepen our understanding of cultural production, cultural phenomena, and the Western cultural tradition. While such literary texts, paintings, and consumer electronics may seem significantly more complex than a one-line BASIC program, undertaking a close study of `10 PRINT` as a cultural artifact can be as fruitful as close readings of other telling cultural artifacts have been.

In many ways, this extremely intense consideration of a single line of code stands opposed to current trends in the digital humanities, which have been dominated by what has been variously called distant reading (Moretti 2007), cultural analytics (Manovich 2009), or culturomics (Michel et al. 2010). These endeavors consider massive amounts of text, images, or data—say, millions of books published in English since 1800 or a million Manga pages—and identify patterns and trends that would otherwise remain hidden. This book takes the opposite approach, operating as if under a centrifugal force, spiraling outward from a single line of text to explore seemingly disparate aspects of culture. Hence its approach is more along the lines of Brian Rotman's *Signifying Nothing* (1987), which documents the cultural importance of the symbol 0. Similarly, it turns out that in the few characters of `10 PRINT`, there is a great deal to discover regarding its texts, contexts, and cultural importance.

By analyzing this short program from multiple viewpoints, the book explains how to read code deeply and shows what benefits can come from such readings. And yet, this work seeks to avoid fetishizing code, an error that Wendy Chun warns about (2011, 51–54), by deeply considering context and the larger systems at play. Instead of discussing software merely as an abstract formulation, this book takes a variorum approach, focusing on a specific program that exists in different printed variants and executes on a particular platform. Focusing on a particular single-line program foregrounds aspects of computer programs that humanistic inquiry has overlooked. Specifically, this one-line program highlights that computer programs typically exist in different versions that serve as seeds for learning, modification, and extension. Consideration of `10 PRINT` offers new ways of thinking about how professional programmers, hobbyists, and humanists write and read code.

The book also considers how the program engages with the cultural imagination of the maze, provides a history of regular repetition and randomness in computing, tells the story of the BASIC programming language, and reflects on the specific design of the Commodore 64. The eponymous program is treated as a distinct cultural artifact, but it also serves as a grain of sand from which entire worlds become visible; as a Rosetta Stone that yields important access to the phenomenon of creative computing and the way computer programs exist in culture.

## CORE CONTRIBUTIONS

The subject of this book—a one-line program for a thirty-year-old microcomputer—may strike some as unusual and esoteric at best, indulgent and perverse at worst. But this treatment of `10 PRINT` was undertaken to offer lessons for the study of digital media more broadly. If they prove persuasive, these arguments will have implications for the interpretation of software of all kinds.

First, to understand code in a critical, humanistic way, the practice of scholarship should include programming: modifications, variations, elaborations, and ports of the original program, for instance. The programs written for this book sketch the range of possibilities for maze generators within Commodore 64 BASIC and across platforms. By writing them, the `10 PRINT` program is illuminated, but so, too, are some of the main plat-

## CRITICAL CODE STUDIES, SOFTWARE STUDIES, PLATFORM STUDIES

Critical Code Studies (CCS) is the application of critical theory and hermeneutics to the interpretation of computer source code, as defined by one of this book's authors (Marino 2006). During an online, collaborative conference, another of this book's authors challenged the 2010 Critical Code Studies Working Group to apply these methodologies to the one-line program that is this book's focus (Montfort 2010). Until then, a number of exemplary readings had taken up software and other encoded objects possessing considerably more code, clear social implications (for example, a knowledge base about terrorists), and more free space for writing of human significance in the form of comments or variable names. Members of the working group had demonstrated they could interpret a large program, a substantial body of code, but could they usefully interpret a very spare program such as this one? What followed, with some false starts, was a great deal of productive discussion, an article in *Emerging Language Practices* (Marino 2010), and eventually this book, with those who replied in the Critical Code Studies Working Group thread being invited to work together as coauthors.

CCS is a set of methodologies for the exegesis of code. Working together with platform studies, software studies, and media archaeology and forensics, critical code studies uses the source code as a means of entering into discussion about the technological object in its fullest context. CCS considers authorship, design process,

forms of home computing, as well as the many distinctions between Commodore 64 BASIC and contemporary programming environments.

Second, there is a fundamental relationship between the formal workings of code and the cultural implications and reception of that code. The program considered in this book is an aesthetic object that invites its authors to learn about computation and to play with possibilities: the importance of considering specific code in many situations. For instance, in order to fully understand the way that redlining (financial discrimination against residents of certain areas) functions, it might be necessary to consider the specific code of a bank's system to approve mortgages, not simply the appearance of neighborhoods or the mortgage readiness of particular populations.

This book explores the essentials of how a computer interprets code function, funding, circulation of the code, programming languages and paradigms, and coding conventions. It involves reading code closely and with sustained and rigorous attention, but is not limited to the sort of close reading that is detached from historical, biographical, and social conditions. CCS invites code-based interpretation that invokes and elucidates contexts.

This book also employs other approaches to the interpretation of technical objects and culture, notably software studies and platform studies. While software studies can include the consideration and reading of code, it generally emphasizes the investigation of processes, focusing on function, form, and cultural context at a higher level of abstraction than any particular code. Platform studies conversely focuses on the lower computational levels, the platforms (hardware system, operating system, virtual machines) on which code runs. Taking the design of platforms into account helps to elucidate how concepts of computing are embodied in particular platforms, and how this specificity influences creative production across all code and software for a particular system. This book examines one line of code as a means of discussing issues of software and platform.

In addition to being approaches, software studies and platform studies also refer to two book series from MIT Press. This book is part of the Software Studies series.

and how particular platforms relate to the code written on them. It is not a general introduction to programming, but instead focuses on the connection of code to material, historical, and cultural factors in light of the particular way this code causes its computer to operate.

Third, code is ultimately understandable. Programs cause a computer to operate in a particular way, and there is some reason for this operation that is grounded in the design and material reality of the computer, the programming language, and the particular program. This reason can be found. The way code works is not a divine mystery or an imponderable. Code is not like losing your keys and never knowing if they're under the couch or have been swept out to sea through a storm sewer. The working of code is knowable. It definitely *can* be understood with adequate time and effort. Any line of code from any program can be as thoroughly explicated as the eponymous line of this book.

Finally, code is a cultural resource, not trivial and only instrumental, but bound up in social change, aesthetic projects, and the relationship of people to computers. Instead of being dismissed as cryptic and irrelevant to human concerns such as art and user experience, code should be valued as text with machine and human meanings, something produced and operating within culture.

## 10 PRINT CHR$(205.5+RND(1)); : GOTO 10

The pattern produced by this program is represented on the endpapers of this book. When the program runs, the characters appear one at a time, left to right and then top to bottom, and the image scrolls up by two lines each time the screen is filled. It takes about fifteen seconds for the maze to fill the screen when the program is first run; it takes a bit more than a second for each two-line jump to happen as the maze scrolls upward.

Before going through different perspectives on this program, it is useful to consider not only the output but also the specifics of the code—what exactly it is, a single token at a time. This will be a way to begin to look at how much lies behind this one short line.

### 10

The only line number is this program is 10, which is the most conventional starting line number in BASIC. Most of the programs in the *Commodore 64 User's Guide* start with line 10, a choice that was typical in other books and magazines, not only ones for this system. Numbering lines in increments of 10, rather than simply as 1, 2, 3, . . . , allows for additional lines to be inserted more easily if the need arises during program development: the lines after the insertion point will not have to be renumbered, and references to them (in GOTO and GOSUB commands) will not have to be changed.

The standard version of BASIC for the Commodore 64, BASIC version 2 by Microsoft, invited this sort of line numbering practice. Some extensions to this BASIC later provided a RENUMBER or RENUM command that would automatically redo the line numbering as 10, 20, 30, and so on.

This convenience had a downside: if the line numbers were spaced out in a meaningful way so that part of the work was done beginning at 100, another segment beginning at 200, and so on, that thoughtful segmentation would be obliterated. In any case, `RENUMBER` was *not* provided with the version of BASIC that shipped on the Commodore 64.

One variant of this program, which was published in the Commodore-specific magazine *RUN*, uses 8 as its line number. This makes this variant of the program more concise in its textual representation, although it does not change its function and saves only one byte of memory—for each line of BASIC stored in RAM, two bytes are allocated for the line number, whether it is 1 or the maximum value allowed, 63999. The only savings in memory comes from `GOTO 10` being shortened to `GOTO 8`. Any single digit including 1 and even 0 could have been used instead. Line number variation in the *RUN* variants attests to its arbitrariness for function, demonstrating that 10 was a line-numbering convention, but was not required. That 8 was both arbitrary and a specific departure from convention may then suggest specific grist for interpretation. For a one-line program that loops forever, it is perhaps appealing to number that line 8, the endlessly looping shape of an infinity symbol turned upon its side. However, whether the program is numbered 8 or 10, the use of a number greater than 0 always signals that `10 PRINT` (or `8 PRINT`) is, like Barthes's "work," "a fragment of substance," partial with potential for more to be inserted and with the potential to be extended (Barthes 1977, 142).

Why are typed line numbers required at all in a BASIC program? Programs written today in C, Perl, Python, Ruby, and other languages don't use line numbers as a language construct: they aren't necessary in BASIC either, as demonstrated by QBasic and Visual Basic, which don't make use of them. If one wants a program to branch to a particular statement, the language can simply allow a label to be attached to the target line instead of a line number. Where line numbers particularly helped was in the act of editing a program, particularly when using a line editor or without access to a scrolling full-screen editor. The Commodore 64 does allow limited screen editing when programming in BASIC: the arrow keys can be used to move the cursor to any visible line, that line can be edited, and the new version of the line can be saved by pressing RETURN. This is a better editing capability than comes standard on the Apple II, but there is still no scrollback (no ability to go back past the current beginning of the screen) in BASIC on the

Commodore 64. Line numbers provide a convenient way to get back to an earlier part of the program and to list a particular line or range of lines. Typing a line number by itself will delete the corresponding line, if one exists in memory. The interactive editing abilities that were based on line numbers were well represented even in very early versions of BASIC, including the first version of the BASIC that ran on the Dartmouth Time-Sharing System. Line numbers thus represent not just an organizational scheme, but also an interactive affordance developed in a particular context.

## {SPACE}

The space between the line number 10 and the keyword `PRINT` is actually optional, as are all of the spaces in this program. The variant line **`10PRINT CHR$(205.5+RND(1));:GOTO10`** will function exactly as the standard **`10 PRINT`** with spaces does. The spaces are of course helpful to the person trying to type in this line of code correctly: they make it more legible and more understandable.

Even in this exceedingly short program, which has no variables (and thus no variable names) and no comments, the presence of these optional spaces indicates some concern for the people who will deal with this code, rather than merely the machine that will process it. Spaces acknowledge that the code is both something to be automatically translated to machine instructions and something to be read, understood, and potentially modified and built upon by human programmers. The same acknowledgment is seen in the way that the keywords are presented in their canonical form. Instead of `PRINT` the short form `?` could be used instead, and there are Commodore-specific two-character abbreviations that allow the other keywords to be entered quickly (e.g., `GOTO` can typed as G followed by SHIFT-O.) Still, for clarity, the longer (but easier-to-read) version of these keywords is shown in this program, as it is in printed variants.

## PRINT

The statement `PRINT` causes its argument to be displayed on the screen. The argument to `PRINT` can take a variety of forms, but here it is a string that is in many ways like the famous string "HELLO WORLD." In `PRINT "HELLO WORLD"` the output of the statement is simply the string literal, the text between double quotes. The string in the maze-generating program is generated by a function, and the output of each PRINT execution consists of only a single character, but it is nevertheless a string.

Today the PRINT command is well known, as are many similarly named print commands in many other programming languages. It is easy to overlook that, as it is used here, PRINT does not literally "print" anything in the way the word normally is used to indicate reproduction by marking a medium, as with paper and ink—instead, it displays. To send output to a printer, PRINT must be followed by # and the appropriate device number, then a comma, and then the argument that is to be printed. By default, without a device number, the output goes to the screen—in the case of the Commodore 64, a television or composite video monitor.

When BASIC was first developed in 1964 at Dartmouth College, however, the physical interface was different. Remarkably, the language was designed for college students to use in interactive sessions, so that they would not have to submit batch jobs on punch cards as was common at the time. However, the users and programmers at Dartmouth worked not at screens but at print terminals, initially Teletypes. A PRINT command that executed successfully did actually cause something to be printed. Although BASIC was less than twenty years old when a version of it was made for the Commodore 64, that version nevertheless has a residue of history, leftover terms from before a change in the standard output technology. Video displays replaced scrolls of paper with printed output, but the keyword PRINT remained.

### CHR$

This function takes a numeric code and returns the corresponding character, which may be a digit, a letter, a punctuation mark, a space, or a "character graphic," a nontypographical tile typically displayed alongside others to create an image. The standard numerical representation of characters in the 1980s, still in wide use today, is ASCII (the American Standard Code for Information Interchange), a seven-bit code that represents 128 characters. On the Commodore 64 and previous Commodore computers, this representation was extended, as it often was in different ways on different systems. In extensions to ASCII, the other 128 numbers that can be represented in eight bits are used for character graphics and other symbols.

The Commodore 64's character set, which had been used previously on the Commodore PET, was nicknamed PETSCII.

The complement to CHR$ is the function ASC which takes a quoted character and returns the corresponding numeric value. A user who is curious about the numeric value of a particular character, such as the capital letter A, can type PRINT ASC("A") and see the result, 65. A program can also use ASC to convert a character to a numeric representation, perform arithmetic on the number that results, and then convert the new number back to a character using CHR$. In lowercase mode, this can be used to shift character between uppercase and lowercase, or this sort of manipulation might be used to implement a substitution cipher.

Character graphics exist as special tiles that are more graphical than typographical, more like elements of a mosaic than like pieces of type to be composed on a press. That is, they are mainly intended to be assembled into larger graphical images rather than "typeset" or placed alongside letters, digits, and punctuation. But these special tiles do exist in a typographical framework: a textual system, built on top of a bitmapped graphic display, is reused for graphical purposes. This type of abstraction may not be a smooth, clean way of accomplishing new capabilities, but it represents a rather typical way in which a system, adapted for a new, particular purpose, can be retrofitted to do something else.

## (

CHR$ and RND are both functions, so the keyword is followed in both cases by an argument in parentheses. CHR$ ends with the dollar sign to indicate that it is a string function (it takes a numeric argument and returns a string), while RND does not, since it is an arithmetic function (it takes a numeric argument and returns a number). The parentheses here also make clear the order of arithmetic operations. For instance, RND(1-2) is the same as RND(-1), while RND(1)-2 is two subtracted from the whatever value is returned by RND(1).

## 205.5

All math in Commodore BASIC is done on floating point numbers (numbers with decimal places). When an integer result is needed (as it is in the case of CHR$), the conversion is done by BASIC automatically. If this value, 205.5, were to be converted into an integer directly, it would be truncated (rounded down) to become 205. If more than .5 and less than 1 is added to 205.5, the integer result will be 206.

This means the character printed will either be the one corresponding to 205 or the one corresponding to 206: ╲ or ╱. A quirk of the Commodore 64 character set is that these two characters, and a run of several character graphics, have two numeric representations. Characters 109 and 110 duplicate 205 and 206, meaning that 109.5 could replace 205.5 in this program and the identical output would be produced.

## +

This symbol indicates addition, of course. It is less obvious that this is the addition of two floating point numbers with a floating point result; Commodore 64 BASIC always treats numbers as floating point values when it does arithmetic. The first number to be added is 205.5; the second is whatever value that RND returns, a value that will be between 0 and 1. On the one hand, because all arithmetic is done in floating point, figuring out a simple 2 + 2 involves more number crunching and takes longer than it would if integer arithmetic was used. On the other hand, the universal use of floating point math means that an easy-to-apply, one-size-fits-all mathematical operation is provided for the programmer by BASIC. Whether the programmer wishes to add temperatures, prices, tomato soup cans, or anything else, "+" will work.

The mathematical symbol "+" originated, like "&," as an abbreviation for "and." As is still conventional on today's computers, the Commodore 64 has a special "plus" or addition key but does not have any way to type a multiplication sign or a division sign. While they appear in some eight-bit codes that extend ASCII and in Unicode, the multiplication and division signs are absent from ASCII and from PETSCII. Instead, the asterisk (*) and the slash, virgule, or solidus (/) are used. Given the computer's development as a machine for the manipulation of numbers, it is curious that typographical symbols have to be borrowed from their textual uses ("*" indicating a footnote, "/" a line break or a juxtaposition of terms) and pressed into service as mathematical symbols. But this has to do with the history of computer input devices, which in early days included teletypewriters, devices that were not originally made for mathematical communication.

### RND

This function returns a (more or less) random number, one which is between 0 and 1. The number returned is, more precisely, pseudorandom. While the sequence of numbers generated has no easily discernible pattern and is hard for a person to predict, it is actually the same sequence each time. This is not entirely a failing; the consistent quality of this "random" output allows other programs to be tested time and time again by a programmer and for their output to be compared for consistency.

It is convenient that the number is always between 0 and 1; this allows it to easily be multiplied by another value and scaled to a different range. If one wishes to pick between two options at random, however, one can also simply test the random value to see if it is greater than 0.5. Or, as is done in this program, one can add 205.5 and convert to an integer so that 205 is produced with probability 0.5 and 206 with probability 0.5.

More can be said about randomness, and much more is said in the chapter on the topic.

### 1

When RND is given any positive value (such as this 1) as an argument, it produces a number using the current seed. This means that when `RND(1)` is invoked immediately after startup, or before any other invocation of RND, it will always produce the same result: 0.185564016. The next invocation will also be the same, no matter which Commodore 64 is used or at what time, and the next will be the same, too. Since the sequence is deterministic, the pattern produced by the `10 PRINT` program, when run before any other invocation of RND, is a complex-looking one that is always the same.

### ;

Using a semicolon after a string in a `PRINT` statement causes the next string to be printed immediately after the previous one, without a newline or any spaces between them. Other options include the use of a comma, which moves to the next tab stop (10 spaces), or the use of no symbol at all, which causes a new line to be printed and advances printing to the next line. Although this use of the semicolon for output formatting was not original to BASIC, the semicolon was introduced very early on at Dartmouth, in version 2, a minor update that had only one other change. The semicolon here is enough to show that not only short computer programs like this one, but also the languages in which they are written, change over time.

### :

The colon separates two BASIC statements that could have been placed on different lines. In a program like this on the original Dartmouth version of BASIC, each statement would have to be on its own line, since, to keep programs clear and uncluttered, only a single statement per line is allowed. The colon was introduced by Microsoft, the leading developer of microcomputer BASIC interpreters, as one of several moves to allow more code to be packed onto home computers.

### GOTO

This is an unconditional branch to the line indicated—the program's only line, line 10. The GOTO keyword and line number function here to return control to an earlier point, causing the first statement to be executed endlessly, or at least until the program is interrupted, either by a user pressing the STOP key or by shutting off the power.

GOTO, although not original to BASIC, came to be very strongly associated with BASIC. A denunciation of GOTO is possibly the most-discussed document in the history of programming languages; this letter (discussed in the "Regularity" chapter) plays an important part in the move from unstructured high-level languages such as BASIC to structured languages such as ALGOL, Pascal, Ada, and today's object-oriented programming languages, which incorporate the control structures and principles of these languages.

### RUN

Once a BASIC program is entered into the Commodore 64, it is set into motion, executed, by the RUN command. Until RUN is typed, the program lies dormant, full of potential but inert. RUN is therefore an essential token yet is not itself part of the program. RUN is what is needed to actualize the program.

In a similar fashion, describing the purpose of each of the twelve tokens in 10 PRINT does address the underlying complexity of the program. A token-by-token explanation is like a clumsy translation from BASIC into English, naively hewing to a literal interpretation of every single character. Translation can happen this way, of course, but it glosses over nuance, ambiguity, and most important, the cultural, computational, and historical depth hidden within this one line of code. Plumbing those depths is precisely the goal of the rest of this book. The rest of this book is the RUN to the introduction here. So, as the Commodore 64 says . . .

READY.

## PLAN OF THE BOOK

The more general discussions in this book are organized in five chapters and a conclusion. Preceding each of the five chapters and before the conclusion are six "Remarks." These are more specific discussions of particular computer programs directly related to 10 PRINT; they are programs that the authors have found or (in the spirit of early Commodore 64 BASIC programmers, who were encouraged to modify, port, and elaborate code and who often did so) ones that the authors have developed to shed light on how 10 PRINT works. These remarks are indicated with "REM" to refer to the BASIC statement of that name, one that allows programmers to use a line of a program to write a remark or comment, such as 55 REM START OF MAIN LOOP.

The first chapter, Mazes, offers the cultural context for reading a maze pattern in 1982. The chapter plumbs cultural and scientific associations with the maze and some of the history of mazes in computing as well. Regularity, the second chapter, considers the aspects of 10 PRINT that repeat in space, in time, and in the program's flow of control. The aesthetic and computational nature of repetition is discussed as well as the interplay between regularity and randomness. The third chapter, Randomness, offers a look at cultural uses and understandings of randomness and chance, as they are generated in games, by artists, and in simulations. It aims to show that behind a simple, commonly used capability of the computer lie numerous historical associations and uses, from the playful to the extraordinarily violent. BASIC, the fourth chapter, explains the origins of BASIC and describes how this language came to home computing. The ways in which short BASIC programs were circulated is also discussed. The fifth chapter, The Commodore 64, delves into the computer's history, exploring the machine on which `10 PRINT` runs. The most relevant technical topics, including the PETSCII character set, the VIC-II video chip, and the KERNAL (the Commodore 64's operating system, stored in 8K of ROM) are also discussed. This chapter situates `10 PRINT` in the context of its platform and that platform's rich cultural contexts.

The remarks reflect on a series of slight variations in the original BASIC program, all of which are also in Commodore 64 BASIC; on ports of `10 PRINT` to different languages and computers; on several ports and elaborations of `10 PRINT` on the Processing platform; on a collection of one-liners, including some Commodore 64 BASIC one-liners found in early 1980s print sources; on an Atari VCS port of the program; and on some greatly elaborated versions of the program in Commodore 64 BASIC. The last remark includes elaborations that generate stable full-screen mazes, allow a user to navigate a symbol around those mazes, and test those generated mazes for solubility.

One line of code gives rise here to an assemblage of readings by ten authors, offering a hint of what the future could hold—should personal computers once again invite novice programmers to RUN.

# 15
# REM VARIATIONS IN BASIC

EMULATING THE COMMODORE 64
UNBALANCED
WEAVE
CORNERS
CORNERS AND DIAGONALS
FOUR WALLS
TWO WALLS
POKE
RANDOM SOUNDS

Even small changes to the **10 PRINT** code can have a significant impact on the visual output and the pattern produced. The output of **10 PRINT** has a unique visual appeal that can be understood in terms of design (a diagonal vs. an orthogonal composition, for instance), and in terms of how it plays against the contextual expectations of the historical period when it emerged (all-text BASIC programs on the one hand and graphical software, particularly videogames, on the other).

To understand more about this, it's possible not only to read the program the way one might go over a poem or other literary text, but also to modify the program and see what happens, as the *Commodore 64 User's Guide* and *RUN* magazine explicitly invite programmers to do. Writing code can be a method of reading it more closely, as was recognized decades ago. The text accompanying the first two printed variants suggested modifying the distribution of characters (in *Commodore 64 User's Guide*) and adding code to cause random color changes (in the magazine *RUN*). This section shows the results of doing the first of these, explores what happens if other PETSCII characters are chosen for display, and finally gives a one-line variation that uses POKE to directly write to screen memory.

As tweaking the program will show, **10 PRINT** is a kind of optimal solution that is uniquely elegant in its design space, that of the Commodore 64 BASIC one-line maze generator. Any similar attempt is both less concise (it requires more code) and less expressive (it resembles a maze less or produces a less interesting visual pattern). In fact, the concision of the code and the expressiveness of the image are tightly related. They arise out of a unique set of constraints and interactions, particularly the interaction between the desire to constrain the program code to a single line and the sequence of adjacent characters in the PETSCII table.

## EMULATING THE COMMODORE 64

The Commodore 64 was an extremely popular computer; many millions of units were sold and many remain in working condition. It is still possible to cheaply acquire a Commodore 64, hook it to a television, and operate it as users of the 1980s did. When one's goal is to provide a classroom of students with access to the platform, however, or when one wishes to be able to play with and program for the Commodore 64 in many different locations on one's own contemporary notebook computer, there is a more practical alternative to finding, setting up, and starting up the classic taupe unit.

This alternative is a Commodore 64 emulator, a software version of the computer that runs on contemporary hardware and functions in the way the original Commodore 64 did. In 1983, a Commodore 64 could be purchased for $600. Today, for those who already have Internet-connected computers, it costs nothing to download and use an emulator. Emulators have been disparaged as inadequate attempts to mimic computers; while they do not capture the material aspects of older computers, they need not be considered as poor substitutes. Instead, an emulator can be usefully conceptualized as an edition of a computer.

When developers produce a program, such as the free software emulator VICE, that operates like a Commodore 64, it can be considered as a software edition of the Commodore 64. It isn't an official or authorized edition—only being a product of Commodore would allow for that. (There are official, authorized emulators for some systems, but VICE and many of the most frequently used emulators are not official.) An emulator like this is an attempt—more or less successful—to produce a system that functions like a Commodore 64. The development of an emulator typically takes a great deal of effort and can be extremely effective, as it is in the case of VICE. Thinking of this as an edition of the system seems to be a useful way to frame emulation, as it allows users to compare editions and usefully understand differences and similarities. Some emulators (like some editions) may be better for teaching, for casual reading or play, or for research and study. Instead of dismissing the emulator as useless because it isn't the original hardware, it makes more sense to consider how it works and what it affords, to look at what sort of edition it is.

The BASIC programs printed in this chapter can be run on a Commodore 64 emulator. The reader is encouraged to download an emulator, run the programs, and imagine how various differences between emulation and the original hardware influence the experience. For instance, the modern PC keyboard does not have the Commodore 64 graphics characters printed on the keys, and mapping the Commodore 64 keys to a modern keyboard layout is not straightforward. Graphically, a composite video monitor or television display attached to a Commodore 64 do not function exactly like a modern LED flat panel; the pixels drawn by an emulator are

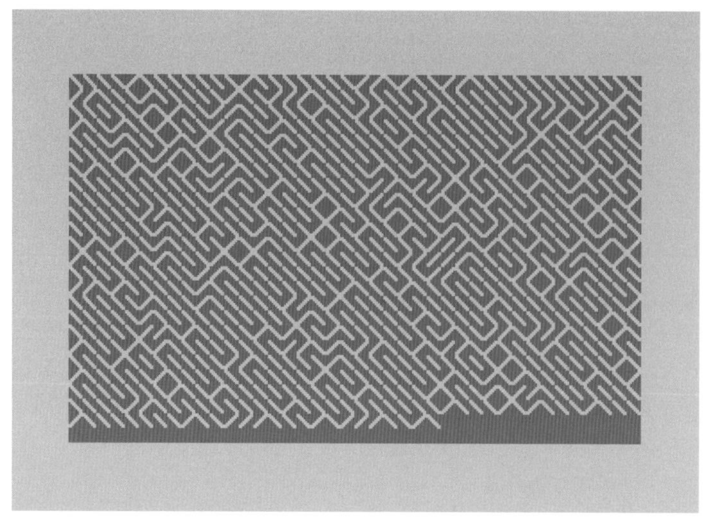

Figure 15.1

```
10 PRINT CHR$(205.25+RND(1)); : GOTO 10
```

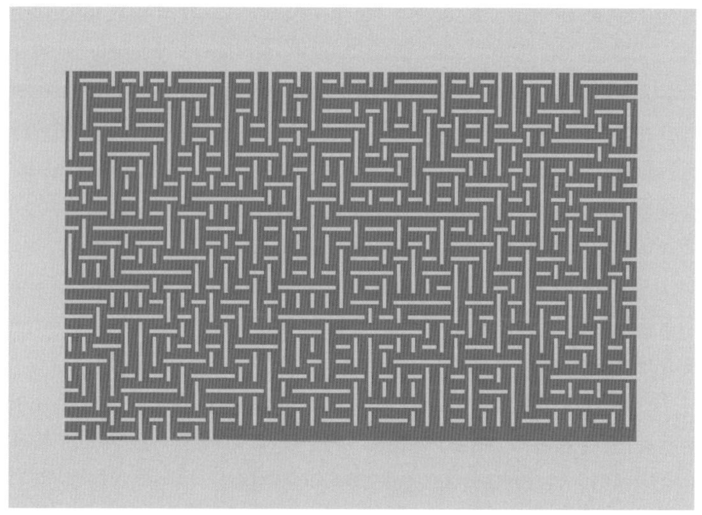

Figure 15.2

```
10 PRINT CHR$(198.5+RND(1)); : GOTO 10
```

overly crisp when compared to those seen on an early display. An emulator lets the user to save the current state of memory, registers, and so on more easily than BASIC programs can be saved to and loaded from disk on the hardware Commodore 64.

## UNBALANCED

The *Commodore 64 User's Guide* encourages users to modify its version of `10 PRINT` in this way: "If you'd like to experiment with this program, try changing 205.5 by adding or subtracting a couple tenths from it. This will give either character a greater chance of being selected" (1982, 53).

Figure 15.1 shows the effect of changing the ".5" to ".25." As one diagonal predominates, the perceived architecture of the maze tends to long corridors along that direction. More extreme variations, such as going to or beyond 0.95 or below 0.05, present what looks like a regular diagonal pattern with a very few lines going the other way, as if they were occasional defects.

## WEAVE

There are no other adjacent characters in the PETSCII data set that, when substituted for the diagonal ╲ and ╱, will result in the construction of a traditional orthogonal maze, one that is aligned to the vertical and horizontal axes of the screen. Using vertical and horizontal bars, for example, results in a disconnected weave (figure 15.2), while solid and empty squares result in a pattern similar to rough static.

Though the result certainly does not suggest a maze as strongly, this "Weave" version of the program is not without visual interest. The output imparts a three-dimensional impression, as if someone had woven bands of material over and under one another.

## CORNERS

The Commodore 64 PETSCII character set includes corner characters, such as 204 and 207, which correspond to lower-left and upper-right corner pieces. Randomly selecting either 204 or 207, as is done in this program, produces an image similar to a honeycomb. Diagonal mazes are particularly efficient ones to produce on a Cartesian grid. If a diagonal line is used, four characters can meet at the corners, whereas only two meet along an edge when tiles touch left-to-right or top-to-bottom. This pattern (see figure 15.3) does not offer as many meeting points, but has some of its own interesting visual properties.

## CORNERS AND DIAGONALS

A simplification of the program above involves dropping the `INT` function, so that the program chooses at random between other characters in addition to 204 and 207, the two corners; this "Corners and Diagonals" version can also choose the two characters in between. These characters are, of course, 205 and 206, which are the ╲ and ╱ characters that are invoked by `10 PRINT`. The result (see figure 15.4) does not have the clear structure of the `10 PRINT` maze and its pathways run for shorter stretches, appearing to be blocked more frequently. Nevertheless, the pattern that is produced is somewhat compelling in its confusion of elements.

## FOUR WALLS

A reasonably intuitive method of constructing a maze-grid is to fill in one edge of each square on a sheet of graph paper. That is, when considering any specific square, fill in the top, right, bottom, or left to form a "wall," then move to the next square and repeat. The four characters in this program correspond to a top-wall, bottom-wall, left-wall or right-wall. Such characters exist in PETSCII in both "thick" and "thin" variants; the ones used in figure 15.5 are the thick ones. Such a process is unfortunately less elegant, as these characters are not (in either variety) placed adjacent to one another in the PETSCII character set—for instance, the ones used here

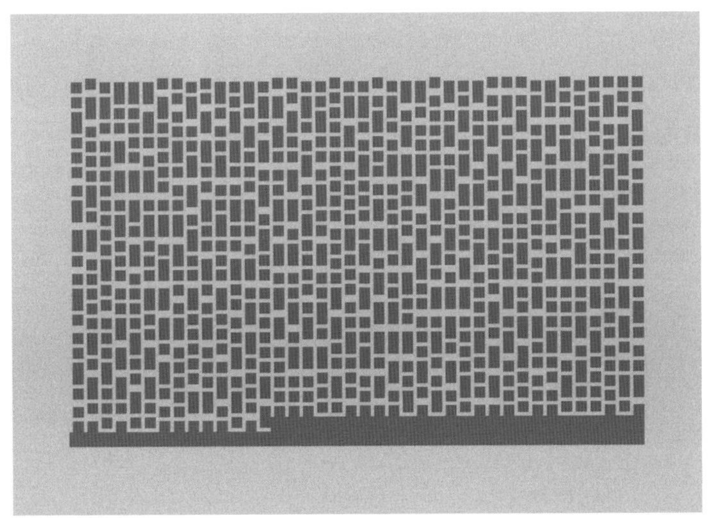

Figure 15.3

```
10 PRINT CHR$(204+(INT(RND(1)+.5)*3)); : GOTO 10
```

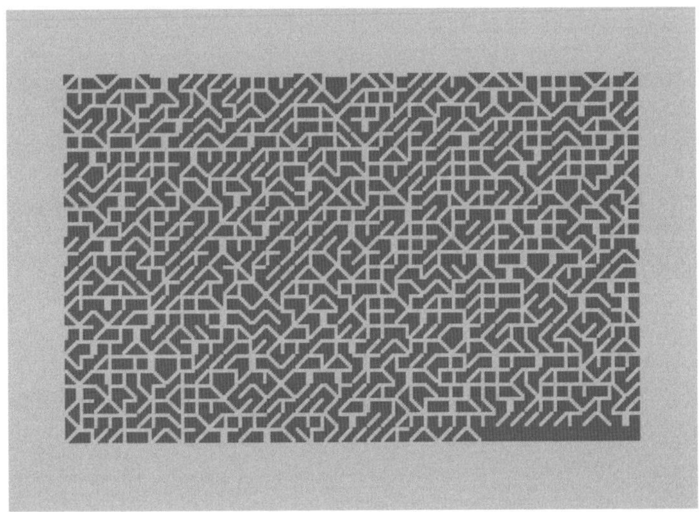

Figure 15.4

```
10 PRINT CHR$(204+(RND(1)+.5)*3); : GOTO 10
```

Figure 15.5

```
10 PRINT CHR$(181+(INT(RND(1)+.5)*3)+(INT(RND(1)+.5))); : GOTO 10
```

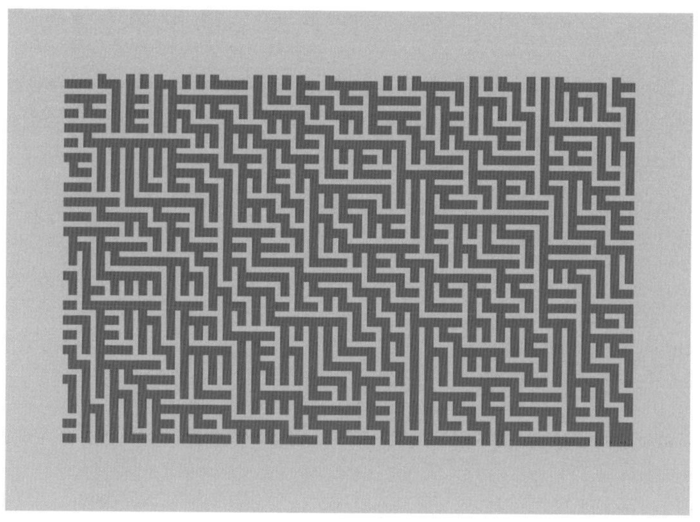

Figure 15.6

```
10 PRINT CHR$(181+(INT(RND(1)+.5)*3)); : GOTO 10
```

are 181, 182, 184, and 185—and so cannot be addressed with a single base value plus an offset, as was done in the previous program.

The image that emerges is indeed mazelike, but this image, like the underlying code, lacks simplicity and elegance. Since top and bottom and left and right lines can be printed up against each other, a variation in the thickness of the walls appears—a noticable but potentially distracting implication of messiness and texture.

## TWO WALLS

The selection of characters 181 and 184, a thick left line and thick top line (figure 15.6), provides the best approximation of the classic orthogonal maze that is seen in arcade, console, and computer games. Producing it is still less elegant than selecting between 205 and 206 as PETSCII values. The characters used are not adjacent, so some trick, such as this one involving the use of `INT`, must be used to select one of the two at random. The resulting output is less visually interesting. It is a maze, but is both less formally dynamic (being aligned to the screen) and less contextually unexpected (being typical of familiar game mazes).

## POKE

A similar maze pattern can be drawn by directly placing characters in video memory using the `POKE` command, which writes directly to memory—screen memory, in this case, which is mapped to the decimal addresses 1024–2024 (see figure 15.7). The `1024+RND(1)*1000` selects a random number in this range as the first argument to `POKE`, pointing that command at some specific location on the screen. The `77.5+RND(1)` selects ╱ or ╲. It should seem odd that after using 205.5 (and thus the values 205 and 206) to refer to these two characters, this program refers to them using the values 77 and 78. It is, indeed, odd. This difference is due to the PETSCII codes for characters not corresponding to their *screen codes*—each character has a different address for `PRINT`ing and for `POKE`ing into screen memory. This rather esoteric feature of the Commodore 64 is discussed in the final chapter of this book, The Commodore 64.

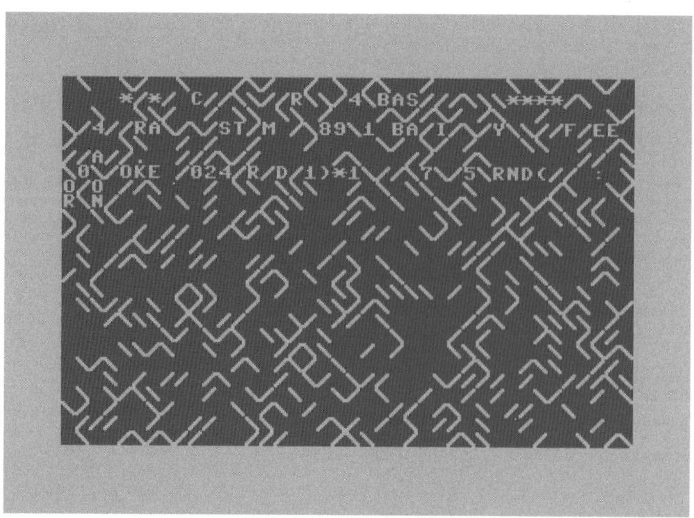

Figure 15.7

```
10 POKE 1024+RND(1)*1000,77.5+RND(1) : GOTO 10
```

This "POKE" program works by randomly selecting one of the one thousand positions on the screen, randomly selecting the screen code for ╱ or ╲, and placing that code in that memory location. Then, of course, it uses `GOTO 10` to loop back to the beginning and do everything again. While the steady-state output is a full screen of characters changing one at time, the program overwrites the existing contents of the screen slowly, filling in the maze pattern at random.

## RANDOM SOUNDS

Finally, consider this considerably more complex program, an audio analogue of 10 PRINT. It plays a sequence of tones chosen from a distribution of two, both of which have the same timbre that approximates that of a piano. The selection is done using the same pseudorandom pattern that 10 PRINT uses, thanks to the invocation of RND(1) in line 30:

```
10 S=54272 : POKE S+24,15 : POKE S+5,190 : POKE S+6,248
20 A(0)=17 : A(1)=37 : A(2)=21 : A(3)=76
30 Q=INT(.5+RND(1)) : POKE S+1,A(Q*2) : POKE S,A(Q*2+1)
40 POKE S+4,17 : FOR T=1 TO 75 : NEXT
50 POKE S+4,16 : FOR T=1 TO 150 : NEXT
60 GOTO 30
```

In Commodore 64 BASIC, one can point into a table of PETSCII characters by simply using 205 and 206 as indices. But there is no similar built-in way to index into a table of notes. After setting up the sound chip in line 10, this program builds such a table using the array A in line 20. Furthermore, the sound chip requires two POKE commands—the ones on line 30—to change the note frequency. Although this is because the chip is extremely accurate in its pitch control, it does make for longer and more involved programs.

This book does not cover arrays (which are not part of the canonical 10 PRINT) in any detail; it would move the discussion quite far afield to explain exactly what is happening in each invocation of POKE in this program. Suffice it to say that POKE is being used to set the sound chip's registers, causing the Commodore 64 to emit musical sounds in a strightforward way—the standard way one would produce music in BASIC. The invocations of POKE are not simply storing values in memory for later use, nor are they placing values in screen memory, as in the previous example—yet all of this is necessary to move from a randomized generator of block graphics to a randomized generator of tones. This program shows how much easier it is for Commodore 64 BASIC to work on graphic, rather than musical, elements.

# 20 MAZES

WHAT IS A MAZE?
MYTH, RITUAL, AND ALLEGORY
THE LABORATORY MAZE
THE COMPUTERIZED MAZE
ENTERING THE MAZE

What is the pattern produced by 10 PRINT? The 1982 *Commodore 64 User's Guide* says the program uses the two graphical characters "for the maze" (53). And the programmer who submitted the one-line version in the magazine *RUN* also described it as "drawing a continuous maze" (13). Surely, the program would be less interesting if framed as "Random Pattern of Lines." But if it is a maze, what kind of maze is it and what cultural associations does that evoke?

An adult seeing a maze appear on the screen, after a young programmer has typed in and run 10 PRINT, could easily trivialize and dismiss it as simply a childish amusement. It is easy to overlook the cultural resonance and historical depth of the maze, which could be seen as nothing more than a flat, empty, puzzle-book diversion. The same dismissal can be leveled against short, recreational BASIC programs, which can seem trivial and of no importance. This chapter rejects that view and looks deeper into the maze—in part, to look deeper into 10 PRINT and the surrounding culture of creative, exploratory computing.

The maze synthesizes the program's output as a visual trope that evokes a long history of meaningful mazes. Mazes can be visual renderings, textual artifacts, horticultural expanses, and architectural spaces. Situated as amusing puzzles, places of terror, behavioral proving grounds, or invitations to contemplative meanderings, in the West the maze's meanings date back to the legend of Theseus and the Minotaur in the labyrinth of Knossos, a bewildering and life-threatening space. In more recent times, mazes have served as spaces for playful movement and as commonplace diversions in puzzle books. Sometimes, mazes are abstract mathematical objects or scientific tools for studying animal behavior. And in computer games, the maze takes on an archetypal, structural frame for adventure, chase, and combat. A full cultural history of mazes throughout the centuries is outside of the scope of this book (for in-depth historical accounts of mazes, see Doob 1990, Kern 2000, and Matthews 1922). Instead, this chapter highlights the mazes throughout history that Commodore 64 users in the 1980s would have been likely to associate with the output they saw after running 10 PRINT.

## WHAT IS A MAZE?

A maze can mean a structure, a network of connected passages that contains a navigable route as well as dead ends and backtracks. Or, a maze can have a more abstract meaning: a complex network of paths with or without a solution. In popular use, the meaning of the term "maze" has been stretched to cover intellectual puzzles, tangled legal code, and confusing, labyrinthine situations. 10 PRINT's output can thus evoke a rich collection of associations by means of a simple yet resonant figure.

10 PRINT meets some of the criteria that William Henry Matthews establishes for mazes in his *Mazes and Labyrinths* (1922): they are "works of artifice," not "'labyrinths' of nature, such as forests, caverns, and so forth"; they are endowed with "an element of purposefulness in the design" (182). They also betray "a certain degree of complexity" (183). Finally, he requires "communication" among the maze's component parts and between its "interior and exterior" (183).

This short program is, indeed, a complex work of artifice. However, ironically, the compelling and captivating quality of 10 PRINT arises from the lack of an obvious, purposeful designer. Someone wrote the line of code, certainly, but the specific person who was the author was not named. The purposefulness of the design arises from a set of accidents, including the BASIC RND function and the appearance of the two diagonal line characters, elements that were themselves created anonymously. Furthermore, in 10 PRINT, communication among the component parts is established by accident, from gaps that appear between slashes. Overall, the construction of 10 PRINT's maze is considerably more muddled than Matthews' criteria would seem to demand.

As material, architectural structures, mazes have a finite size. But there is no limit to how long 10 PRINT can be left running. As an endless production, 10 PRINT suggests the form of a maze, but it does not always offer a path or solution. As such, the program exists in between the two definitions of maze: a physical structure on the one hand and an intricate confusion on the other.

Mazes typically offer at least one path; the key structural difference is whether they offer more than one—whether they are unicursal or multicursal. A unicursal maze offers a single path along which walkers proceed, never making a choice about where to turn. A multicursal maze, by

## MAZE VS. LABYRINTH

The terms "maze" and "labyrinth" are generally synonyms in colloquial English. Still, many scholars and historians have argued over the distinction between these two terms. In the most popular proposed distinction, "labyrinth" refers only to single-path (unicursal) structures, while "maze" refers only to branching-path (multicursal) structures.

In this book, the terms "maze" and "labyrinth" are not used to distinguish two different categories of structure or image. Instead, the two terms indicate a single conceptual category, with this book primarily using the term "maze" for both.

contrast, invites wrong turns, has dead ends, and may even have multiple paths to the exit or center.

In unicursal mazes, the navigable space is bounded and a single path is set; users have no directional decisions to make, save to follow the meanderings of the path, leaving their attention, mind, or emotions free to wander or focus elsewhere, while continuing to the end at the center of the maze or to a unique exit. The unicursal maze sometimes allegorizes temporality, offering a spiritual and contemplative space to the walker. Unicursal mazes can be traversed repeatedly and ritualistically for peace and spiritual comfort. In unicursal hedge mazes the hedges often limit one's vision to an immediate and foreshortened horizon, suggesting enclosure and protection.

Multicursal mazes, by contrast, ask to be solved. Instead of following the unicursal maze's predetermined path, visitors to a multicursal maze run the risk of getting lost as they attempt to find the exit.

The `10 PRINT` program *itself* (not its output) can be seen as a unicursal maze. When inputting this program, beginning programmers follow a series of characters, copying them from manual or magazine to computer terminal. The program starts as a puzzle for those who have some understanding but not complete knowledge of BASIC and the Commodore 64. Once the code has been typed and executed and the programmer witnesses the maze, there is no returning to a naive view of this line of code—it is impossible to read the line without imagining its output. With some study, it becomes clear how the program produces this output: the single path through this short but initially tangled program is revealed.

Yet the program's output also suggests a multicursal maze, because the patterm can apparently be traversed, or at least attempted, in several ways. Even though the maze generates itself anew line by line, it does so slowly, and at any given point a single screen can be interpreted and one can consider whether a solution is possible. To do so does require that the viewer make some assumptions about where the maze starts and ends as well as about other matters. (An exploration of this process appears in the remark Maze Walker in BASIC). In any case, the invitation to see this as a multicursal maze is clear to many.

## MYTH, RITUAL, AND ALLEGORY

The novice programmers of the Commodore 64, particularly those who were young, would have no doubt been enticed by the depiction of mazes as sites for adventure. Mazelike environments, printed in modules and drawn by hand, were a part of *Dungeons & Dragons,* the popular role-playing game that began in the mid-1970s. Dungeon masters in that game plotted spaces, commonly on graph paper, full of monsters and fiends that were inspired by several fantastic and legendary sources, including the myths of ancient Rome and Greece.

The most famous ancient maze of myth is the labyrinth of Knossos, Crete, in which Theseus encounters the Minotaur, a horrifying hybrid, the cursed offspring of Minos's wife and a bull (*Minos* + *tauros*). Like a basement or attic in Gothic literature (see Gilbert and Gubar 2000), the Knossos labyrinth is the hiding place for a defective, dangerous family member. Theseus arrives at Knossos and wins the affection of the king's daughter Ariadne, who offeres him a means of returning from the labyrinth after he enters it to defeat the Minotaur. She suggests he tie a string to the entrance and unravel it as he proceeds through the maze so that he can follow it back to the entrance. Thanks to Ariadne's thread, Theseus successfully makes his way through the maze, slays the Minotaur, and escapes. The allegory here invokes the danger of illicit desire; it also shows that those who hold tight to a predetermined path can succeed.

The Knossos maze is best understood in terms of Theseus's narrative path through it, not as the space of the labyrinth itself. This transforma-

Figure 20.1
The central labyrinth and maze patterns of Amiens Cathedral were built in the thirteenth century. Courtesy of Stephen Murray.

tion from multicursal, unknowable confusion to a marked and bounded pathway reflects the mastery of any system, from challenging, mysterious, threatening, and deadly to easy, known, mapped, and tamed. This original labyrinthine myth underscores the reality of many puzzles: when the solution is known, the puzzle seems simpler if not trivial. Rather than the fantasy of a warrior moving freely through an open map, the tale of Theseus teaches that success comes from adhering to a string, a particularly useful analogy in the unforgiving corridors of programming syntax.

The morphing of the maze from complex to simple (or at least understandable) is part of the Commodore 64 user's ideal encounter with `10 PRINT`, but the user is more like the creator of a maze than its explorer. Daedalus, the architect of the labyrinth at Knossos, holds a place of honor as puzzle maker supreme. Daedalus understands that planning, intentionality, and construction are integral characteristics of the mystique of the maze. `10 PRINT` thus channels Daedalus more than Theseus: the program is a blueprint for a maze, not just a structure or image that appears without any history or trace of its making. And at the same time, `10 PRINT` *itself* takes the role of maze creator: the programmer may be the maze's architect, but the program is its builder.

The associations evoked by `10 PRINT` may begin with the Minotaur's maze, but they continue through history, adding to the complex symbology and sacred rites of Christian churches and then rising in the turf and hedges of the countryside. Mazes take on religious import on the floors of cathedrals and basilicas. Among the largest and most famous church labyrinths is at Chartres, France, built circa 1200 CE. It is a walkable, eleven-circuit labyrinth ornamented around its outer ring with lunations (Kern 2000, 153), and has been an object of endless speculation, from rumors of treasure buried under its center to theories about its functioning as a lunar calculator.

Church mazes are usually meant to be walked or crawled on the path to penance. The names of these include Labyrinth of Sin, The Path to Redemption, and The Path to Jerusalem. These pathways symbolized paths to Christian salvation, relating a Paschal instead of a Minoan mystery. Interestingly, the path of the meanderings in the labyrinths at the cathedrals at Chartres and at Amiens are exactly the same, even though the former is circular and the latter octagonal, as seen in figure 20.1 (Wright 2001, 60).

`10 PRINT` retains a dimension of spiritual mystery. The program certainly doesn't seem to be part of any religious practice, but as code,

## DANCING A COMPLEX STRUCTURE

Mazes are usually imagined as architectural, material, and fixed, but cultures have long noticed that they can correspond directly to a human activity, dance. In *The Iliad*, Homer credits Daedalus both with a dance floor and a labyrinth. Kern speculates that the labyrinth was a choros, which has the double meaning of dance and dance surface. Given that no labyrinthine buildings survive in Crete, the depictions of labyrinths on coins may indicate the path of a dance—particularly since maze dances have survived. Theseus meets the Minotaur in a Minoan maze, but he and his men immortalize that adventure in dance on the way back. As Matthews explains, "On the island of Delos they performed a peculiar dance called the Geranos, or 'Crane Dane,' in which they went through the motions of threading the Labyrinth, and . . . this dance was perpetuated by the natives of that island until fairly recently" (1922, 19). These dances have continued to be performed elsewhere, and numerous other labyrinthine dances are known, some with military purposes and some tied to rites of spring. Martha Graham adapted the motifs of the Cretan maze story in "Errand into a Maze" (1949), where it is Ariadne who is trapped by the Minotaur. After contemplating her escape from the labyrinth—represented by a rope on the floor—"she breaks her pattern and breaks her tormentor. The maze of rope reflects the maze of her mind and the maze of the myth" (Zlokower 2005).

The dancer's relationship to the maze is analogous to that of the amateur learning BASIC. As the novice programmer prepares to face the Minotaur machine, a single line of code serves as a clue leading to safety. As with the maze dance, it is in tracing this labyrinth by typing and running `10 PRINT` that the very corridors are created.

The maze dance has not been completely forgotten in digital media. It may seem odd to think of *Dance Dance Revolution* as a maze game, but its arrows do show a labyrinthine path that the dancer, standing in place, is supposed to navigate. Missing a step is allowed, but the perfect performance will be as ritualized a motion through space as a *Pac-Man* pattern. Looking beyond the arcade, Diana Slattery has created a work called *The Maze Game* that brings together the maze as a site of meaningful dance. In her digital work and companion novel, moving through a lethal maze takes grace and literacy, since the maze is constructed out of glyphs from Slattery's created visual language "glide." Slattery's work stands at the intersection of dance, maze, and narrative, showing a new connection.

10 PRINT taps into the mazelike mystery that visual symbols and glyphs evoke: to type in a program from a manual is to follow the twisted line from code to output and back again. The programmer follows the single path of the code from ignorance to knowledge, a pilgrim's path. 10 PRINT may not help programmers attain salvation, but it does offer an accessible means by which novice programmers can trace the steps of writing code to be initiated into the mysteries of a magic box, the personal computer.

As with a rosary and the Stations of the Cross, the Christian labyrinth is unicursal. None included dead ends or choice points until the fifteenth century, when multicursal aberrations appeared, as Helmut Birkhan explains, as a "symptom of the secularization of the labyrinth idea" (quoted in Kern 2000, 146). With this secular turn, the maze becomes a space of leisure as well as ritual, and is lined with hedges, marked by rocks, and surrounded by grooves. Church-like mazes and mazes that invite a ritual attitude surfaced throughout Europe, although several of these were more related to pagan rites of spring than to Christianity. In *A Midsummer Night's Dream*, the faerie queen Titania ponders the ghostly outlines of abandoned turf mazes:

> The nine men's morris is fill'd up with mud,
> And the quaint mazes in the wanton green
> For lack of tread are undistinguishable. (2.1.98–100)

As more and more pagan and secular mazes emerged alongside church and other labyrinth traditions, they retained some of their profound, sacred nature while also offering puzzle play and leisure.

Hedge mazes and 10 PRINT possess affinities that their material differences obscure. Hedge mazes need to be planned and plotted, but unlike most other mazes, they must grow in order to fulfill that plan. 10 PRINT's maze does as well, albeit in a different way than bushes do: once seeded, the computer-generated maze grows without tending, growing until the viewer interrupts it.

Hedge mazes offer decoration in a garden, but as leisure devices instead of religious rituals, they also offer exhilaration and vertigo when they are "run." Writing of a famous half-mile hedge maze at Hampton Court Palace near London, Matthews describes it as an "undiluted delight" to "scores of hundred of children, not to mention a fair sprinkling of their elders" (1922, 129). This way of encountering the maze was carried into video games such as *Doom* (1993) and *Pac-Man* (1980). 10 PRINT's continuously cascading display echoes the playful zigzagging of children gamboling through the hedges.

## THE LABORATORY MAZE

The maze traveler has had many manifestations: the brave warrior facing obstacles, the penitent disciple undertaking a divine ritual, the Elizabethan child experiencing vertiginous pleasure. But no discussion of the cultural touchstones of mazes (and their resonances for maze creators) would be complete without that humbler maze walker, or crawler, the laboratory rat. In the context of psychological testing, the rat's encounter with the maze does not prove bravery, piety, or ingenuity so much as it *reduces* human agency and learning to behavioral conditioning.

The first maze constructed for rats by researchers was built in the late 1890s—but it was not originally used for testing the creatures. Willard Small of Clark University built a maze environment to allow rats to eat and exercise when they *weren't* taking part in experiments. Small wanted the environment to simulate the burrows that rats inhabit in nature, but he modeled the first laboratory rat maze after the Hampton Court Palace maze (Lemov 2005, 25). The restorative maze is quite consonant with the purposes for which the Hampton Court Palace maze was built, although Small was attending to the constitution of rodents rather than royals.

John B. Watson used maze environments for more familiar research purposes: to determine whether rats could make their way through a maze under different experimental conditions. After his rats had learned their way through a maze, Watson blinded or otherwise maimed the creatures to deprive them of different senses. His work attracted public attention, and he was denounced in a *New York Times* editorial as a torturer. Watson, however, was sure of his behavioral science agenda, and he concluded that the same principles of operant conditioning that apply to rats apply to people as well. By 1916 he had moved on to experiments with infants. In one famous experiment he conditioned a baby, "Little Albert," to fear a furry white rat and furry white things in general (Buckley 1989).

The use of mazes in experiments with rats increased greatly during the 1920s. Behaviorism, the perspective that all animal and human actions are behaviors, is now mainly associated with another American scientist, B. F. Skinner. His operant conditioning chamber, also known as the Skinner box, is another famous environment for laboratory animals that was built decades after Watson's mazes saw their first use. While Skinner's name is better known today, Watson's maze remains emblematic—and similar environments are still used for experiments today.

In 1959, one of the earliest computer programs written for fun—an example of "recreational computing"—depicted an experimenter's maze. The program, perhaps the first computer program to draw a maze of any sort, was written for the TX-0 at MIT by Douglas T. Ross and John E. Ward. The TX-0 was an experimental computer that provided one of the first opportunities for people to program when not working on an official project. It also allowed programmers to work on the machine interactively, much as Commodore 64 programmers later would, rather than submitting batch jobs in the form of decks of punched cards. In the program that became known as "Mouse in the Maze," a mouse moves through a maze, eating cheese. The mouse could also consume martinis, which cause it to become disoriented and degrade its performance. In this case, the environment implemented was not the hedge maze of diversion and fun, but a more staid experimenter's maze. This essentially serious maze was then made playful with the addition of an amusing alcoholic reward and the simulation of appropriate behavior.

10 PRINT picks up on aspects of "Mouse in the Maze." Its output is a regular arrangement of "walls" in a grid—akin to the display of that earlier program and similar to the arrangement of the stereotypical laboratory maze. "Mouse in the Maze" does not present the compelling creation of an inspired Daedalus, but a behaviorist experiment. This maze is a challenge to intelligence—not, however, a romantic, riddling intelligence, but a classically conditioned, animal kind. It also brings in the idea of the scientist, who may be indifferent to the struggles of the creatures lost in the maze.

But who is the user at the interface of 10 PRINT, the scientist or the rodent? When 10 PRINT runs, it may generate its maze relentlessly, but it does not trap the user like a rat. Instead, given the top-down view and the lack of a user-controlled maze walker, the computer presents the programmer with the point of view of the maze designer, offering in a sense to collaborate with the user in creating a new design. Amid the playful and religious connotations of the maze are those things the experimenter's maze

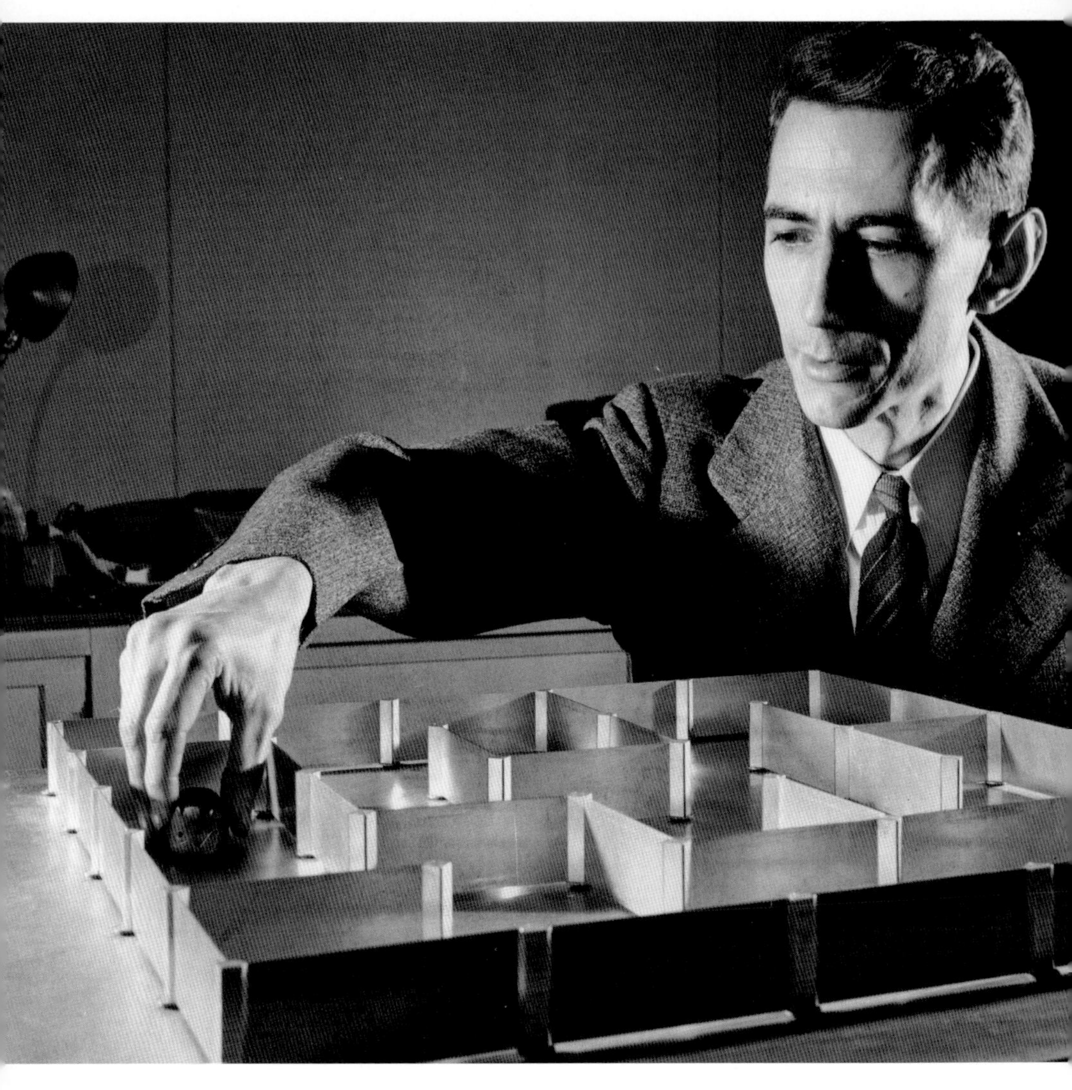

Figure 20.2
Information theory pioneer Claude Shannon pictured ca. 1950 with his mechanical mouse Theseus and its magnetic metal maze. Courtesy of MIT Museum.

hints at: that the computer is a scientific instrument, and the walker of the maze might be not a Greek hero but a small creature driven by hunger.

## THE COMPUTERIZED MAZE

In the early 1950s the mathematician and engineer Claude Shannon designed a mechanical mouse (see figure 20.2) that appears to solve the same kind of maze a real mouse might be expected to navigate in one of Watson's behavioral experiments. Shannon, a foundational figure in modern computing, named the mouse Theseus, collapsing the mythological hero and his noble plight into a mere contraption guided by a mechanized system. Although featured in both *Time* and *Life* ("Mouse with a Memory" 1952; "Better Mouse" 1952), Theseus itself was not a sophisticated piece of artificial intelligence. It was simply a wooden mouse on wheels with a bar magnet inside and copper-wire whiskers. The true magic of this mouse resides underneath the maze, in a system of electronic relays that switch positions when the mouse's whiskers touch corresponding walls in the maze above. The first time through a maze, Theseus blunders randomly, propelled by its magnet, flipping the relays underneath whenever it encountered a passage. The next time, Theseus navigates the maze perfectly, thanks to the relays underneath, which record the correct route.

This means of negotiating the twisting passages of Shannon's maze was not mere novelty. As *Time* explained in 1952, Theseus is "useful in studying telephone switching systems, which are very like labyrinths." Indeed, George Dyson argues that Theseus inspired the RAND Corporation engineer Paul Baran's "adaptive message block switching"—the precursor to what is now known as packet switching, the protocol that defines the way data flows on the Internet (Dyson 1997, 150).

Aside from its significance to network computing, Theseus serves as a vivid example of an early connection between mazes and computers. Furthermore, Theseus shares a procedural resonance with `10 PRINT`. Theseus "learns" through repetition, or looping, the fundamental process that is used to draw the `10 PRINT` maze. And like a computer program, the mouse in Shannon's maze is only the surface-level signifier of much deeper processes. Theseus in fact is not only dumb but, by itself, inert. The "brain" of Theseus lies in the relays hidden underneath the surface of the maze, much in the same way the on-screen design of `10 PRINT` is generated by a piece of code, initially not very clear, which depends upon an invisible, low-level call to a pseudorandom number generator.

Computers did not completely change the cultural idea of the maze, but they did provide new ways to represent, generate, solve, and play in mazes. And, as computers came into the home and became widely accessible, they helped to bring mazes into daily life once again. In part, this happened thanks to the work of early computer scientists who wrote programs to generate mazes. But many popular mazes were not as computationally sophisticated. They were, however, integrated cleverly into enjoyable computer games that reached a mass audience.

It is useful to group these computer mazes by the point of view they offer to their interactors. There are first-person mazes, partially represented on a screen, which show the wall or passageway directly in front of the maze walker. There are also second-person mazes, textually represented, in which the maze walker is the "you" to whom the traversal of the maze is narrated. And, there are third-person mazes, sometimes fully represented mazes, in which the maze walker maintains a large-scale or omniscient view.

A significant early maze program is *Maze,* which presents a 3D view of a maze in which a player can see (and shoot) opponents. This program was created in 1973 at the NASA Ames Research Center by Steve Colley and Howard Palmer and later made into a multiplayer game by Greg Thompson. In 1974 the program was then expanded at MIT; Dave Lebling wrote a server that provided text messaging and supported up to eight players or robots. The same program was later ported to the Xerox Alto as *Maze War.*

The *Maze* environment was created for entertainment, but it was really little more than a convoluted battlefield—not a space to be explored or solved and certainly nothing like the entirely nonviolent English hedge maze. Other terrifying maze environments became a staple of early home computer mazes, and some contained a Minotaur-like threat. *3D Monster Maze* was an early example, developed in 1981 and released the following year on the Sinclair ZX81. The game uses character graphics and features a randomly generated 16 × 16 maze with a Tyrannosaurus Rex.

Although 3D mazes with some more exploratory aspects were offered in the *Ultima, Wizardry,* and *Bard's Tale* series, the maze is more a frightening site for combat than a playful place of discovery in many first-person games. This can be seen as early as 1984 in the Commodore 64 game *Skull*, which allows the player to search for treasure and sends threatening skulls into the maze as opponents. *Wolfenstein 3D* (1992) and *Doom* (1993) make this perspective on a mazelike environment even more fearsome. Sound design, darkness, and the use of conventions from horror films that give the effect of seeing without peripheral vision all contribute to this effect. The first-person maze, in addition to connecting players to the perspective and to some extent the subjective experience of their maze-bound characters, is likely to inspire close and constant attention.

Many of the earliest computer-presented mazes are not visual; they are described textually, narrated to the player from a second-person perspective. Second-person mazes of a sort are found in early text-based games such as *Hunt the Wumpus*, a 1973 BASIC program by Gregory Yob. *Hunt the Wumpus* departs from the standard grid-based BASIC game by providing a playing field of a different topology, a dodecahedron. The player stalks and is stalked by a formidable opponent, much as the dinosaur later pursues the player of *3D Monster Maze*.

Textually described mazes developed into their most complex and confusing configurations in text-based adventure games of the sort now called interactive fiction. The genre began with the groundbreaking *Adventure*, written by Will Crowther for the PDP-10 in 1976 and later expanded by Don Woods into a full-fledged underground adventure. Basing the game in part on his own caving experience in the Mammoth Cave system, Crowther includes a ten-room maze introduced with "YOU ARE IN A MAZE OF TWISTY LITTLE PASSAGES, ALL ALIKE." "YOU" works to connect the player to the character in the maze, although in a different way than first-person 3D games do. For one thing, that pronoun sometimes is explicitly used to address the operator of the program rather than to indicate the main character, as when *Adventure* outputs "IF YOU PREFER, SIMPLY TYPE W RATHER THAN WEST."

From *Hunt the Wumpus* through *Adventure*, another notable difference is that second-person mazes are typically turn-based rather offering real-time play. They also are embedded in a broader context of simulated spaces. Sometimes these are confusing ones that, even if they are not called mazes, require that players map them on paper. In any case, they usually invite different forms of systematic, high-level thinking that allows the environment to be figured or puzzled out. The player's activity is thoughtful and paced at the player's discretion rather than being based on twitch reflexes.

When players draw maps of the mazes in *Adventure, Zork,* or other interactive fictions, they transform textually represented second-person mazes into visually represented third-person mazes. Such maps convey a sense of mastery of the maze even though a third-person perspective on a maze does not guarantee its safety or solubility.

Shannon's *Mouse in the Maze* offered an early glimpse of the third-person computer maze, but this form truly erupted in the Unites States less than two years before the release of the Commodore 64, in October 1980. This is when the original *Pac-Man* arcade game arrived from Japan. In Japan, the genre of games inspired by *Pac-Man* is called "dot-eat" games (ドットイート), but in the United States such games are called maze or maze chase games.

Pac-Man cannot thread his way through the environment to find an exit—except for the tunnel that links the left and right side of the screen together. The playing field may be better described as being littered with obstacles rather than as being "a maze" in the sense that church labyrinths and hedge mazes are usually understood. Nevertheless, the playing field *was* called a maze from the beginning. *The New York Times* called Pac-Man "a circle with a big mouth that eats up dots in a maze while other big mouths try to eat it up" (Latham 1981), while *Newsweek* mentioned the "maddening Pac-Man maze" (Langway 1981). The puzzle the game poses to the voracious Pac-Man is not to get out of the maze, but to run through all of it while avoiding the pursing monsters.

*Pac-Man's* maze is aligned to the axes of the display: the paths are either horizontal or vertical. But just as the tanks in *Tank* (1974) and the player's ship in *Asteroids* (1979) can turn and fire in many different directions, it is possible to represent a maze that is not "orthogonal" in this way: `10 PRINT` provides a very simple alternative, a diagonal maze. Third-person videogame mazes, in contrast, are almost always aligned as in *Pac-Man,* even those that predate the dot eater.

Magnavox's infamous *K. C. Munchkin* (1981) is something of a *Pac-Man* knock-off that was itself knocked off shelves by a famous court ruling, *Atari v. Philips.* To players today, the game looks like just another maze game. With doors that open and close, only twelve dots on the screen, and other notable differences, it now seems impossible to confuse with *Pac-*

*Man*. The two games are similar in that they both feature mazes that are orthogonally aligned. But among *K. C. Munchkin*'s differences are that it allows players to take on the role of Daedalus, designing their own levels.

Other videogame mazes, and games with mazy environments, quickly made their way into the home, too. The game bundled with the classic cartridge-based Atari VCS in 1977 was *Combat*, which brought the convoluted battlefields of *Tank* into the home. Soon after, that console featured *Maze Craze* (1978), which allows players to compete in several different challenges in maze environments that were automatically generated.

All of these games treat the screen display as a single complete visual unit, like the board of a board game. The continuously scrolling maze of `10 PRINT` at least suggests a maze that is larger than the screen, even if one cannot navigate around to see what is offscreen. Another interesting contrast to the single-screen maze is a close-up design that puts the player in a larger-scale maze, seen in the 1979 Atari VCS game *Adventure* (see figure 20.3). This console game is loosely based on the interactive fiction work of the same name, and features a hero who can collect treasure despite the efforts of three dragons. Unlike *Pac-Man*, in which the player can guide Pac-Man out a warp gate on one side of the screen and see him enter on the other side, *Adventure* contains numerous topologically impossible warps that are always hidden from view and can only be deduced. Instead of an overview map of the total maze, each screen is a closeup of simple paths, often emphasizing discontinuous fragments of other paths that can't easily be reached.

Diagonal orientation of the sort produced by `10 PRINT` did have a place in the design of early mazelike games. It emerged through isometric video games that introduced diagonal motion at the same time they challenged the picture plane through the pseudo-3D effect of isometric perspective. Two isometric games came to arcades in 1982: *Q*bert*, a completion/avoidance platformer on an isometric pyramid, and *Zaxxon*, an obstacle-racer emphasizing pseudo-3D elements. Neither is particularly mazelike compared to later isometric games from years after the first version of `10 PRINT`. *Ant Attack* (1983) and *Marble Madness* (1984) are examples of games with more convoluted obstacle courses on fields that were larger than the screen.

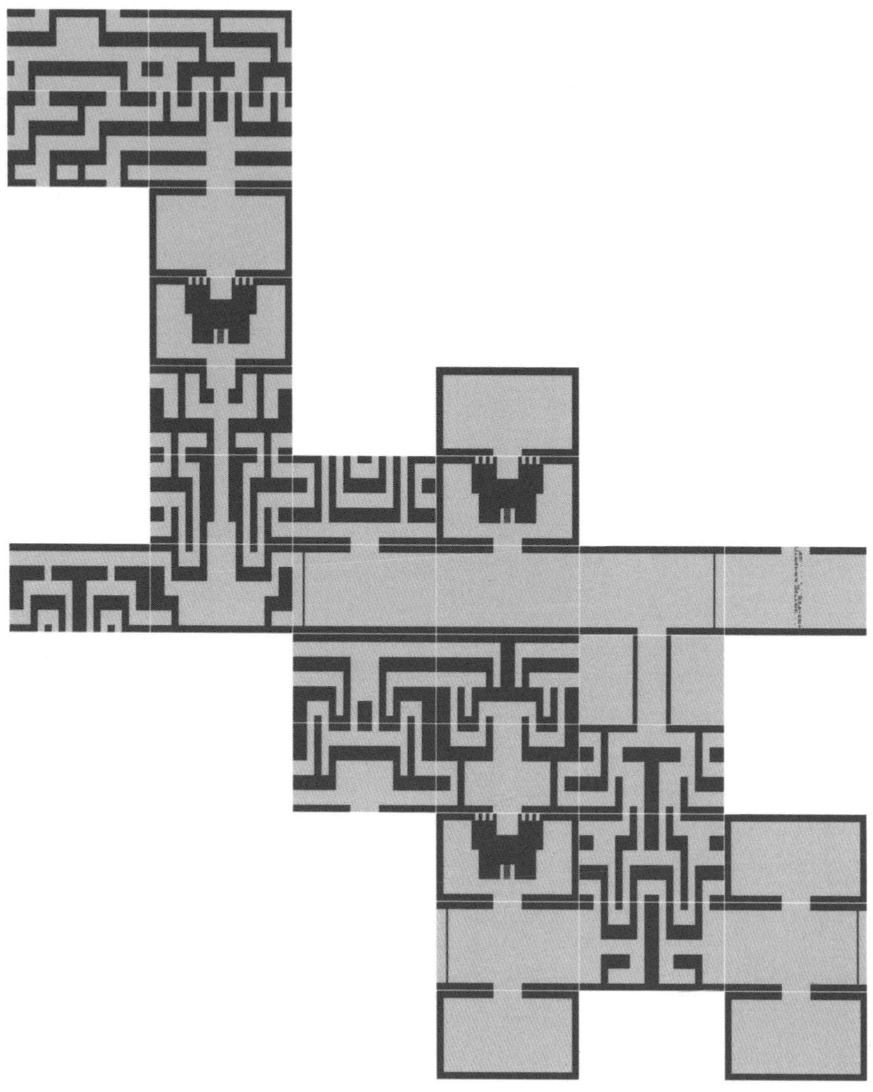

Figure 20.3

*Adventure* (1979) for the Atari VCS featured a maze to navigate while fighting dragons and searching for keys to enter castles.

## ENTERING THE MAZE

While 10 PRINT seems to be a noninteractive 2D third-person maze, its single line of code produces an unusual twist on this form of maze, shifting it to a different axis than is traditionally used. This is accomplished by the simple selection of two diagonal character graphics. That design element introduces another complexity: even though the maze is built from left to right and down the screen, the walls and paths do not follow this axis of construction.

In the mid-1980s, it would be impossible for most users to consider a maze-generating computer program without thinking of the many computer games that take place in mazes. But, for many, the maze would also be associated with different types of terror, contemplation, experimentation, and play. Would the user be Theseus or Daedalus? The scientist or the rat? Pac-Man or Zaxxon? And would programming be meditating, dancing, escaping, solving, or architecting a maze? This richness seems to be part of what encouraged new Commodore 64 programmers to "enter the maze" by entering this program on their computer, to work at solving and understanding this code only to revise, extend, and reimagine it in their own programs.

Considering 10 PRINT in light of the cultural history of mazes situates the program's output in a space of symbolic meanings and design principles—the many ways in which something can be seen as mazelike or designed to be mazelike. This view sheds light on the specific ways in which 10 PRINT both echoes and alters earlier notions of a maze. The output is not unicursal, after the fashion of early labyrinths, nor is it marked for traversal with clear entrances and exits, as in a meditative or hedge maze, nor is its system of paths continuous and fully explorable, as in a laboratory run for rats. Instead, 10 PRINT produces something of the visual complexity of later mazes, but this complexity does not address a particular purpose, and instead emerges out of an absolute simplicity of design. If 10 PRINT is a maze in a new and different way, this difference is based in deep similarity to the precursors it resembles, in particular, the way that all mazes arise out of shared principles of regularity on the one hand and randomness on the other.

# 25 REM PORTS TO OTHER PLATFORMS

APPLESOFT BASIC AND TANDY COLOR BASIC
PERL AND JAVASCRIPT: MODERN ONE-LINERS
PATH: MAZE AS PERVERSE PROGRAM
WHAT PORTING REVEALS

Adapting a program from one hardware system to another is "porting," a term derived from the Classical Latin portāre—to carry or bear, not unlike the carrying across (trans + lātus) of translation. A port is borne from one platform to another, and the bearer is the programmer, who must gather up the details of the original and find places for them amid the particulars of the destination, attempting to identify and preserve the program's essential properties. The translator faces these same sorts of problems when encountering a text, and such problems are particularly acute when the text is a poem. Where does the poetry of the poem lie? In its rhythm? Its rhyme? Its diction? Its constraints? Its meanings? Which of these must be carried over from one language to another in order to produce the most faithful translation?

In *Nineteen Ways of Looking at Wang Wei*, a study of the act and art of translation, Eliot Weinberger (1987) reads nineteen versions of a four-line, 1,200-year-old poem by the Chinese master Wang Wei, attentive to the way translators have reinterpreted the poem over the centuries, even as they attempted to be faithful to the original. With a single word, a translator may create a perspective unseen in Wei's original, radically shift the mood of the poem, or transform it into complete tripe. Many times these changes come about as the translator tries to improve the original in some way. Yet translation, Weinberger writes, "is dependent on the dissolution of the translator's ego: an absolute humility toward the text" (17).

The programmer who ports faces similar challenges. What must be preserved when a program is carried across to a new platform: The program's interface? Its usability? Its gameplay? Its aesthetic design? The underlying algorithm? The effects of the constraints of the original? And should the programmer try to improve the original? The ethos of adaptation will vary from project to project and programmer to programmer; what a programmer chooses to prioritize will help to determine the qualities of the final port and its relationship to the original program.

In this remark, a number of ports—translations—are presented. These are ports from Commodore 64 BASIC to other platforms and languages, developed specifically for this book. Other ports can be found elsewhere in this book. By striving to design accurate adaptations, and to capture qualities of the original code as well as the output, nuances of the original that might otherwise be overlooked can be revealed. Just as the variations of `10 PRINT` in the previous remark illustrate the consequences of choosing one particular set of parameters among the many that were possible on the Commodore 64, ports of `10 PRINT` can highlight the constraints and affordances of individual platforms. The ports provide a tightly focused comparison of the Commodore 64 to other systems, emphasizing the unique suitability of the Commodore 64 for this particular program.

## APPLESOFT BASIC AND TANDY COLOR BASIC

Applesoft BASIC is one of two standard BASIC implementations for the Apple II; Applesoft is the one that supports floating point math and seems very similar to Commodore 64 BASIC. The Apple II family of computers was of the same era and uses the same processor as did the Commodore 64, the MOS 6502. Applesoft BASIC, like Commodore 64 BASIC, was written by Microsoft and based on its 6502 BASIC, a version (as discussed in the chapter on BASIC) that derives from Microsoft's Altair BASIC. The Apple II computers and the Commodore 64 were really quite alike, almost as if they were siblings separated by corporate circumstance.

This makes the Apple II a good starting point for a series of `10 PRINT` ports. The same BASIC statements and keywords can be used in a version for this computer, and the same sort of scrolling will push the maze continually up the screen.

On the Apple II, however, the slash and backslash characters must serve as the maze walls, since the PETSCII diagonal-line characters are not available. The codes for those Apple II characters are not adjacent; they have the ASCII values 47 and 92. This means that a more elaborate expression for the selection of a character must be used. The first step is selecting the value 0 or 1. This first selection is accomplished in `INT(RND(1)*2)`, which in the inner expression produces a floating point number that is at least 0 and less than 2, such as 0.492332 or 1.987772; then, using INT, this value is truncated to either 0 or 1. The next step is to multiply that value by 45 and add 47 so that either 47 or 92 results. This is a reasonably simple way to make this selection, but, as with certain Commodore 64 BASIC variants, the code that is needed is more elaborate and less pleasing than in the canonical `10 PRINT`:

```
10 PRINT CHR$(47+(INT(RND(1)*2)*45)); : GOTO 10
```

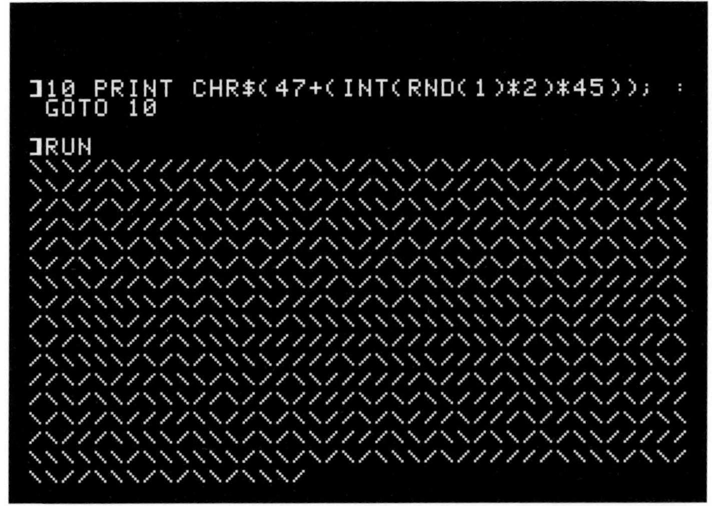


Figure 25.1

Screen capture from the Apple II port of **10 PRINT**.

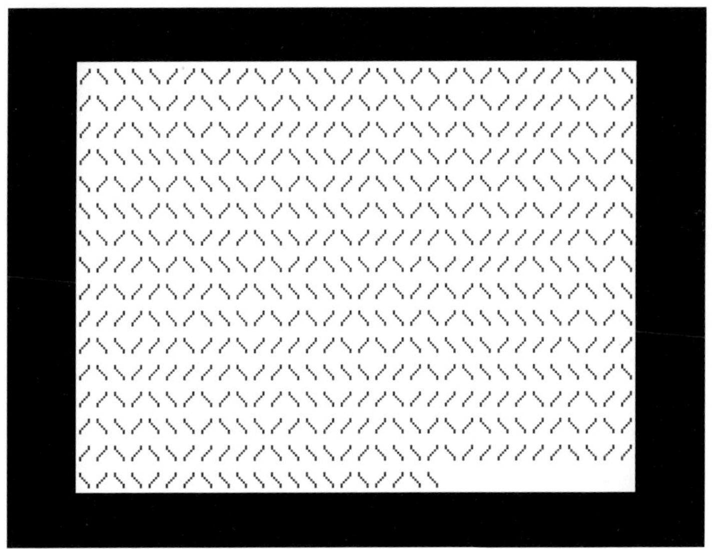

Figure 25.2

Screen capture from the TRS-80 Color Computer port of **10 PRINT**.

The output of the program is less satisfying, too (figure 25.1). Although the "/" and "\" characters on Apple II computers are exactly diagonal, they do not span the entire square that bounds a character. This means that the "walls" do not meet either horizontally or vertically. Each Apple II character is five pixels wide and seven pixels tall, so the perfect diagonals of the slash and backslash have a pixel of empty space at the top and another at the bottom. In any case, Apple II characters cannot be drawn directly against one another, as all characters on the system are printed with a one-pixel-wide space on either side of them and a one-pixel space below.

This space between characters is even more evident in the port of 10 PRINT to another competitor of the Commodore 64 in the 1980s—the TRS-80 Color Computer (or "CoCo"), sold through Radio Shack. If the Apple II was the Commodore 64's sibling, raised by another corporation, then the Color Computer, with the Motorola 6809 and a different version of Microsoft BASIC, was the eccentric cousin. Just as with Applesoft BASIC, the Color BASIC port of 10 PRINT requires the use of ASCII characters 47 and 92; one significant change, however, must be made to the program:

```
10 PRINT CHR$(47+INT(RND(0)*2)*45);:GOTO 10
```

Note the change from RND(1) to RND(0). This revision is due to the Color Computer's implementation of RND, which diverges quite a bit from that in other BASICs. In a move to make the RND command more intuitive, the TRS-80 chooses a random number between 1 and the argument, X. So RND(6) chooses a random number between 1 and 6. RND(1) in Color BASIC will only ever choose the number 1, making for a decidedly nonrandom pattern. RND(0), however, selects a floating point number between 0 and 1, which, multiplied by 2, can serve as the numerical basis for the random pattern. The execution of the program reveals, though, that randomness is not the only essential element of 10 PRINT (figure 25.2). Even when compared to the Apple II, the TRS-80's text display is poorly suited for the transformation of typographical symbols into graphical patterns. The Color Computer's slash and backslash characters each occupy a 5 × 7 region on a larger grid of 8 × 12, leaving so much space between the characters that they can never resolve themselves into the suggestion of a connected pattern, much less a maze.

While the Apple II and Color Computer had many interesting BASIC programs written for them and shares features with the Commodore 64, the way these computers handle text display means that neither can host a one-line BASIC version of `10 PRINT` that is as satisfying as the Commodore version.

## PERL AND JAVASCRIPT: MODERN ONE-LINERS

Perl and JavaScript programs were devised that are parts of `10 PRINT` and output the ASCII slash and backslash characters. The JavaScript program is chiefly interesting because it presents a graphical, or typographical, problem that is even worse than the ones seen on the Apple II and the Tandy Color Computer. The default font on a Web page, viewed in a graphical user interface browser, is proportional—different letterforms have different widths. While slash and backslash are the same width, differences in kerning mean that the pair "/\" is wider than either "//" or "\\". So the two symbols do not line up in a grid, and the result is even less like a maze.

A first version of the Perl one-liner follows; it's shown in figure 25.3:

```
while (print int(rand(2)) ? "/" : "\\") {}
```

The "\" character (the backslash) is used in combination with another character in Perl to print special characters such as the newline, which is indicated as "\n". (The same is true in JavaScript.) Because of this, it is necessary to use "\\" to print a single backslash character. This Perl port uses the `while` construct to create an infinite loop. The condition of this loop prints either "/" or "\" at random. The `print` statement, which should always succeed, will return a value of 1, corresponding to true—so the loop will always continue. The body of the `while` loop is empty; nothing else except printing a character needs to be done, and that is already accomplished within the condition. The resulting output is similar to that of the Apple II program: random slashes are produced that line up in a grid but don't meet horizontally or vertically.

There are a few ways to tweak this code to make it more like `10 PRINT` in form and to have it produce output that is more like `10 PRINT`'s. First, the somewhat obscure but more GOTO-like `redo` statement can be

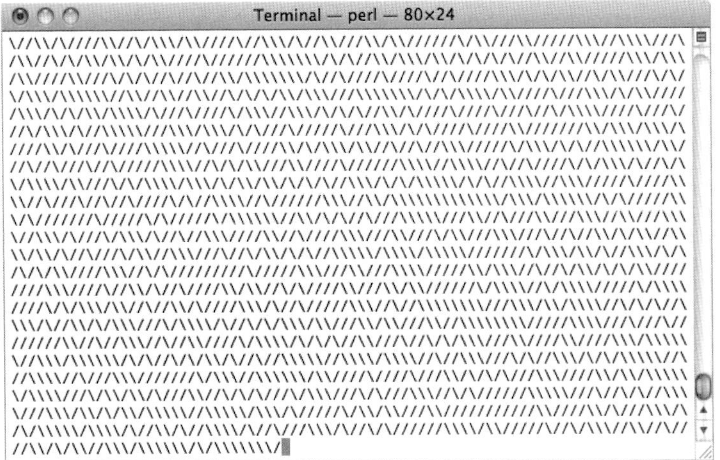


Figure 25.3

Screen capture of the ASCII Perl port of `10 PRINT`, which uses the slash and backslash to approximate the diagonal lines.

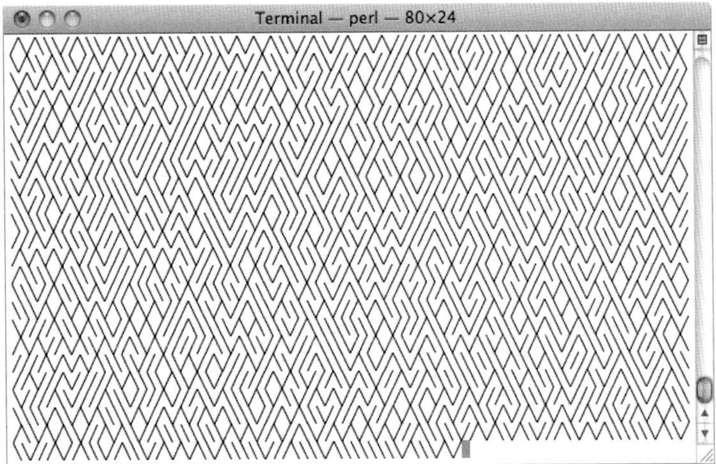


Figure 25.4

Screen capture of the Unicode Perl port of `10 PRINT`, which uses characters 9585 and 9586 to better approximate the PETSCII characters.

used, causing the program to loop back to the beginning of its code block, which is enclosed in curly braces, "{" and "}". Second, the Unicode characters 9585 and 9586 can be used to build the maze. These characters are the two diagonal lines, similar to the PETSCII characters on the Commodore 64, and like those characters they are also adjacent. This means that a trick similar to `205.5+RND(1)` can be used to randomly select between them—in this case, `9585.5+rand`. That expression is used as an argument to Perl's `chr` function, just as the original BASIC program wraps it in the `CHR$` function. Finally, to avoid the production of error messages, a statement needs to be included that tells Perl it can output characters in Unicode. That statement could go outside or inside the loop; the program just runs slightly slower, which is probably desirable, if it is placed inside and executed each time:

```
{binmode STDOUT,"utf8";print chr(9585.5+rand);redo}
```

While the original `10 PRINT` produces a maze with gaps or thin connections at each grid point, this maze (see figure 25.4) has what look like overlaps at each of these junctures. Nevertheless, the use of Unicode's similar characters does a great deal to enhance the appearance of the output.

## PATH: MAZE AS PERVERSE PROGRAM

While computer users may think of programming languages as relatively straightforward instruments used to produce increasingly complex or efficient tools and experiences, `10 PRINT` begins to show that code itself can have aesthetic features.

Some programmers choose to reject—at least for a while—the values of clarity and efficiency in programming in favor of other values. While some of the techniques such programmers use rely on the exploitation of conventions in existing, "normal" programming languages, others involve the invention of entirely new languages with their own aesthetic properties. These "weird languages" (sometimes also called "esoteric languages") test the limits of programming language design and comment on programming languages themselves. One them is the unusual-looking language called PATH.

The sort of weird languages Michael Mateas and Nick Montfort (2005) dub "minimalist" comment on the space of computation itself. As they put it, "Minimalist languages strive to achieve universality while providing the smallest number of language constructs possible. Such languages also often strive for syntactic minimalism, making the textual representation of programs minimal as well." The archetypical minimalist language is Brainfuck, which provides seven commands, each corresponding to a single character of punctuation.

Another style of weird language eschews the usual organization into lines of code and uses a two-dimensional space to hold a program's instructions. One such language is Piet, whose source code resembles abstract paintings (like those by its namesake, Piet Mondrian). Another is Befunge, which uses typographical symbols including "<," "v," and "^" to direct program flow.

PATH is a weird language that borrows from the conventions of Brainfuck and Befunge, offering a syntactically constrained language whose control flow takes place in a two-dimensional space. PATH has a natural connection to `10 PRINT` because the language uses the slash and backslash characters to control program flow. These symbols are reflectors in PATH. As the program counter travels around in 2D space, it bounces off the reflectors in the intuitive way.

In addition to "/" and "\," PATH uses "v," "^," "<," and ">" to move the flow conditionally, down, up, left, and right, if the current memory location is nonzero. Memory locations are arrayed on an infinite tape Turing style, and the program can increment and decrement the current memory focus.

Given PATH's strong typographical similarity to the output of `10 PRINT`, it is possible to implement a port of `10 PRINT` in PATH—a program that generates labyrinths by endlessly walking a labyrinth (figure 25.5).

When the program is run, the result is similar to figure 25.3. Confusing? The point of such a program, and such a programming language, is to confuse and amuse, of course. Without understanding the details of how this program works, one can still appreciate an intriguing property it has. The output of `10 PRINT` in PATH is itself a PATH program. This new program doesn't do anything very interesting; it simply moves the program counter around without producing any output. Still, it demonstrates a general idea: that programs are texts, and there is nothing to keep people from

```
/ /
\ + } } } } } + } } + } } + } + } + } + }    }   } + } +  \
/                                                         /
\ } ++++++++++++++++++++++++++++++++++++++++++++++++ \
/                                                    /
\ } +++++++++++++++++++++++++++++++ \
  / +++++++++++++++++++++++++++++++ /
  \ +++++++++++++++++++++++++++++++++ \
/         {{{{{{{{{{{{{{{{{{{        /
!
/                                                                                                                       \
                  /  - {  \          /  - {  \          /  - {  \          /  - {  \
\} } } } } } } v }^ { !/ !\ !/  { v }^ { !/ !\ !/  { v }^ { !/ !\ !/  { v }^ { !/ !\ !/    \
                       {                  {                  {                  {
               \ }     ^ + { /    \ }     ^ + { /    \ }     ^ + { /    \ }     ^ + { /
           /                                                                               /

                  /  - {  \          /  - {  \          /  - {  \          /  - {  \
           \ { v }^ { !/ !\ !/  { v }^ { !/ !\ !/  { v }^ { !/ !\ !/  { v }^ { !/ !\ !/  v  !/  \
                       {                  {                  {                  {        \ - /
               \ }     ^ + { /    \ }     ^ + { /    \ }     ^ + { /    \ }     ^ + { /


/  {{{{{{{{  v  }}}}}}}}                                                                        /
              \  {{{{{{{{                                                                                       \
   /+                         \             /+ {                        \
   \{{{{{{{{{ \                             \{{{{{{{{{ \
\ v }}}}}}}}} ^ !/ {{{{{{{{{ !\ !/       } v }}}}}}}}} ^ !/ {{{{{{{{{{ !\ !/   \
   /-                           /           /- {                          /
   \{{{{{{{{{ \                              \{{{{{{{{{ \
  \ }}}}}}}}} ^  /                         \  }}}}}}}}} ^ /
/                                                                              /
     /+ {{                          \               /+ {{{                         \
     \{{{{{{{{{ \                                   \{{{{{{{{{ \
\ }} v }}}}}}}}} ^  !/ {{{{{{{{{{{ !\ !/       }}} v }}}}}}}}} ^ !/ {{{{{{{{{{{{ !\ !/   \
      /- {{                            /             /- {{{                          /
      \{{{{{{{{{ \                                   \{{{{{{{{{ \
     \  }}}}}}}}} ^  /                            \  }}}}}}}}} ^ /
/                                                                                        /
       /+ {{{{                            \                /+ {{{{{                         \
       \{{{{{{{{{ \                                        \{{{{{{{{{ \
\ }}}} v }}}}}}}}} ^    !/ {{{{{{{{{{{{{ !\ !/      }}}}} v }}}}}}}}} ^ !/ {{{{{{{{{{{{{{ !\ !/      \
        /- {{{{                              /              /- {{{{{                           /
        \{{{{{{{{{ \                                        \{{{{{{{{{ \
      \  }}}}}}}}} ^    /                                 \  }}}}}}}}} ^ /
/                                                                                                   /
         /+ {{{{{{                            \                  /+ {{{{{{{                         \
         \{{{{{{{{{ \                                            \{{{{{{{{{ \                                    !
\ }}}}}} v }}}}}}}}} ^    !/ {{{{{{{{{{{{{{{ !\ !/      }}}}}}} v }}}}}}}}} ^ !/ {{{{{{{{{{{{{{{{ !\ !/         \
          /- {{{{{{                             /                 /- {{{{{{{                           /
          \{{{{{{{{{ \                                            \{{{{{{{{{ \
        \  }}}}}}}}} ^    /                                     \  }}}}}}}}} ^ /
/                                                                                                              /
\ }}}}}}}} v }}}}}}}}}  .  !/ {{{{{{{{{{{{{{{{{                                                                         /
          \ }}}}}}}}}} . { /
```

Figure 25.5

The PATH port of 10 PRINT, an actual computer program written in an intentionally perverse programming language.

writing programs (such as the much less perverse compilers and interpreters that are in continual use) that accept programs as input and produce programs as output.

## WHAT PORTING REVEALS

Porting a program is always an act of translation and adaptation. As such, porting reveals what in a program is particular to its source context, suggests many potential approaches to what is essential about the program, and explores how that essence may be portable to a specific target context. Each port is unique, whether to a related platform, to a modern scripting language, or even to a weird, minimalist language. Each involves different constraints, and once realized each offers different insights. Sometimes these insights are into the platform itself, such as when different implementations of randomness require a change in how a value is used or a calculation is done. At other times, the new insights may be into the syntax of a particular language, which may afford more or less elegant ways of expressing the same process. Other insights may point to the permeable boundaries between a program and its platform environment, as when the graphic qualities of a particular character are vital to a particular visual effect. Porting to radically different languages can also challenge deeper paradigmatic assumptions about a program's form and function, including how and why output is produced and whether it (in turn) becomes input of some kind. Taken together, the combined insights of many ports may produce a new, different understanding of the original source. Inhabiting the native ecosystem of its platform, articulated in the mother tongue of its language, ports clarify the original source by showing the many ways it might have been other than what it is. Notably, many of these insights are not available through token-by-token analysis of code. They require closely considered reading, writing, *and* execution of code.

Other ports of `10 PRINT` are discussed in detail later in this book. Three of these, discussed in the remark Variations in Processing, are versions of the program that elaborate on the original and are written in the system Processing. Two others ports are in assembly language, written at the lower level of machine instructions and requiring things to be implemented that are taken for granted in other ports. The first of these, also discussed in a remark, is for a system without character graphics or, indeed, without typographical characters at all: the Atari VCS. Finally, the last chapter introduces and explicates a Commodore 64 assembly version of 10 PRINT to show some of the differences between BASIC and assembly programming and to reveal more about the nature of the Commodore 64. These explorations all interrogate the canonical 10 PRINT program, asking what it means to try to write the same program differently or to try to make a program on another platform the same.

# 30
# REGULARITY

REPETITION IN SPACE
THE GRID IN MODERN ART
THE COMPUTER SCREEN
REPETITION IN TIME
REPETITION IN PROCESS
PERFORMING THE LOOP

Figure 30.1
Vera Molnar, *Untitled (Quatre éléments distribués au hasard).* Collage on cardboard, 1959, 75 × 75 cm. Paris, Centre Pompidou-CNAC-MNAM. © bpk | CNAC-MNAM | Georges Meguerditchian.

In 1959 artist Vera Molnar created *Untitled (Quatre éléments distribués au hasard),* a collage similar to `10 PRINT` (figure 30.1). A variant of the `10 PRINT` program shipped with the first Commodore 64s in 1982 (figure 30.2). And in 1987, Cyril Stanley Smith more or less recreated `10 PRINT`'s output from a reduced, random arrangement of Truchet tiles (figure 30.3). How did the same essential mazelike pattern come to appear in all of these different contexts in the twentieth century?

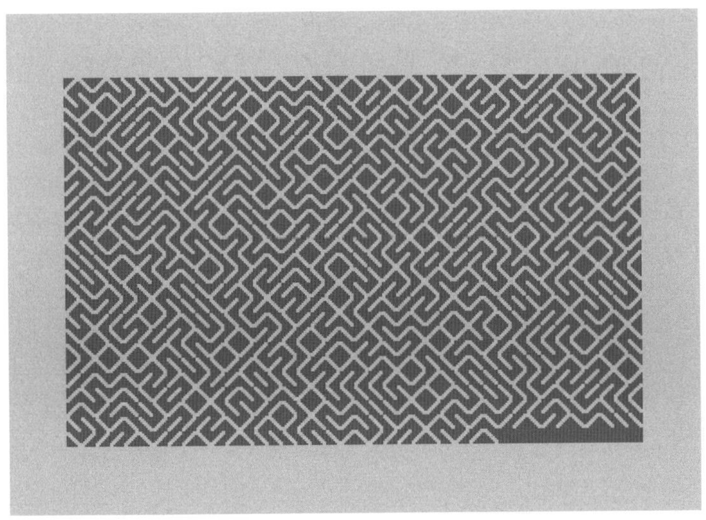

Figure 30.2
Random maze program from the *Commodore 64 User's Guide*, 1982.

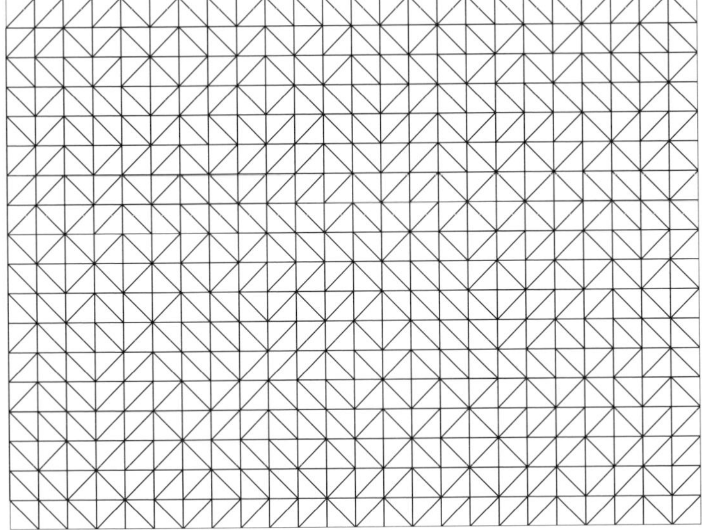

Figure 30.3
Truchet's four tiles placed in random orientations by Cyril Stanley Smith in 1987. The solid coloring was removed to show the formal connection to the `10 PRINT` pattern.

The repetitions of the 10 PRINT process are connected to two categories of artistic tradition and to the flow of control in computer programs. The first tradition within the arts is in the domain of craft, particularly pattern-based crafts such as needlework and ornamental design. The second is the creation of complex patterns using repeated procedures and a small number of elements. In this way, the aesthetic of 10 PRINT parallels experiments in painting, sculpture, sound composition, video art, performance, experimental animation, and dance. In both cases, these artistic practices owe their success to factors that also make 10 PRINT compelling: the continual repetition of a simple rhythmic procedure or rule across a regular space or time signature creating a complex and stimulating gestalt. In its minimalist and constructivist strains the world of art confronts the constraints and regularity of the *technē* of programming, which makes room for a formal definition of a repeating process that a computer can carry out. In all of its newfangled (for the 1980s) sophistication, 10 PRINT ties the computer to the homespun tradition of handicraft: stitching, sewing, and weaving.

This intersection of design craft, art, and computation is not accidental, for 10 PRINT is a demonstration of the generative qualities of repeated procedure. 10 PRINT was written and published at a time when the art world was turning to explore the constraints and possibilities of the systematization of creativity in an age of Taylorism and Fordism, of which the computational machine is itself an expression. Situating 10 PRINT not only within twentieth-century art, but also in the larger traditions of formal experimentation and craft culture can help to explain how the personal computer is a site of procedural craft.

This chapter explores the first of two formal aspects of the 10 PRINT program that give it its compelling visual power. This chapter focuses on regularity, while the next one deals with randomness. Although the pattern of 10 PRINT cannot be established at a glance, the program is nothing if not regular. It works regularly in space, time, and process—and each of these aspects of regularity is examined in the discussion that follows. Spatial regularity is considered, beginning with tilings, continuing through the history of the grid, and ending with a discussion of the computer screen. Artistic repetition in time, particularly in music and performance, is considered next. Then, repeating processes and the programming constructs that support them are discussed.

## REPETITION IN SPACE

In a classic, provocative text, *The Sense of Order*, E. H. Gombrich (1994) wrestles with the tensions between pleasing repetition and uninteresting redundancy. As he reflects on pavement designs he notes the pleasure in encountering one whose pattern cannot be fully grasped. Gombrich explains this desire for variation or complexity in terms of the information theory emerging at the time, which posits that information increases in step with unpredictability (9). He goes on to speculate that the viewer examines patterns by trying to anticipate what comes next. "Delight," he writes, "lies somewhere between boredom and confusion" (9). Consider, again, the Labyrinth at Chartres as one such balance of the two.

`10 PRINT` no doubt offers similar delights, thanks to its creation of a complex pattern from a simple random alternation. As Gombrich later argues, the greatest novelties computers bring to visual design and variation are not only their ability "to follow any complex rule of organization but also to introduce an exactly calculated dose of randomness" (1994, 94). In this view, computers prove to be entrancing weavers, and the design of `10 PRINT`, as a work of pattern rather than paths, may be less like the work of Daedalus than that of Arachne.

Patterns are inextricably tied to a process of repetition. This notion is clearly demonstrated in Gombrich's commentary on "the hierarchical principle" by which units are "grouped to form larger units, which in turn can easily fit together into larger wholes" (1994, 8), or a *gestalt*. The sum of the pattern then is the result of a process. This interrelationship of pattern, perceived whole, and process becomes clear in his discussion of paving and of various methods for selecting stones. By extension, visual design relies on the process of repeating patterns across space, even if these patterns are not drawn as individual units. The regulated backdrop or foundation of these orderly patterns in Euclidean space is the grid.

The grid provides a framework within which human intuition and invention can operate and that it can subvert. Within the chaos of nature, regular patterns provide a contrast and promise of order. From early patterns on pottery to geometric mosaics in Roman baths, people have long used grids to enhance their lives with decoration. In Islamic culture, the focus on mathematics and prohibition on representational images led to the most advanced grid systems of the time, used to decorate buildings and religious texts. Grids have also long been used as the basis for architecture and urban planning. For example, it is impossible to imagine New York, the one-time city of the future, without the regular grid of upper Manhattan. (Broadway breaks this grid in ways that form many of the city's most notable public spaces.) The grid is also the basis for our most intellectual play, from chess to go, whether the design submits to or reacts against it.

The grid has proved essential to the design of computers from the grid of vacuum tubes on the ENIAC (1946) to the latest server farms that feed data to the Internet. A new era of more reliable computing was spawned in the 1950s by a grid of ferrite rings called core memory (figure 30.4). This technology works by addressing each ring on the grid to set its charge to clockwise or counterclockwise to store one bit of information. Because the information is stored as a magnetic force, it maintains its state with or without power. The grid is an essential geometry of computation.

The two-dimensional regularity of the grid is essential to the impact of `10 PRINT`, as removing a single character from the program reveals. Taking out the semicolon that indicates that each character should be drawn immediately to the right of the previous one, the symbol that wraps the program's output continually rightward across the screen, makes the importance of the grid clear (see figure 30.5):

```
10 PRINT CHR$(205.5+RND(1)) : GOTO 10
```

As a column of diagonal lines, the output does not form a maze and the vibrant pattern that encourages our eyes to dance across the screen is not established (figure 30.5). The essential process of `10 PRINT` in time is a single, zero-dimensional coin flip to pick one of two characters; when this recurs in time, it becomes a one-dimensional stream of diagonal lines that either flows quickly down the left side (if the semicolon is omitted) or moves right to wrap around to the next position below the current line and to the left. The visual interest of this program results from wrapping this one-dimensional stream of tiles into the two-dimensional grid.

### Truchet Tiles

Imagine the diagonal character graphics in `10 PRINT` are painted on a set of square ceramic tiles, of the sort used for flooring. Each tile is painted

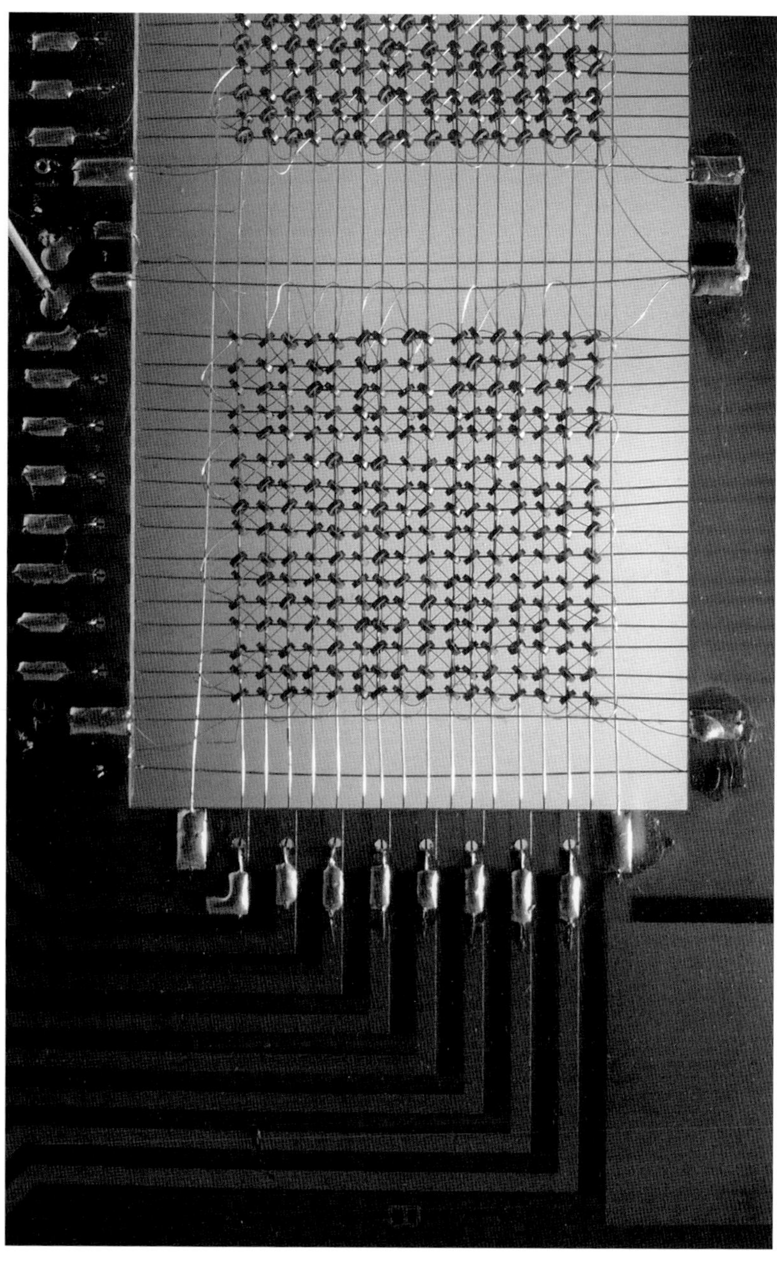

Figure 30.4
Magnetic core memory.

Figure 30.5
This screen capture from the 10 PRINT variation without the semicolon shows the importance of the two-dimensional grid as a defining characteristic of the program.

with a black diagonal line dividing two white triangles. A tile can be rotated in two orientations, so that the diagonal line appears to be a backslash or a forward slash. Now imagine painting one of the two triangles black. Each tile can now be rotated in four different orientations, like a black arrow pointing at each of four corners. Repeatedly placing tiles down in the same orientation will create a pattern (figure 30.6). Two tiles can be placed next to each other to create one of sixteen unique formations, and laying down any such pair repeatedly will again produce patterns. Indeed, any unique grouping of tiles (whether 2 × 1, 4 × 4, etc.) can serve as a building block for larger regularity.

Now, imagine a whole floor or tapestry covered with a regular pattern of these repeating tiles. This thought exercise suggests the power of the Truchet tile, so named because the Dominican priest Sebastien Truchet first described what he called the "fecundity of these combinations" in 1704, after experimenting with some ceramic tiles he came across at a building site for a château near Orléans (Smith and Boucher 1987, 374).

Matching a single Truchet tile with another, and another, and another, and so on, a designer is able to create an incredible array of patterns. The interplay between the direction of each tile and the varying repetition of black and white—of positive and negative—produces symmetrical designs that can range from grid-like patterns to mesmerizing, almost three-dimensional illusions. Unlike earlier, Islamic patterns or Celtic designs, which both relied on multiple-sized shapes, the Truchet tile uses only a single size and a single shape (Smith and Boucher 1987, 378). In his original 1704 essay, Truchet provides examples of thirty different patterns, barely evoking the aesthetic possibilities of his tiles, though he notes that he "found too great a number to report them all" (374). Truchet's work would be the inspiration for a later book, Doüat's modestly named *Methode pour faire une infinite de desseins differents . . .* [*Method for Making an Infinity of Different Designs . . .*] which in turn had a considerable impact on eighteenth-century European art (373).

Yet all of Truchet's and Doüat's examples are regular patterns, symmetrical and repetitive. The historian of science Cyril Stanley Smith observed in 1987 that even more compelling designs can be generated from Truchet tiles if dissymmetries are introduced. What happens when the regularity of a Truchet pattern is interrupted by randomness? Smith provides one example, a block of Truchet tiles arranged at random (figure 30.3). The lattice of the basic grid is still visible, but randomness has made its mark, leaving imperfections that disrupt any nascent pattern. Unlike the symmetrical examples Truchet and Doüat give, there is no resolution to the structure. The center cannot hold, and neither can the margins. Smith next pushes the limits of the Truchet tiles' regularity by omitting solid coloring from the tiles, leaving only the black diagonal line. The four possible orientations of any given tile are then reduced to two.

These modified Truchet tiles generate a design that looks unmistakably like the output of `10 PRINT`, a program published a half decade before Smith and Boucher's article. The grid still remains—indicating the edges of each tile—but the diagonals no longer seem to bound positive or negative space. Instead, they appear to be the walls of a maze, twisty little passages, all different. In this Truchet tile-produced artifact the dynamic between regularity and its opposite come into play, suggesting that regularity is not an aspect of design that exists in isolation, but rather can only be defined by exceptions to it, by those moments when the regular becomes irregular. Rather than celebrating that `10 PRINT` "scooped" Smith,

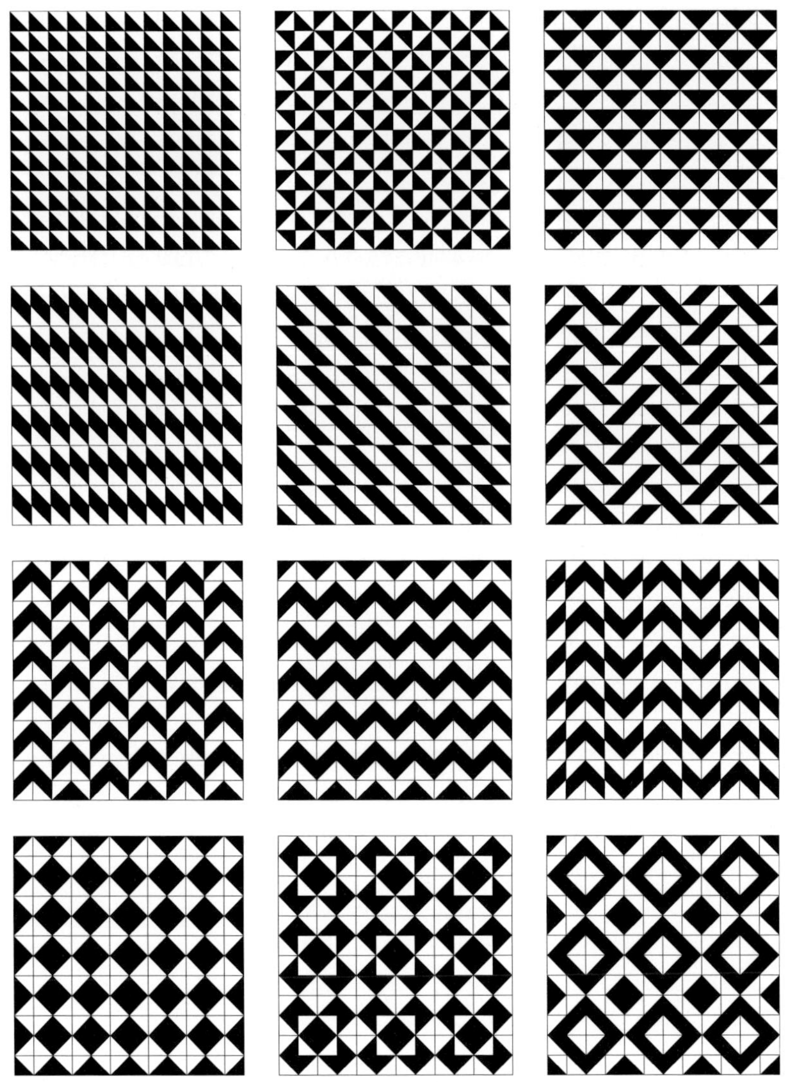

Figure 30.6

Patterns from Sébastien Truchet's "Mémoire sur les combinaisons," 1704. Each 12 × 12 pattern redrawn above is constructed from smaller patterns using one tile design, half black and half white cut across the diagonal.

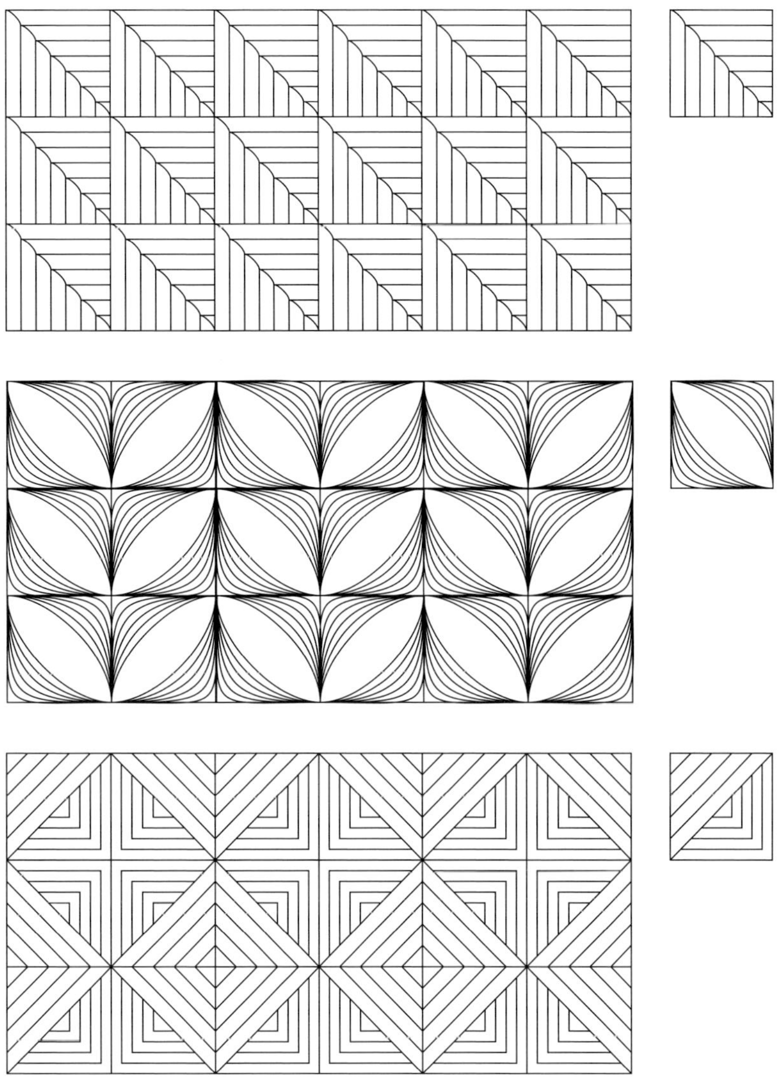

Figure 30.7

Examples of litema patterns from South Africa. These patterns are typically etched into the plastered mud walls on the exterior of homes. The patterns are constructed by repeating and rotating a single square unit.

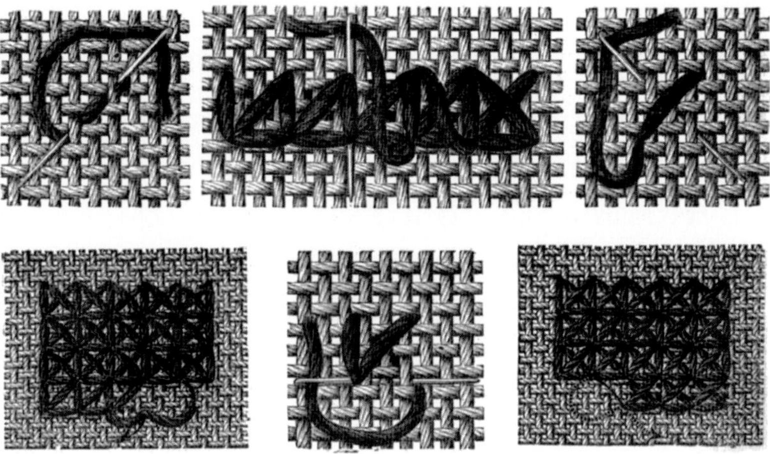

Figure 30.8

Examples of stitchwork from The Square Pattern technique from *The Young Ladies' journal Complete guide to the work-table.*

it seems appropriate to note that there are several ways up the mountain—or into the maze—of this particular random and regular pattern; one was discovered at Commodore, another by taking a mathematical perspective on tiling patterns and their aesthetics.

## Textiles and Craft

The experiments of Truchet and Doüat did not introduce the idea of creating patterns out of simple variations on shapes. Such practice is commonplace across many forms of design, particularly in the realm of ornament, where both regular and irregular patterns have long been created. Franz Boas documented compelling examples of theme and variation of Peruvian weavers, for example (cited in Gombrich 1994, 72). The Kuba of Zaire create patterns of a complexity that has puzzled electrical engineers, patterns with the mazelike passageways of `10 PRINT` and yet of a far greater intricacy (Huang et al. 2005). Or consider the murals of the Sotho women of South Africa, decorative geometric murals known as *litema* (figure 30.7). This technique, documented as early as 1861, involves assembling networks of squares made of painted mud and etched with fingers and sticks

(Gerdes 1998, 87–90). In fact, the decorative arts have long held this secret to 10 PRINT. Such techniques are detailed in the examples of fancy work in the 1885 *The Young Ladies' journal Complete guide to the work-table* (figure 30.8). The examples therein demonstrate the orthogonal basis for stitchwork that is evocative of the grid of the computer screen.

The hundreds of techniques define patterns ranging from simple grids to complex emergent patterns. As Mark Marino argues elsewhere (2010), these pattern books and instructive texts, primarily aimed at young women, provided models of fundamental processes similar to the role of the computer manuals and magazines such as *RUN*. Many of the techniques result from a repeated process with instructions, similar to that indicated by a computer program. For example, the Square Pattern technique (figure 30.8) in the Fancy Netting chapter is defined as a pair of operations that are repeated:

> No. 6.— SQUARE PATTERN
>
> For this pattern:—
> 1st Row: Work one plain row.
> 2nd Row: One ordinary stitch, and twist the thread twice round for the large square. Repeat to the end of the row.
>
> The first and second rows are repeated alternately. Arrange the stitches so that a long stitch always comes under a short stitch.

Such examples demonstrate that while the systematic theorization of patterns such as the one produced by 10 PRINT may emerge periodically, the production of those patterns is deeply woven into the traditions of decorative craft. The fundamental role of shared techniques for process and pattern place computer programming squarely in the realm of *technē*, artistic craft. As in the *Commodore 64 User's Manual*, this text promotes the execution of a set of instructions collected as a technique. On the surface, the parallels between teaching needlecraft and programming are striking. The programmers, however, are not taught to repeat the procedure but instead, initially, to repeat a formal description of the procedure by typing it into the machine—which then does the repeating for them. It is the very automation of the process that makes 10 PRINT possible; the program operates less like handy stitching and more like the machinery of the Jacquard Loom.

Prior to that loom, during or near the second century BCE, China gave birth to a loom "that made it possible to create a pattern in fabric . . . called a drawloom because [it] allowed the warp threads to be drawn up individually to create the design to be woven" (10). That loom, however, was irregular: "the arrangement of the individual warp threads was different for every single row of weaving" (10). By contrast, the loom designed by Joseph-Marie Jacquard was regular and programmable (12). Such a machine relied on an exacting degree of regularity. Of course, much has been made of the Jacquard Loom as the prototypical computer, for example James Essinger's book *Jacquard's Web: How a Hand-Loom Led to the Birth of the Information Age* (2004). The core similarity in these early accounts were the punch cards, which were automatically applied to the control system and which served as patterns for the loom to follow. Earlier punch card looms have been discovered and attributed to J. B. Falcon, B. Bouchon and Vaucanson, whose invention of a mechanical duck is a bit more widely known (Zemanek 1976, 16). According to Essinger, Falcon's punch cards were "clumsily made and unreliable" (36).

Commercial-grade textiles require up to four thousand cards strung together—a far cry from the two statements on the one line of `10 PRINT` (figure 30.9). The cards are applied to a bar, an "elongated cube," full of "hundreds of identical holes . . . to accommodate the tips of needles," which are raised according to the selections on the punch card. As the bar turns with each pick of the shuttle, it moves down the material as if moving down a computer screen. Regularity made it possible for the Jacquard Loom to draw its intricate patterns. But the use of the cards as a pure pattern and the inability to regulate the flow of control meant that patterns have to be defined exhaustively rather than through concise programs. In other words, the number of cards is proportional to the size of the pattern being woven. While needlework instructions demonstrate the role of repeated process and pattern over somewhat regulated space, the loom regulates time and space without, in effect, repeating the process.

`10 PRINT` can be imagined as the complete method of craft programmed into the computer—as it was not fully programmed into the loom. The loop offers a way for the weavers of the computer screen to shift their emphasis from a fixed template, traversed once, to a more intricate

Figure 30.9

Punch card-operated loom at the Sjølingstad Uldvarefabrik in Sjølingstad, Norway. Courtesy of Lars Olaussen, Creative Commons Attribution-NonCommercial-ShareAlike 2.0 Generic.

model of process. `10 PRINT` demonstrates the power of the computational machine to rapidly prototype a repeated pattern, and since it executes the pattern itself, the incipient programmer is freed to experiment with variations and extensions of that process.

## THE GRID IN MODERN ART

In the 1960s and 1970s, artists moved away from abstract expressionism, the dominant current of the 1950s, and its preference for raw emotion. Newer movements such as op-art and minimalism along with the continued line of constructivism in Europe engendered a body of rational, calculated visual art that utilized grids and even spacing to define order. A tour through any major American modern art museum will reveal Frank Stella's canvases of regular lines, Ad Reinhardt's hard-edge grids of barely distinguishable tones, Carl Andre's grids of metal arranged on the floor, Donald Judd's regularly spaced steel fabrications, Dan Flavin's florescent matrices, and Agnes Martin's exquisite, subtle grids on canvas. This list could continue for pages as it moves forward in history; the point has no doubt been made. This American tendency to move toward minimal forms was expressed well by Ad Reinhardt in "Art-as-Art" in 1962: "The one object of fifty years of abstract art is to present art-as-art and as nothing else, to make it into the one thing it is only, separating and defining it more and more, making it purer" (Rose 1991, 53).

In Europe at the same time, a massive number of artists were working with grid systems, and they were often doing so with more explicit focus and rigor. This energy was frequently channeled into groups that formed in different cities. For example, there was GRAV (François Morellet, Julio Le Parc, et al.) in Paris, ZERO (Heinz Mack, Otto Piene, et al.) based in Düsseldorf and extending a wide net across Europe, The Systems Group (Jeffrey Steele, Peter Lowe, et al.) in London, and the Allianz in Zurich (Max Bill, Richard Paul Lohse, et al.). The most iconic artist to work with grids might be the optical artist Victor Vasarely, whose grids were mesmerizingly distorted. His work was so systemized that he invented a notation system to enable a team of assistants to assemble his works using instructions and modular, prefabricated colored pieces. Although it is difficult to discern by just looking at the work, there was tension between the artists who worked toward the primacy of mathematical form and those who maintained a desire to imbue subjectivity and emotion in their geometric compositions.

In critiquing of the former category of art, Ferreira Gullar, a Brazilian poet and essayist, wrote the 1959 "Neo-Concrete Manifesto" declaring that it was dangerous for art to be concerned only with "objective problems of composition, of chromatic reactions, of the development of serial rhythms, of lines or surfaces" (Zelevanksy 2004, 57). Gullar's manifesto harkens back and reimagines works of the early twentieth century by artists such as Wassily Kandinsky, Kasimir Malevich, and Alexander Rodchenko. Within the specific context of the grid, pioneers Piet Mondrian, Theo Van Doesburg, and other artists affiliated with De Stijl abandoned representation entirely. Van Doesburg et al. coined the term "concrete art" to categorize works that are conceived without reference to nature and symbolism. The manifesto "The Basis of Concrete Painting" published in April 1930 stated, "The work of art should be fully conceived and spiritually formed before it is produced. It should not contain any natural form, sensuality, or sentimentality. We wish to exclude lyricism, dramaticism, symbolism and so forth" (Fabre and Wintgens Hotte 2009, 187). Van Doesburg continued in "Elementarism (The Elements of the New Painting)" from 1932: "One must not hesitate to surrender our personality. The universal transcends it. . . . The approach to universal form is based on calculation of measure and number" (187). Representative works such as Mondrian's *Composition with Red, Blue, Black, Yellow, and Gray* (1921) and Van Doesburg's *Counter-Composition VI* (1925) were composed exclusively with orthogonal lines to form a grid. Works from this time also experiment with rotating the grid 45 degrees to create a more dynamic composition. This formal technique manifests itself, of course, in `10 PRINT`.

While the `10 PRINT` program came out of the computer culture and not the art world, it has an uncanny visual resemblance to prior works of twentieth-century art. Paul Klee, a Bauhaus professor and highly influential artist (1879–1940), produced works in the 1920s that seemed to resume Truchet's and Doüat's experiments. In his concise *Pedagogical Sketchbook,* published in 1925, Klee presents his thoughts on quantitative structure, rhythm, repetition, and variation. His *Variations (Progressive Motif),* painted in 1927, demonstrated his theories as a visual composition. He divided the 40cm-square canvas into a grid of nine units, where each unit contains a pattern of parallel lines, with some exceptions, which run vertical, horizontal, or diagonal. More insight into this painting is found in his notebooks, as published in *The Thinking Eye* in 1964. Klee discusses the difference between natural and artificial measurement as the difference between idiosyncratic and rational order. More important, he discusses tension and dynamic density through the linear and progressive spacing of parallel lines. Through these visual contrasts in *Variations,* Klee explores the same aesthetics questions that can arise from `10 PRINT`. First he created an artificial grid to work within; then he populated each square with ordered but variable patterns. Klee didn't have the advantage of motion that is afforded to `10 PRINT`, but he simulated it through the expansion and contraction of parallel lines within his grid.

In France, a group of like-minded artists within and around GRAV (Groupe de Recherche d'Art Visuel) were exploring variations within grids. François Molnar and Vera Molnar worked on a series of images in 1959 that presented a visual system strikingly similar to `10 PRINT`. In the essay "Towards Science in Art," published in the anthology *DATA: Directions in Art, Theory and Aesthetics* in 1968, François Molnar published the images *Simulation d'une série de divisions de Mondrian à partir de trois au hasard* and *Quatre éléments au hasard.* Both are 24 × 24 unit grids with one of a few possible forms painted into each grid unit with black gouache. As the titles suggest, a random process defines the elements in each square. Their *Composition Stochastique* of the same year systematizes the random component by producing a modular set of two elements—left and right diagonals that are placed within a 10 × 10 unit grid. In the illustrations for the essay, they feature a 1 percent, 5 percent, 30 percent, and 50 percent ratio of left to right diagonal lines to show the result of chaos intruding upon order. Given that this is a 100 unit grid, these percentages correspond to precisely 1, 5, 30, and 50 units in each figure. In the 50 percent figure, the only substantive difference with our `10 PRINT` program is the variation on the core elements. So, just as a mathematician independently described the output of `10 PRINT` in 1987, a team of artists working in Paris produced the fundamental algorithm for `10 PRINT` in 1959—twenty-three years prior to the printing of the *Commodore 64 User's Guide.*

In her 1990 essay entitled "Inconceivable Images," Vera Molnar wrote that she was thinking about *Composition Stochastique* as a computer program, because she had access to a machine:

> To genuinely systematize my research series I initially used a technique which I called machine imaginaire. I imagined I had a computer. I designed a programme and then, step by step, I realized simple, limited series which were completed within, meaning they did not exclude a single possible combination of form. As soon as possible I replaced the imaginary computer, the make-believe machine by a real one.

Across the Atlantic in the 1960s the American artist Sol LeWitt embarked on decades of work exploring grids and regular structures. In 1968, LeWitt started making drawings directly on walls, rather than on paper or canvas that would be placed on the wall. In this return to the scale of frescos, his drawings within grids integrated into architecture to transform the space (Singer 1984). His *Wall Drawing 291* from 1976 is a striking work, with a strong similarity to `10 PRINT`. Instead of the binary decision within `10 PRINT`, LeWitt's drawing allows for horizontal and vertical lines, to create four choices for each grid element. LeWitt's work is encoded as an algorithm—another similarity with `10 PRINT`. A difference is that the instructions are in English, rather than BASIC:

> 291. A 12" (30cm) grid covering a black wall. Within each 12" (30cm) square, a vertical, horizontal, diagonal right or diagonal left line bisecting the square. All squares are filled. (The direction of the line in each square is determined by the draftsman.)

This grid-based wall drawing wasn't an isolated work within LeWitt's output. He created dozens of similar drawings, each with slightly different rules and allowing for varied lines including arcs and dotted lines.

While many artists and critics in the twentieth century were clearly obsessed with the grid, not all have celebrated it. The critic Rosalind Krauss put the grid into a different context in her 1979 essay "Grids" (Krauss 1979). She acknowledges the proliferation of the grid but criticizes it as a dead end: "It is not just the sheer number of careers that have been devoted to the exploration of the grid that is impressive, but the fact that never could exploration have chosen less fertile ground." She continues, "The grid declares the space of art to be at once autonomous and autotelic." Through pursuing pure visual exploration like variations on grids, Krauss argued that

## SCREENSAVERS AND COMPUTER DREAMS

While no one has ever claimed that **10 PRINT** might be used as a screensaver to prevent phosphor burn-in on CRT monitors and televisions, its noninteractive, endlessly looping nature coupled with its pleasing and changing image make it a close cousin to this type of program. If one had to place **10 PRINT** into a familiar software category, "screensaver" would not be a bad one to choose.

The earliest screensaver dates to 1968, when researchers at Stanford University programmed the text "Take Me, I'm Yours" to appear at random locations on an open terminal screen of Stanford's Artificial Intelligence Lab's time-sharing system, signaling the terminal was free to use. In 1973, engineers at the famed Xerox PARC lab created screensavers with bouncing and zooming graphics, moving screensavers beyond mere text (Davenport 2002, 65). In the early 1980s, commercial screensavers followed, such as Berkeley Systems' bestselling *After Dark* collection. By the height of the screensaver craze in 1996, the design of computer monitors made phosphor burn-in nearly impossible. Yet screensavers lived on in roles that went beyond their original utilitarian or aesthetic function. The SETI (Search for Extraterrestrial Intelligence) project released software for PCs that harnessed unused computer cycles to process radio waves from outer space—all the while displaying a screensaver on the computer display. Along different lines, Nancy Davenport created the "May Day" screensaver that captures the repetitive and often image-based nature of contemporary political protests.

There are provocative parallels of the screensaver in the history of art. David Reinfurt (2009) considers a wide variety of moving visual and mechanical pieces, including Marcel Duchamp's *Precision Optics* projects, Alexander Calder's mobiles, phased oscilloscope displays, Brion Gysin and Ian Sommerville's *Dreammachine*, and generated visual and sound art. Reinfurt sought to find interesting connections and not to trace a genealogy or demonstrate influence, but there appears to be a compelling pre-war antecedent of these programs.

Perhaps the most intriguing protoscreensavers are found even earlier, in the form of Duchamp's 1933 *Rotoreliefs*. This set of six discs, each printed on both sides with offset lithography, allowed the purchaser to do something with a 33 RPM turntable when it was not being used for its primary purpose: listening to music. Of course, the disc caused additional wear on one's turntable and did not "save" it, but screensavers have seldom been truly valued as savers. Just as a screensaver pack offers several options to suit the mood of the non-computer-using viewer, *Rotoreliefs* offered twelve options for the viewer, the nonlistener. One side of the third disc features "Poisson Japonais" and—just as the screensaver would later make the monitor into a simulation of a fish tank—makes the turntable into a fish bowl.

This twist on the electronic device (initially the turntable, later the television or computer monitor) calls attention to its being a piece of furniture; it also simulates the activity of a living creature using electricity and technology. It shows us our powerful media technologies made mute, circling, and amusingly off-kilter. The relationship to technology that is suggested by the aquarium screensaver (or fish Rotorelief) is one of odd juxtaposition and low-key looping motion, probably not far off from the effect of spinning a bicycle wheel that has been fixed in a stool.

One very emblematic screensaver combines life and technology in an even more curious way. In Berkeley Systems' *After Dark 2.0*, the "Flying Toasters" screensaver features toasters flitting across the screen using their small (birdlike) wings. The toaster, that single-purpose device used only to cause bread to undergo the Maillard reaction, drifts lazily through space alongside . . . pieces of toast. This screensaver suggests that androids *do* dream of electric sheep and that computers, when they snooze, have visions of lower forms of technology in flight. The *After Dark 2.0* toasters, remarkably, are not pure technological artifacts—they are cyborg toasters with organic wings. While the scene they take part in is amusing, it also at least risks calling attention to the limitations of the computer, which, despite its general-purpose capabilities, does not help to prepare food, is entirely inorganic, and, of course, does not fly. The computer may be capable of symbolic manipulations and machine dreams, but there are realms into which it cannot go, realms towards which it is left to aspire. Perhaps all of this is not imagined by the average computer nonuser observing toasters in flight, but any of it which is will contribute to the absurdity of the image and the pleasure of the onlooker.

Some screensavers create very abstract patterns that have no simple interpretation, even as something like an abstract maze. Others, like the early Windows "Starfield" and the Windows 95 "Maze" (which shows movement through a 3D, RPG-like maze) suggest that the computer is a vehicle for exploration. These screensavers live alongside those that play with our perceptions of life, inviting us to think about how technologies relate to creatures like fish and birds. But in addition to all of these, there are screensavers that accumulate structures in a way that suggest industrious, technical production. The Windows 95 "Pipes" screensaver is a fairly famous example. It assembles 3D tangles of multicolored pipes which become impossibly dense and intricate. This screensaver does more plumbing work in a few minutes than Nintendo's Mario has done in his lifetime. The busy visuals show that the computer is hard at work, even though its user is not interacting with it. While the image is pleasing to look at, it also projects a more serious image than the frivolous flying toaster or simulated fish tank.

While 10 PRINT is extremely abstract, its generation process seems to be one of furious and constant construction. 10 PRINT suggests that the computer is a maker of structures, is tireless at producing these at a regular rate, and can create patterns that are both pleasing to view and perplexing to walk through. While the Windows 95 "Maze" screensaver provides the viewpoint of Theseus (or perhaps the Minotaur), 10 PRINT shows us the maze as seen by Daedalus: from the mind's eye of the architect, the viewer shares the imagination of a structure that is continually in the process of being built.

the visual arts abandoned narrative and discourse and moved into cultural isolation.

During the era of our 10 PRINT program, in wake of the Vietnam war and social movements of the late 1960s and early 1970s, the larger emphases within visual arts communities had moved away from minimalism and constructivism (and their variants) to focus back on expressive and realistic painting and the emerging acceptance of photography. The visual work created for early home computers and games systems like the Atari VCS and Commodore 64, however, were highly constrained by the technical limitations of the hardware and therefore had more in common with the visual art of prior decades.

A chief explanation for these uncanny similarities is the grid itself. In "Designing Programmes," the Swiss designer Karl Gerstner (1964) asks, "Is the grid a programme? Let me put it more specifically: if the grid is considered as a proportional regulator, a system, it is a programme par excellence." Gerstner's encounters with the computer led him to theorize the regulated space as a program itself. The grid systematizes artistic creation even as it presents a challenging and yet generative platform for experimentation, whether on canvas, the dance floor, or a computer screen.

## THE COMPUTER SCREEN

While the traditions of twentieth-century art and earlier craft traditions are significant for `10 PRINT`, the program functions the way it does because of the circumstances of technology, the history of the Commodore 64's display, and the types of regularity it supports. Again, the grid acts as a program to determine the final output.

The Commodore 64's video image is a grid 320 pixels wide and 200 pixels tall. This accommodates an array of characters or, in the terminology of Commodore 64 hi-res graphics, attribute cells. Specifically, the grid is 40 attribute cells wide and 25 high. (There are other graphics modes that offer advantages, but for understanding 10 PRINT, this array of characters or attribute cells is most important.) The 40 × 25 grid contains exactly 1,000 characters, each represented by a byte. This fits nicely into one kilobyte (which equals 1024 bytes)—in fact, it is the largest grid that is forty characters wide and occupies 1024 bytes or less.

Economically and conveniently, the Commodore 64 could be taken out of its box and hooked to an ordinary television. It was an idea that could be seen in Steve Wozniak's Apple I, introduced in April 1976. Later, the more widespread Apple II could also be connected to a television if one used an inexpensive RF modulator, purchased separately. (This component was left off the Apple II as a workaround; the FCC would not otherwise approve the computer, which would have produced too much interference.) The Apple II was the main precedent in home computing—other early home computers such as the TRS-80 Model II and Commodore PET had built-in monitors—but the idea was not original to Apple. At Atari, television engineer and employee #1 Al Alcorn had designed a *Pong* cabinet that, rather than using an expensive commercial CRT (cathode ray tube), incorporated an ordinary black-and-white television that was initially bought from a retail store. Wozniak, who did the original design for the Atari arcade game *Breakout*, knew about this trick of using a TV as a monitor. Videogame consoles (including Atari's 1977 VCS, later called the

Atari 2600, and the Magnavox Odyssey by Ralph Baer, introduced in 1972) would typically hook to televisions, too.

The rectangular form of the television image had its origins in the movie screen, which was rectangular due to the material nature of film and apparently obtained its 4:3 aspect ratio thanks to a gesture by Thomas Edison, one which resulted in a frame that was four perforations high. While the aspect ratio of film changed and diversified over the years, television in the United States (standardized in the NTSC format in 1953) and many computer monitors, through the 1980s and 1990s, used the 4:3 ratio.

Although composite monitors were available for the Commodore 64, the relationship between that system and the television was clear and was the default for those setting up their computer and hooking it up to a display. For a Commodore 64 purchased in the United States, the system's video output usually terminated in a NTSC television. But the computer display did not begin there: it has a heritage that included at least two output methods, ones that seem unusual today.

As one of this book's ten coauthors has noted, "Early interaction with computers happened largely on paper: on paper tape, on punch cards, and on print terminals and teletypewriters, with their scroll-like supplies of continuous paper for printing output and input both" (Montfort 2004). The standard output devices for computers through much of the 1970s were print terminals and teletypes. Output was not typically produced on pages of the sort that come from today's laser printers, but on scrolls of standard or thermal paper. The form factor for such output was not a standard 8½ × 11-inch page, but an essentially endless scroll that was typically 80 columns wide.

Teletypes were used to present the results of the first BASIC programs written at Dartmouth in the 1960s, and they were the typical means of interacting with important early programs such as *Eliza* and *Adventure*. With such a system for output, there was no need for an automated means of saving and viewing the "scrollback"—a user could actually pick up the scroll of output and look at it. Of course, this sort of output device meant that animation and other effects specific to video were impossible.

An argument has been advanced that the modern computer screen also has an important heritage in the round CRT display of the radar screen (Gere 2006). The SAGE early warning system, the PDP-1, and the system on which Douglas Engelbart did the "mother of all demos" all sported round CRTs, as did early televisions. It is notable that the first two systems that may have been videogames in the modern sense, *Tennis for Two* by William Higginbotham and *Spacewar* by Steve "Slug" Russell, Martin "Shag" Graetz, Alan Kotok, and others were both created for circular CRT displays. While radar and some other images were actually round, as the early cathode ray tube was, the television signal and the page were not. What was, for radar, a radial display eventually gave way in computing to the rectangular, grid format that was adhered to by both page and television image.

## REPETITION IN TIME

While `10 PRINT` would be impossible without the regularity of space, it would also be wholly other without regularity of time and process. The program is as much the product of ordered isometric shapes across a grid as it is the repeated placement of those shapes. Gombrich notes that "Everything . . . points to the fact that temporal and spatial orders converge in our experience. No wonder language speaks of patterns in time and of rhythms in space" (1994, 10). He continues to examine simple mechanical temporal rhythms from the pendulum's swing to the turn of the cog. As a bridging example between spatiality and temporality, he notes the way a regular configuration of stairs' height and depth in a staircase lead to a regular climb up the steps.

As Gombrich develops the notion of temporal repetition and regularity, he quickly transitions into a discussion of process. Whether a clock ticking or a person climbing the stairs, the temporal regularity is the result of a repeated process. Gombrich then moves to a discussion of work, by referencing K. Bucher's *Work and Rhythm,* which insists "on the need for timed movement in the execution of joint tasks," for example workers loading bricks onto wheelbarrows (Gombrich 1994, 10). The ticking clock does more than set the hours of labor on the factory floor: it epitomizes the regular movement of the workers. Gombrich continues, "And here again it is not only the simultaneous movement that is ensured by rigid timing. Even more important is the possibility inherent in any order of constructing a hierarchy of movements or routines to ensure the performance of more complex tasks" (10). This formulation suggests the relationship between regulated time and instruction, hierarchies of movements and routines, which recalls Taylorist models of production as well as programming. While a full investigation of those connections lies outside the aim of this book, it is important to note the fundamental role of processed instructions in producing rhythms in time and space.

Process and the appearance of motion are essential to 10 PRINT. The still images that show a moment in the program's run, the sort that are reproduced in this book, document the program to some extent but are an incomplete representation. A full understanding of the program comes only through experiencing the pattern building one unit at a time and the surprise of the unexpected sequences and connections that form into a maze as the left or right line is randomly drawn.

The visual arts at their most traditional, represented by frescoes, stone and bronze sculptures, and canvases, are static. A viewer creates motion by moving around a work, eyes exploring the surface, but the object is still. The thrust of machines into life at the beginning of the twentieth century was an inspiration to painters (the Futurists), photographers (Étienne-Jules Marey, Eadweard Muybridge), and sculptors who used motors to create motion. The origin of integrating physical movement into artworks in the twentieth century is often credited to Naum Gabo for his *Kinetic Construction (Standing Wave)* from 1919–1920. This sculpture created a virtual volume in space by mechanically hitting a metal rod near the base to send a wave through the object. Gabo was thrilled to bring motion into his art and his enthusiasm led to "The Realistic Manifesto," cowritten with his brother, Antoine Pevsner, in 1920. After rejecting the traditional foundations of art they declared:

> We renounce the thousand-year-old delusion in art that held the static rhythms as the only elements of the plastic and pictorial arts. We affirm in these arts a new element, the kinetic rhythms as the basic forms of our perceptions of real time. (Quoted in Brett and Nash 2000, 228)

With kinetic rhythm as the base of all new art, Gabo's *Kinetic Construction* is an ideal demonstration. It is a machine without visual interest or relation to the sculpture of the time. It performs the same motion precisely over and over. The work of art is reduced to a rhythmic repetition. While other pioneers of motion in art such as Marcel Duchamp and Alexander Calder worked with motors to create regular machines, by the middle of the century the dominant form of motion had shifted to the type of chance motion experience through the wind moving a Calder or Rickey mobile or the anarchic mechanical chaos of Jean Tingely. The essence of 10 PRINT lies in the relationship between both forms.

The next phase of the pairing motion and repetition in visual art brings us closer to 10 PRINT. Artists began to create works for screens, first with film and later for CRT screen with video. Akin to the minimalist sculptures referenced above, there was a proliferation of minimal gestures within experimental film and animation. Starting in the 1960s, artists including Lillian Schwartz, John Whitney, Norman McLaren, Bruce Nauman, Richard Serra, and Paul Sharits explored repetitive physical movements and abstract motion with rigor. *The Flicker* (1965), a film by Tony Conrad, stands out for its clarity. As shown earlier, without the semicolon in 10 PRINT, each diagonal line could be seen as a panel of a film strip. It's only a small leap to imagine the left line of the program as an unexposed film frame (clear) and the right line as the maximum exposure (black) to bring the fundamental mechanism of 10 PRINT close to *The Flicker*. The fundamental difference is the larger arc within Conrad's work. The pace at which the projection flips from pure light to black is slower at the beginning and end of the film to give it a beginning and end, while 10 PRINT maintains the same pace, does not vary in any way as it begins, and continues running until interrupted.

Simultaneously with the exploration of repetition in film, a host of composers based musical works on repetition. Like film and video, musical performance is temporal, but unlike these linear media, performances and 10 PRINT unfold in real time, each step happening in the moment and potentially informed by the present state. *Piano Phase* (1967) by Steve Reich is an iconic sound work built on repetition. In this approximately twenty-minute-long composition, two pianists start by playing the same twelve-note melody continuously. One pianist plays the sequence faster so it moves out of phase until they are back in phase, but the faster pianist is playing the second note, while the slower is on the first note. This continues until the faster pianist has complete a full loop and both are again playing the same sequence at the same time. The piece iterates further from that point, but the same phasing technique is used until the end. The concept is the same as in Reich's later and simpler piece *Clapping Music* (1972), which is clapped by two performers and varies only in rhythm. In 10 PRINT, new forms emerge from the program's decision to display the left or right line, but in *Piano Phase* and *Clapping Music*, new sonic forms emerge by playing the same sequence over and over, with performers playing at a different speeds.

## REPETITION IN PROCESS

The artworks in this chapter engage with regularity as a style and technique; computers employ regularity as a necessary paradigm of their existence. The execution of a computer program, even one that is riddled with bugs or does numerous complex and interesting things, is nothing if not regular. In fact, it is the regularity of computer processes that many of the artworks discussed in the chapter are reacting to and against. Even more than in the Ford factory, regularity becomes a paradigm of the computational age, to be explored and resisted because it is the central logic for even the most basic computational literacy. While the assembly line might put many goods in the hands of twentieth-century consumers, families did not need to contemplate assembly lines to consume these goods. Even for workers actually in a factory, the flow of the factory would be defined elsewhere. However, to write even the most rudimentary program, a person must understand and engage the regularity of the machine. Consequently, it is worthwhile to articulate the process of flow and control that allows this regularity to become such a generative space.

Part of what gives programs their power is that they can be made even more regular by repeating a sequence of instructions. This repetition can be accomplished in two main ways: in a loop that continues for a certain number of iterations or in an unbounded loop. These two loops correspond to two types of branching, the conditional and unconditional branch. To understand the unbounded loop of `10 PRINT` and the specific legacy of `GOTO` is to understand the essentials of the flow of control in computer programs.

To explain the loop, it is necessary to first juxtapose it with the alternative: not having a loop and letting a program progress in the usual sequence. In any imperative programming language, commands are processed in a particular order that relates to the left-to-right then top-to-bottom path that Western readers' eyes take along a page. If one types two

PRINT commands directly into the Commodore 64's BASIC interpreter, with a colon between them, like so:

```
PRINT "FIRST": PRINT "SECOND"
```

the result is

```
FIRST
SECOND
```

The command on the left is executed first, then, the command on the right. In executing the following program, the top-most, left-most command is run first, then the one to the right, and then the one on the next line, so that

```
10 PRINT "FIRST": PRINT "SECOND"
20 PRINT "THIRD"
```

prints FIRST, SECOND, and THIRD, in that order. Since BASIC uses line numbers to determine the sequence, the order in which these two lines are typed is completely irrelevant to how the program runs.

There are some important ways to complicate this straightforward program flow. All of these ways involve branching, which causes program flow to shift to some other command rather than continuing along to the subsequent one. The same could be said of the low level of machine code and its execution by the processor. A machine language program is a sequence of numbers typically processed in order of appearance. An executing machine language program, however, like a high-level program in BASIC or another imperative language, can either continue to process the next instruction or can move out of sequence to process a different instruction. The standard case is when a processor continues to the next machine language instruction, just as the reader of a text moves to the next word or line. This involves incrementing the program counter so that it points to the place where the next instruction is located in memory. If the current instruction is one that can change the flow of control, however, the program may jump to a new memory location and a new piece of code. The branch or jump is the key operation that is used to build a loop.

### Conditional and Unconditional Branching

There are two essential ways that the flow of control can change and a program can branch, continuing from a new point. An unconditional branch always directs the program to jump to a new location, like the instruction "Go directly to Jail. Do not pass Go" in Monopoly. The assembly mnemonic for an unconditional branch is `jmp`; the corresponding BASIC keyword is `GOTO`; packaging together a branch away from a line of code and then a subsequent branch that returns to the original line constitutes a subroutine, implemented in BASIC using `GOSUB` and `RETURN`. When an unconditional branch is used to point back to an earlier instruction, it can cause repetition in process as in the case of `10 PRINT`.

The other type of branch is a conditional branch, a type of instruction that is critical to general-purpose computing. There are many different types of conditional branches in assembly, since there are many different types of conditions. `beq` is "branch if equal," for instance: when used after a comparison (`cmp`), the branch will be taken only if the compared values are equal. `bmi`, "branch if minus," checks to see if the last computation resulted in a negative value. In BASIC, using the `IF . . . THEN` statement is the most straightforward way to accomplish a conditional branch, as this program demonstrates:

```
10 INPUT A$
20 IF A$ = "1" THEN PRINT "YOU TYPED ONE!" : END
30 PRINT "SOMETHING ELSE..."
```

If, after running this program, the user types just the digit "1" and then presses RETURN, all of the statements on line 20 will be executed. "YOU TYPED ONE!" will be printed and then the program will terminate as `END` instructs. This is another way to change the flow of the program, of course: use `END` or `STOP` to terminate the program. If `STOP` is used, the `CONTINUE` command can be issued to pick up where the program left off.

If the user types nothing or anything other than a single "1" before pressing RETURN, the flow of control moves to line 30; both the first `PRINT` statement and the `END` are skipped. "SOMETHING ELSE . . ." is printed instead. This program, although written differently, does exactly the same thing:

```
10 INPUT A$
20 IF A$ = "1" THEN GOTO 40
30 PRINT "SOMETHING ELSE..." : END
40 PRINT "YOU TYPED ONE!"
```

Instead of using the IF . . . THEN to directly determine whether two statements (the PRINT and END statements) should be executed, this one changes the flow of control with GOTO. The GOTO statement is used to skip ahead past PRINT "SOMETHING ELSE..." and END to line 40. Although this isn't a very exciting program, it shows that unconditional branching can be used to jump *ahead* in the sequence of lines; there is nothing about GOTO that means it *must* be used to repeat or loop.

Although there is no IF . . . THEN statement in 10 PRINT, and the program does not by any interpretation contain a conditional branch, this short program does accomplish a very small-scale sort of variation. By computing 205.5+RND(1) and passing that value to the function CHR$, the program prints either PETSCII character 205 or PETSCII character 206. This variation between two characters is a one-bit variation, a selection from the smallest possible set of options. Yet, in combination with the regularity of a repeating processes and the regularity of the Commodore 64's screen grid, these selections take shape as something evocative and visually interesting.

### The Harmfulness of GOTO

Those aware of the discourse in computer science might turn to 10 PRINT with some trepidation, thanks to a 1968 letter to the editor from famous computer scientist Edsger W. Dijkstra, one that was headlined "Go To Statement Considered Harmful" (EWD 215). Although the title was actually written by the editor—Dijkstra called this article "A Case against the GO TO Statement"—the letter and the sentiment behind it have gained lasting fame. One author called it "probably the most often cited document about any type of programming" (Tribble 2005). As this author explains, Dijkstra's exhortation was written at a time when the accepted way of programming was to code iterative loops, if-thens, and other control structures by hand using goto statements. Most programming languages of the time did not support the basic control flow statements that we take for granted today, or only provided very limited forms of them. Dijkstra did not mean that *all* uses of goto were bad, but rather that superior control structures should exist and should replace most uses of goto popular at the time.

Indeed, there is an obvious control structure, unfortunately absent from BASIC, which would accomplish the purpose of 10 PRINT's GOTO without requiring the use of GOTO. This is the while or do . . . while loop, which in this case could simply be used with a condition that is always true so that the loop would always repeat. For instance, if Commodore 64 BASIC had a DO . . . WHILE statement and a keyword TRUE, one could write:

```
10 DO : PRINT CHR$(205.5+RND(1)); : WHILE TRUE
```

This would certainly be a clearer way to write the program, and it would be widely recognized today as clearer because Dijkstra's view of programming has prevailed. When the creators of BASIC introduced True BASIC in 1983 they included the DO loop; its syntax was a bit different from the preceding, but the essential construct was the same.

Although this important construct is missing from early versions of BASIC, it's not obvious that the tiny program 10 PRINT would have particularly offended Dijkstra. In his letter, he objects to the "unbridled use of the go to statement," but he does not state that *every* use of it is unambiguously bad. He describes the GOTO-related problems that arise when programmers are not able to track and understand the values of variables. But 10 PRINT has no variables, so this particular problem with GOTO is not an issue in this particular case.

As mentioned, GOTO has a assembly language equivalent, jmp. Dijkstra essentially exempted assembly language from his critique of GOTO. He recognized that computer programs written in a high-level language are more complicated and nuanced ways of expressing thought, not tied directly to machine function. By creating a new sort of language that does not directly mimic the operation of the processor, it is possible for programmers to think more flexibly and powerfully. Although Dijkstra objected to the way BASIC was designed, he, like the original designers of BASIC, worked strenuously to describe how high-level languages, useful for thinking about computation, could work in machine-independent ways.

### Bounded and Unbounded Loops

10 PRINT works as it does because of its repetition of the PRINT statement, repetition that is unconditional: it will continue until something outside the program interrupts it, such as the user pressing the key labeled RUN STOP or unplugging the computer. This ability to repeat endlessly differentiates the program from its artistic parallels in other media.

At a high level, programs can contain two types of loops: bounded (also called "finite") and unbounded (or "infinite"). 10 PRINT has the latter kind. If one is writing a program that is intended to produce some result and exit, it would be a mistake to include an unbounded loop, creating a bug that would make the program hang on a particular set of operations. Even among comparisons to repetitions in fine art and craft work, the computer stands alone as a system capable of infinite looping. Nonetheless, the unbounded loop does have legitimate uses. It can be used to keep an application, usually an interactive one, running and possibly accepting input until the system is shut off, rebooted, or interrupted. This can be done, and is done, even on a Commodore 64.

Bounded loops are those that end under certain conditions. The exact conditions vary; some will continue until the program reaches a predefined exit state, while others execute a specific number of times. If there are exit conditions for a loop at all, that suggests the programmer expected some kind of change to be introduced as the program executes.

A common use of finite loops is to create an iterative process. Iteration is a special type of looping where the result of one pass through the loop influences the result of succeeding passes. The simplest example of an iterative process is nothing more than counting: beginning with an initial value of 1, adding 1 to this (that is, incrementing it) to produce 2, performing the same incrementing operation again to yield 3, and so on. If the program goes to some limit, say 10, the loop is bounded:

```
10 A=1
20 PRINT A
30 A=A+1
40 IF A<=10 GOTO 20
```

If line 40 is replaced with 40 GOTO 20, the loop becomes unbounded. A

## BASIC CONSIDERED HARMFUL

Edsger W. Dijkstra, of "Go To Statement Considered Harmful," was not at all a fan of the BASIC programming language in which 10 PRINT is written. He wrote in a 1975 letter, "How do we tell truths that might hurt?," published in 1982: "It is practically impossible to teach good programming to students that have had a prior exposure to BASIC: as potential programmers they are mentally mutilated beyond hope of regeneration" (EWD 498).

The statement appears amid other one-sentence jabs at programming languages (FORTRAN, PL/I, COBOL, and APL), IBM, and projects to allow "natural language" programming. In a 1984 keynote address, "The Threats to Computing Science," Dijkstra said, similarly, that "the teaching of BASIC should be rated as a criminal offence: it mutilates the mind beyond recovery" (EWD 898). In both cases, his statements are not part of arguments, nor are they elaborated at all. They are simple denunciations of BASIC—no doubt resonant with many computer scientists and no doubt of some tactical value at the time, when the structured programming that predominates today and that Dijkstra was advocating was still being questioned.

Dijkstra's papers contain a single reference to BASIC coinventor John Kemeny. Dijkstra read Kemeny's 1983 article in *Daedalus,* an article that discussed the idea of computer literacy and declared that "the development of 'structured languages' in recent years has been a giant step forward." Dijkstra simply wrote a dismissive

conditional branch is what makes loop bounded—it ends when the condition is met. Therefore, an unconditional branch to earlier in the program corresponds to an unbounded loop.

The bounded loop, and counting up or down to a particular value, is so important in programming that BASIC has its own special syntax for specifying that sort of loop, using the FOR . . . TO and NEXT statements. The bounded program above could also be written:

```
10 FOR A=1 TO 10
20 PRINT A
30 NEXT
```

sentence about the article, saying it "gave a striking example of superficiality" by comparing computer languages to natural languages (EWD 858).

The context for these statements was a time of formation and fortification of the discipline of computer science. Also important was that at this time, computer scientists were undertaking the development and use of languages that might support first formal verification (the provability of programs) and later the weaker, but still potentially very useful, technique of program derivation (Tribble 2005). BASIC, created for quick interactive use and very amenable to creative production, was not a suitable language for Dijkstra's goals.

Much of Dijkstra's influential thinking (about stepwise programming, for instance) applies most clearly to programs of some complexity. It would be difficult to develop a program as simple as **10 PRINT** using stepwise programming, since it may take about one step to write it. As mentioned, **10 PRINT** is in a sense exempt from Dijkstra's critique of GOTO because of its lack of variables. But in another sense, it is one of many extremely simplified programs that could lead programmers to learn programming methods that don't scale. The risk of learning programming via one-liners is that one learns tricks and particular methods instead of gaining an understanding of programming methodologies.

The same program could be written in yet another way:

```
10 A=1
20 PRINT A
30 A=A+1
40 PRINT A
50 A=A+1
...
200 PRINT A
```

Doing so is an inefficient and error-prone way to write a process. The programmer is forced to do a repetitive task that the computer is extremely well suited to accomplish on its own. Modifying the program to count to 50 takes four times as long as writing the original program, if this way is chosen. In the previous program, one simply changes "10" to "50" in line 10.

### Looping and Iterating

10 PRINT's unbounded loop produces iterative effects, even if it is not enacting a purely iterative process. The unconditional branch at the end is what accomplishes this: **10 PRINT** clearly repeats. There is nothing in the code, however, to indicate that **10 PRINT** is an example of iteration in the more mathematical or computational sense. There are no variables that change value from one pass to the next—there are no variables at all, in fact—and the code inside the loop, and the way that code works, never changes. In the most straightforward computing sense, the BASIC program `10 PRINT CHR$(205.5+RND(1)); : GOTO 10` does not iterate.

Nonetheless, watching the program execute on screen shows hints that there is something changing as it runs: the position where a new character is displayed changes every time the loop executes, moving one location to the right until it reaches the fortieth column; then, the display of characters continues on the next line in column 1. The entire contents of the screen also moves up by two lines, with the top two lines disappearing, once the display of characters reaches the bottom left position.

None of this is a direct result of any BASIC statements included in **10 PRINT**. Displaying strings on the screen generally has this effect, since BASIC's PRINT command calls the Commodore 64 KERNAL's CHROUT routine to produce output. So, while **10 PRINT** is not an iterative program, it invokes the iterative behavior of `PRINT`. **10 PRINT** exposes the power of using simple, iterative steps to create a complex construction.

Computing is full of iterations and simple loops. The highest level of an application program is typically the "main loop" that checks for user input and for other events. Turn-based games, such as a chess program that plays against a human player, will typically have a conditional loop for each turn, conditioned upon whether or not the game is over. And frames of a graphics window or the screen overall, whether drawn in OpenGL, Processing, or by some other means, are drawn within a loop that repeats more or less rapidly depending upon the framework.

## PERFORMING THE LOOP

*Step Piece* by Vito Acconci is a performance work based on repetition that is interesting to compare and contrast with 10 PRINT; it is a defined, repetitive procedure that is carried out by a person rather than a computer. Acconci defined this work in a brief text: "An 18-inch stool is set up in my apartment and used as a step. Each morning, during the designated months, I step up and down the stool at the rate of 30 steps a minute; each morning, the activity lasts as long as I can perform it without stopping."

Since there are months designated for the performance, Acconci defined a bounded loop. *Step Piece* was certainly meant to be the same every morning in particular ways during these months. But it was not the same at every point for a viewer or for Acconci, and will not be the same at every point for someone considering the piece years later. How is repeating the same thing over and over not repetitive? A person's repetitive performance cannot be exactly the same each time. Acconci no doubt stepped more rapidly at some times and then needed to slow down; his foot struck the stool in a slightly different way, producing a different sound. There is no close analogue to this in 10 PRINT, since a Commodore 64 runs the program the same way each time and the symbols are presented in the same way on the same well-functioning television. The photographic documentation of *Step Piece* shows Acconci in action with one foot on the stool and the other on the way up or down. Just as different screen captures from 10 PRINT are different, each photo is different—they differ even more in some large-scale ways since they are images of the same person in different postures, not a 40 × 25 grid with different elements in it.

Additionally, as the days pass, Acconci gets better at his repetitions (like a weightlifter doing "reps" to improve strength) while 10 PRINT writes characters to the screen at the same rhythm and in the same manner as long as the program runs. Some computer programs do actually improve over time—for example, because they cache frequent operations or use machine learning to classify inputs better. A one-line program like 10 PRINT, however, is an exemplar of the legacy of computers as basic calculating machines that do the same thing with symbols each time they are run. Finally, the repetition does not have the same effect on the viewer because the context of life changes from day to day. Thus, repetitive motion may elicit different thoughts at different times.

### FOR . . . TO . . . STEP

The FOR loop in BASIC is a bit more general than is shown in the example on page 96. It can be used not only to increment a variable, but also to change its value each time by any amount. A different increment is set using the STEP keyword. To show only the even numbers between 2 and 10:

```
10 FOR A=2 TO 10 STEP 2
20 PRINT A
30 NEXT
```

If STEP is omitted, it's the same as adding STEP 1. The step value can be set to a negative number or even to zero. By setting the value to 0, an unbounded FOR loop can be created:

```
10 FOR A=1 TO 10 STEP 0
20 PRINT "FOREVER!"
30 NEXT
```

This allows for an alternate version of 10 PRINT that uses a FOR loop instead of GOTO:

```
10 FOR A=1 TO 2 STEP 0 : PRINT CHR$(205.5+RND(1)); : NEXT
```

This one is slightly longer and exceeds the forty characters of a physical line but still a "one-liner" in the sense that it fits into the eighty-character logical line.

In this version, the "10" at the beginning is optional. The three statements can be entered together in immediate mode, just as one can type PRINT "HELLO" and have the PRINT statement executed immediately:

```
FOR A=1 TO 2 STEP 0 : PRINT CHR$(205.5+RND(1)); : NEXT
```

The only reason the line number is needed in the original program is as a point to branch back to. As GOTO goes, so goes the line number.

So, these are at least four ways that *Step Piece* changes through its repetition: (1) human performance changes in subtle ways from repetition to repetition; (2) documentation shows different, nonrepetitive moments; (3) human performance improves over time; and (4) the work is perceived in different contexts, even by the same viewer. *Step Piece* is exemplary here because it seems to be the more or less pure repetition of pure repetition, but actors putting on the same play on different nights encounter a similar type of nonrepeating repetition and all of these four points also apply to the case of plays that run for several performances. Even though 10 PRINT is a performance by a digital machine, (2) and (4) still apply, so that its repetition also varies in these ways.

The performance piece *Dance*, a collaboration between choreographer Lucinda Childs, composer Phillip Glass, and artist Sol LeWitt, interweaves these performance strands together. Like all of the works already discussed, narrative is absent and the subject is literally movement, hearing, and seeing through variation and repetition (figure 30.10). For three of the five sections of the performance, LeWitt created films of the dancers performing the same sequence of motions that they perform live on stage. He filmed them on top of a grid to reinforce the structure within the choreography. The film is projected onto a scrim at the front of the stage during the performance, and it is synchronized to a recorded version of Glass's score. At times the projected image is enlarged and at times it is slowed down as the film echoes the movements of the live performance. Glass's music for *Dance* features his signature style of repeating and transforming brief passages. The foundation of *Dance* is Lucinda Childs's choreography, which she has referred to as stripped-down ballet. In the first and strongest movement, the dancers move along straight lines from left to right and right to left across the stage. As they quickly follow the line in a mix of running, skipping, and turning, they move through a series of tilts. The perception is they are moving through every permutation within the grammar of movements created for the dance. As with 10 PRINT, the sound and motion are hypnotic and emphasize the details of the variation rather than larger global structural changes. *Dance,* however, is unlike 10 PRINT in that it works across multiple media to synthesize a powerful and at times overwhelming aesthetic experience.

Regularity is an important technique of the mid-to-late twentieth century in part because artists explored systematic production and repeated

Figure 30.10

Image from the 2009 revival of *Dance*, a 1979 collaboration of Lucinda Childs, Phillip Glass, and Sol Lewitt. Photo by Sally Cohn, ©2009. Courtesy of Sally Cohn.

processes as epitomized by computer programs. The impact of those art forms is in the stripping away of their representational and expressive possibilities, the minimalism in their constructivist techniques. By contrast, `10 PRINT`, as an initial and initiating example for novices at the Commodore 64, does not strip away but offers an introductory glimpse of the effects of the flow and control of computer systems processing an unbounded loop within the constraints of regulated time and space. If the art world was moving away from representation and expression to this minimalism, the novice programmer was encountering `10 PRINT` as the beginning of a movement toward representation and expression, in this case within the world of computer graphics.

In the cases discussed, regularity in time, space, and process becomes programmatic, a proportional regulator that proves to be a generative constraint, producing larger patterns that can be quite unexpected. Through the unrelenting predictability of regularity, the repeated random presentation of two diagonal lines across a grid becomes a quite unanticipated scroll of mazes. As a pedagogical example in the *technē* of programming, `10 PRINT` is both a product of and a demonstration of the force of computational regularity.

# 35

# REM VARIATIONS IN PROCESSING

Building a high-resolution, interactive program that is inspired by 10 PRINT allows visual design variations that might not be easy or even possible within a Commodore 64 program. Computational visual art has been created on a variety of platforms and in many systems and languages over the last fifty years, but the last decade has seen an explosion in the use of commercial tools for designers with embedded programming languages (most notably, Adobe Flash) along with programming environments designed by visual artists. John Maeda's Design by Numbers system from 2001 offers one example of the latter; a far more influential tool is Ben Fry and Casey Reas's Processing, itself inspired by Maeda's work and started within his research group at the MIT Media Lab.

While a simple BASIC program writes some text to the screen with `10 PRINT "HELLO WORLD"`, a simple Processing program draws a square to the screen with `rect(20, 30, 80, 60);`. This one-line Processing program draws the rectangle with its upper-left corner at coordinate (20, 30) and with a width of 80 pixels and height of 60 pixels. Essentially, Processing is an image-making programming language that builds on knowledge of geometry, photography, typography, animation, and interaction. Under the hood, Processing is based on Java with a specialized toolkit, program framework, and authoring environment, all suited to the development of interactive visual sketches. Because Processing is situated between programming and the visual arts, it serves as a bridge between two professional cultures. Those who approach Processing with a programming background are encouraged to learn more about making sophisticated visual images. From the other side, visual artists learn the fundamentals of procedural literacy.

The algorithm underlying 10 PRINT is of course not specific to the Commodore 64; it can be executed with a sheet of graph paper, a pen, and a coin to toss. The act of running the algorithm on a number of different platforms reveals what is essential to the algorithm, on the one hand, and to the specific constraints and affordances of the system on the other: lines produced by PRINT wrap and scroll automatically, for instance, so characters can accumulate and fill the screen without being addressed by x and y coordinates. More subtle defaults of the Commodore 64 include the color (light blue on blue) and the speed at which each new section of the maze is added. When 10 PRINT is ported to another platform, certain features of the Commodore 64 must be defined consciously or at least approximated within the new platform; the programmer can renegotiate the precise color, resolution, and speed of the maze. While many elements and aspects of the original program can be modified in BASIC on the Commodore 64, some are more firmly fixed. Primarily, the 40 × 25 character screen that defines the resolution of the grid is fundamental to the computer's video system and defines the number of units that make up the maze.

The first Processing port of 10 PRINT was written to take advantage of the increased resolution of contemporary screens. It does this by making the thickness and ends of the lines into variables that can be changed while the program runs. The lines of the maze can range in width from 0.5 to 10 pixels, and the lines can terminate with a rounded or square end. Like `10 PRINT`, this Processing port maintains the grid of lines at 40 × 25 units, but, unlike `10 PRINT`, it doesn't add each grid unit in sequence from left to right and top to bottom. In the new high-resolution version, the entire maze is refreshed at once. Using the default Processing colors to create white lines and a black background confers a mood similar to that of the original lower-contrast blues of the Commodore 64 (see figure 35.1).

While creating these variations, some additional quick changes were introduced to explore the visual aspects of the `10 PRINT` maze. First, the 50–50 chance to draw a left or right line was altered so it could be reweighted while the program runs to increase the chance of drawing one line instead of the other. The result is shown in figure 35.2. Then, graphic symbols different from the original diagonal lines were used to expose part of the program's structure.

The optical effect of the maze is created as these diagonals align themselves to produce walls and paths. The viewer's eyes dance across the image as they attempt to find their way through the structure. Some symbols also create a strong, but different optical effect, while other symbols generate a boring, flat graphic. Figure 35.3 shows the result of using a blank image (space) and circle in place of the diagonals. This exploration into applying a different visual skin to the fundamental coin-toss structure of the `10 PRINT` program reveals that the appeal of `10 PRINT` derives from the random choice among two or more elements, the precise selection of which optically activates the viewer to create an interesting and culturally relevant image—in this case, the maze.

The changes just discussed can be explored directly on the Commo-

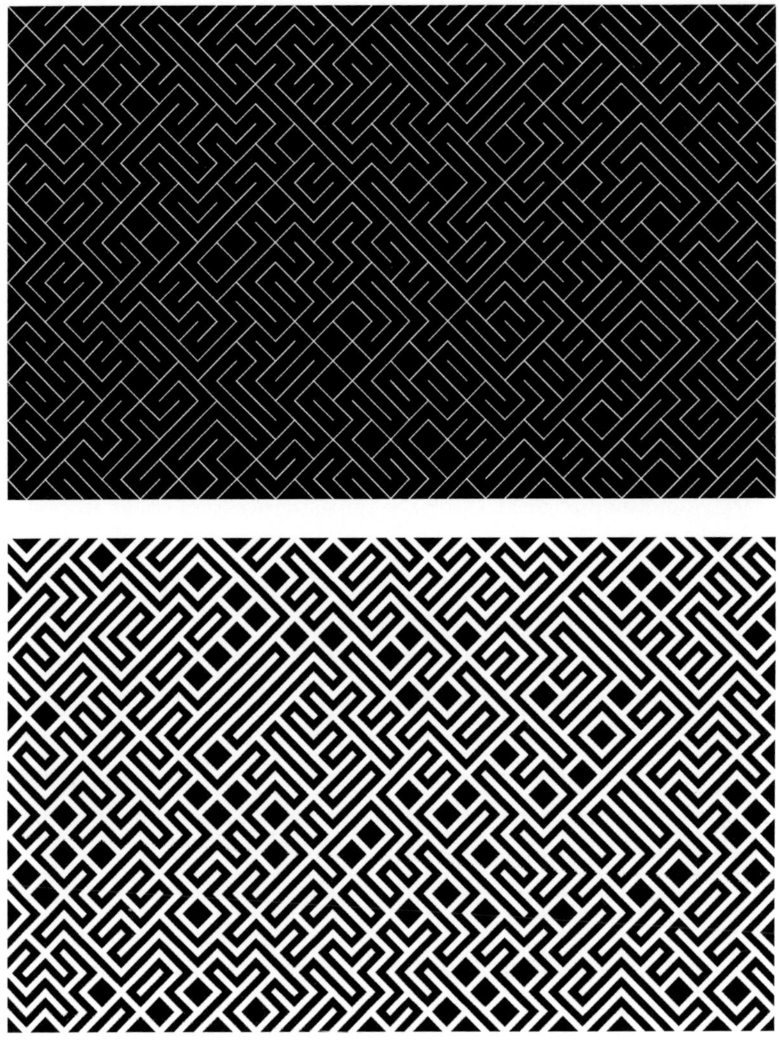

Figure 35.1

Processing ports of 10 PRINT that explore the effects of changing the line weights and endings.

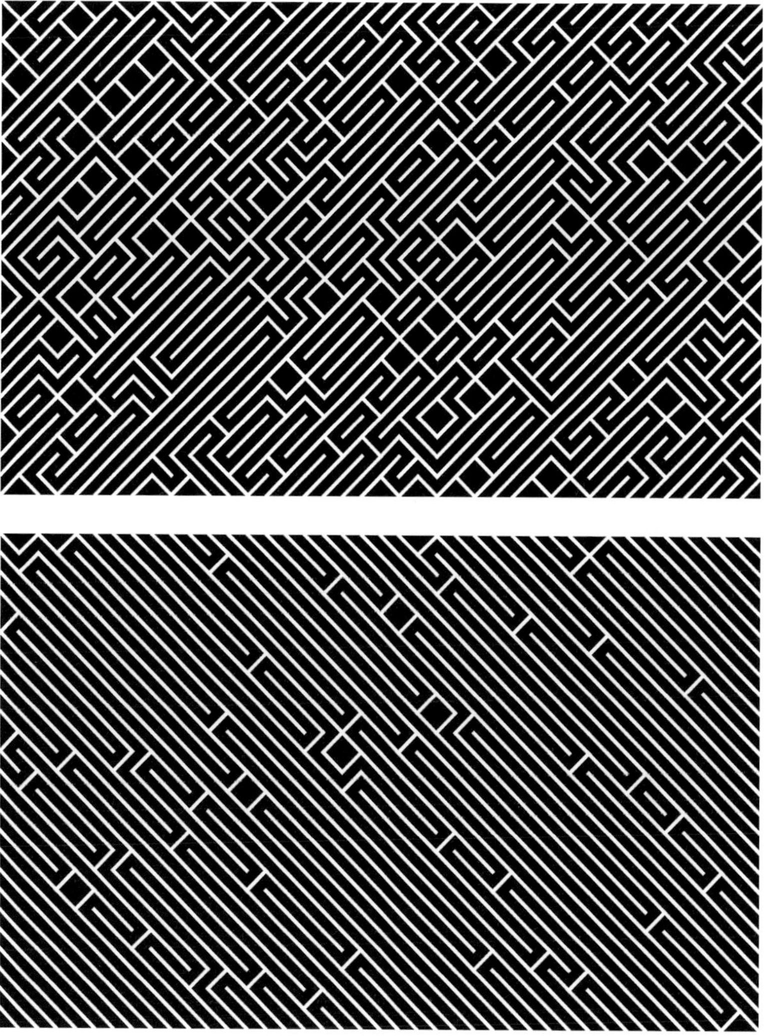

Figure 35.2

Processing ports of `10 PRINT` that explore different weightings for the random values. The top image has a 25 percent chance of drawing a left-leaning diagonal line and the bottom image has a 95 percent chance.

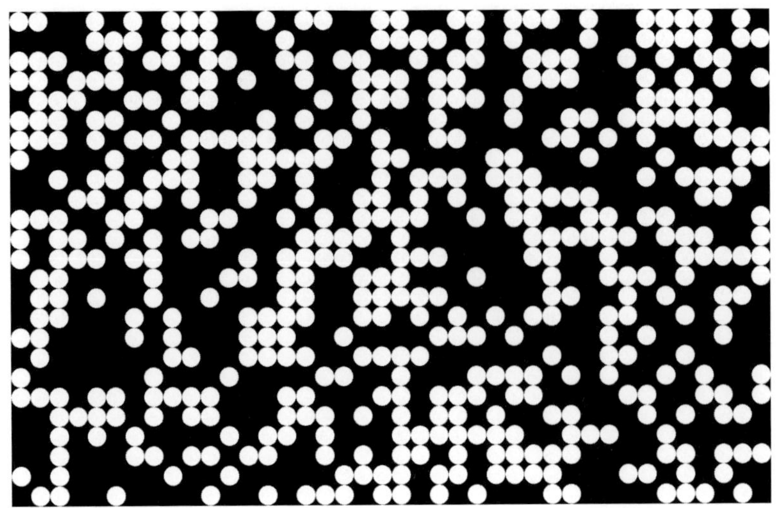

Figure 35.3

Processing port of `10 PRINT` that replaces the lines with circles and blank spaces.

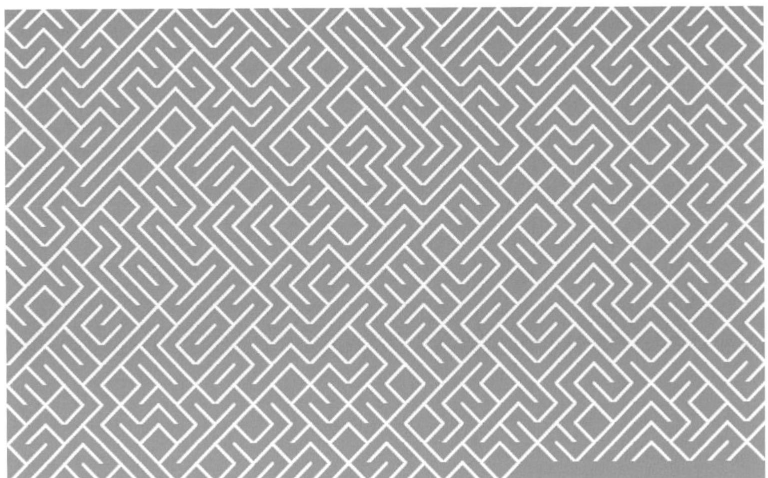

Figure 35.4

Processing port of `10 PRINT` focused on closely imitating the behavior of the Commodore 64.

dore 64, some more easily and some less so, as has been shown to some extent in the remark Variations in BASIC. It is convenient to explore these changes in Processing, however. For one thing, Processing exposes many dimensions of variation, down to the pixel level, which would be difficult to change on the original platform. For another, a programmer who is highly fluent in Processing can work through ideas and problems easily using that system.

Some variations that are most easily accomplished on the Commodore 64 are the ones involving reweighting the distribution of lines and replacing the lines with spaces and circles. As discussed earlier, **10 PRINT**'s distribution of ╱ and ╲ can be altered by simply changing the ".5" in "205.5," for instance:

```
10 PRINT CHR$(205.25+RND(1)); : GOTO 10
```

The **10 PRINT** variation to show spaces and circles instead of diagonal lines also changes the selection of value 205 or 206 to choose between the numerical code of the space character, 32, and that for a circle character, 113:

```
10 PRINT CHR$(32+(INT(RND(1)+.5)*81)); : GOTO 10
```

Writing and running this first Processing port, which focuses entirely on the image of the maze and on allowing runtime changes in parameters, points out an important visual aspect of the original **10 PRINT**: watching the maze building up or accumulating one unit at a time on the Commodore 64 is a major component of the experience. This behavior doesn't naturally take place with Processing because the entire screen updates at once, not character by character. Processing makes more extensive use of the computer's double-buffered graphics system. This allows graphics to be drawn to an off-screen image buffer, stored in RAM, and, once completed, pushed across to the computer screen. For programs that feature animation or interaction, and thanks to today's much faster hardware, the result is a new image written and drawn to the screen about sixty times per second.

The lines of Processing programs do not begin with numbers, as they do in Commodore 64 BASIC. Each line is executed in order from top to bottom and according to some higher-level rules. This can be seen in the following Processing port of **10 PRINT**. This program does not allow the user to interactively vary parameters, but it does reproduce the character-at-a-time construction of the original:

```
int w = 16;
int h = 16;
int index = 0;

void setup() {
  size(640, 384);
  background(#0000ff);
  strokeWeight(3);
  stroke(224);
  smooth();
}

void draw() {
  int x1 = w*index;
  int x2 = x1 + w;
  int y1 = h*23;
  int y2 = h*24;

  if (random(2) < 1) {
    line(x2, y1, x1, y2);
  } else {
    line(x1, y1, x2, y2);
  }

  index++;
  if (index == width/w) {
    PImage p = get(0, h, width, h*23);
    background(#0000ff);
    set(0, 0, p);
    index = 0;
  }
}
```

The primary structure of the program is defined by the `setup()` and `draw()` blocks. Variables may be defined outside of these blocks, but everything else is sequenced through them. When the program starts, the variables outside of the blocks are declared and assigned. Next, the lines of code inside of `setup()` are read from top to bottom. Here, the size of the display window is set to be 640 pixels wide and 384 pixels high, and the colors for the background and lines are defined. Next, the code inside `draw()` runs from top to bottom. Whatever code is inside the `draw()` block runs, from top to bottom, once for each frame until the program is terminated. The code within the `if` statement, inside `draw()`, samples a random value and then draws one of the two possible lines. The code in the `if` block at the bottom of `draw()` moves the maze up when the maze line that is currently drawing is filled. This code behaves and looks more similar to the canonical Commodore 64 `10 PRINT` (see figure 35.4), but the process is defined differently.

There is a way within Processing to make a `10 PRINT` port that is in some ways a better approximation of the program on the Commodore 64. This method uses the text console of the Processing Development Environment (PDE) instead of the pixels in the display window; this console is typically used for error messages and writing debug statements through the `print()` and `println()` functions, which are similar to `PRINT` in BASIC. The console, however, can only print text; programs themselves are not typed in this area, and graphics cannot be drawn there. The other significant difference is that the graphic characters of PETSCII are not available in the native console font for the PDE. As a result the "/" and "\" (slash and backslash) characters need to be used in place of diagonal graphics ╱ and ╲. This results in space between the lines which prevents the illusion of a continuous maze. The output is similar to that of the first `10 PRINT` port in Perl, shown in figure 25.3. A Processing program that produces this approximation of `10 PRINT` can also be realized in one line:

```
void draw() { print((random(1)<0.5) ?'/' :'\\'); }
```

When the program is run in Processing, an empty display window opens and the text is printed to the console as seen in figure 35.5. This exploration raises a crucial difference between writing this program in Commodore 64 BASIC and writing it in Processing. The one-line Processing program is

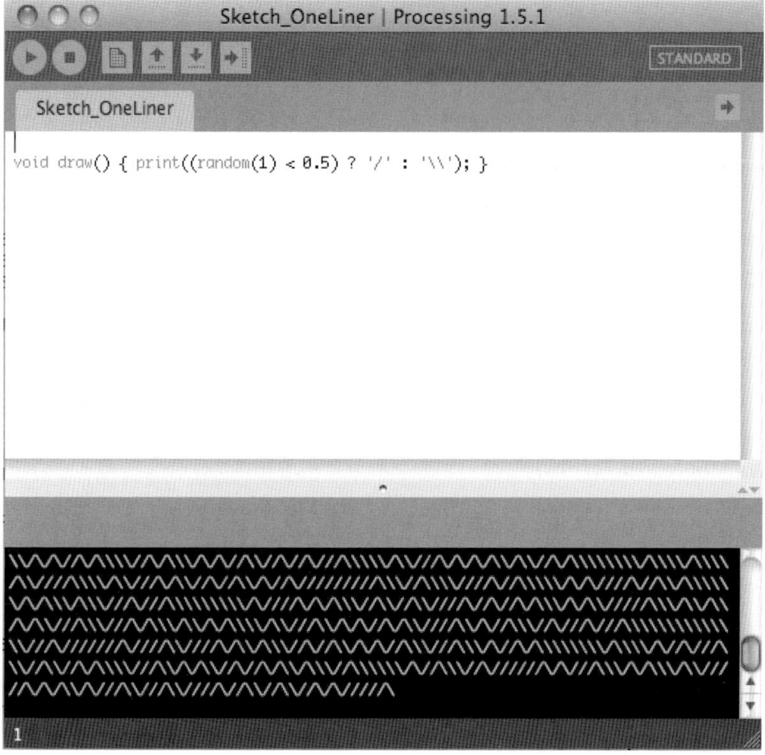


Figure 35.5

This one-line Processing `10 PRINT` port is algorithmically more similar to the Commodore 64 program, but the visual output is extremely different. The code is written in the text editor and the output is drawn to the console rather than opening a new display window.

quite similar as code but produces a divergent result, one that looks a great deal like that of the first Perl one-liner and the Apple II one-liner discussed in the previous remark.

Evaluating the similarities and differences between the Commodore 64 `10 PRINT` program and the Processing port shows that the shape of the small component lines, and specifically the shape of their ends, is a subtle but crucial factor. In the Commodore 64 `10 PRINT` image, each single-character diagonal line comes to a point on both ends. This is a result of the characters being 8 × 8 pixel tiles with thick lines that run all the way to the corners. This maze is created by tiling these 64-pixel squares.

In the Processing program, each added line is free to extend beyond any particular box within the window. A Processing window is a continuous surface of pixels, each of which can be addressed precisely with an x- and y-coordinate. The `10 PRINT` program comprises 320 × 200 pixels, but the controllable resolution is 40 × 25, for a total of 1000 elements. A Processing version of the program can utilize all of the pixels in a window—and in a screen-filling window on a large, contemporary display, this can mean millions of pixels. A 1080p high-definition display, for example, is composed of 2,073,600 pixels.

With this enhanced resolution in mind, a third version of `10 PRINT` in Processing follows—one that takes more liberties with the original program. The number of rows and columns in the grid is variable, the direction of the line defines its color (black or white), each line is defined as a quadrilateral to give the shape more flexibility, and a third color is used for the background. Each time the code is run, the size of the grid unit is defined at random as a power of 2 (2, 4, 8, 16, or 32), and the thickness of the lines is set randomly to 2, 4, or 8. Figure 35.6 shows some of the varied results. With the ability to further define the graphics, the code becomes longer than a one-liner, but still fairly compact.

The decision to display one direction of lines as white and the other as black triggers the viewer's evolved perception to create depth within this two-dimensional image. The ordinary process of visual perception indicates that there is a light source that is reflecting off one directional edge and creating a shadow on the other. The angle at which the lines terminate in this program enhances the effect by occlusion and termination at the edge. This creates an isometric perspective that further enhances the perceived dimensionality. These effects work well in some randomly determined con-

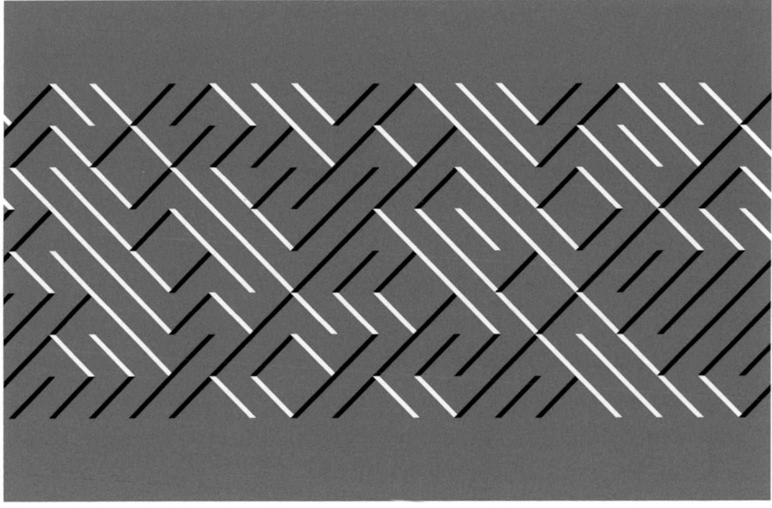

Figure 35.6

Processing port of 10 PRINT that adds a new line shape, colors, and variation of grid units.

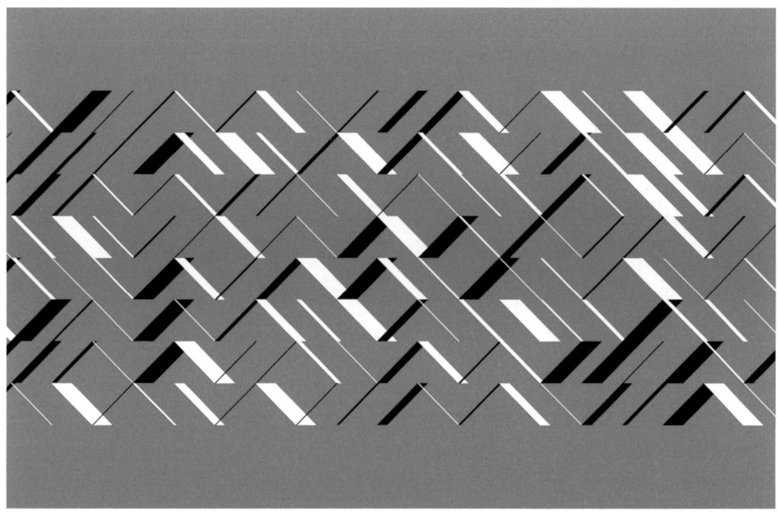

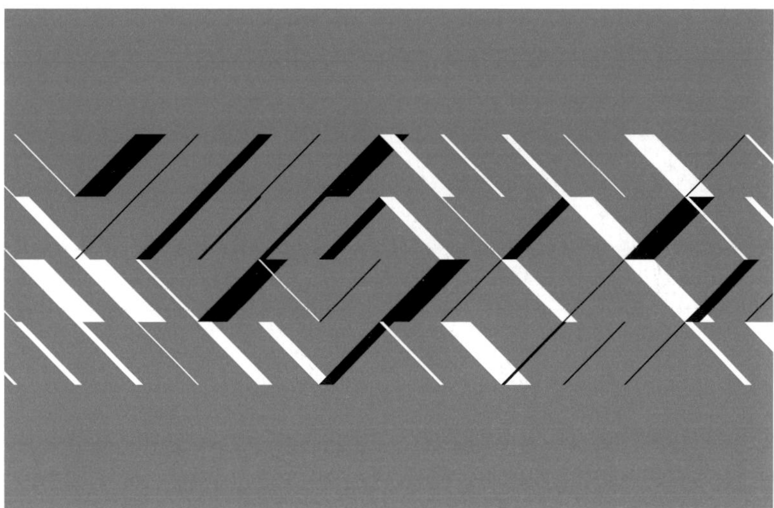

Figure 35.7

Processing program based on `10 PRINT`, but significantly different, in which each line has a random thickness.

figurations and are subverted by others (figure 35.6). This is accomplished with the following program:

```
size(1020, 680);
noStroke();
background(0, 0, 255);
int rows = int(pow(2, int(random(1, 6))));
int u = height / (rows + 4);
int thickness = int(pow(2, int(random(1, 4))));
int uth1 = u / thickness;
int uth2 = u + uth1;
int startX = int(-u * 0.75);
int startY = height/2 - rows/2 * u;
int endX = width+u;
int endY = height/2 + rows/2 * u;
for (int x = startX; x < endX; x += u) {
  for (int y = startY; y < endY; y += u) {
    if (random(1) > 0.5) {
      fill(255);
      quad(x, y, x+u, y+u, x+uth2, y+u, x+uth1, y);
    }
    else {
      fill(0);
      quad(x, y+u, x+u, y, x+uth2, y, x+uth1, y+u);
    }
  }
}
```

It is worth noting that, despite all of the random options in the newly defined program, the line weight remains constant throughout. To check the visual effect of selecting a random line weight, one can simply move lines 6–8 of the program (declaring and defining `thickness`, `uth1`, and `uth2`) right underneath the second line beginning with `for`, so they are within that `for` loop. The results are shown in figure 35.7. At this stage, the program distinguishes itself significantly from its parent and emerges as a qualitatively unique algorithm.

# 40 RANDOMNESS

GAMES OF CHANCE
RANDOMNESS BEFORE COMPUTING
RANDOMNESS COMES TO COMPUTING
COMPUTATIONAL RANDOMNESS IN THE ARTS
THE COMMODORE 64 RND FUNCTION

An essential element of 10 PRINT is randomness; the program could not produce its mesmerizing visual effect without it. This randomness comes by way of RND, a standard function in BASIC. RND has been part of the BASIC lexicon since the language's early days at Dartmouth. What the function does is easily characterized, yet behind those three letters lie decades, even centuries, of a history bound up in mathematics, art, and less abstract realms of culture. This chapter explores randomness in computing and beyond. The role of randomness in games, literature, and the arts is considered, as are the origins of random number generation in modern mathematics, engineering, and computer science. Also discussed is the significance of "pseudorandomness"—the production of random-like values that may appear at first to be some sad, failed attempt at randomness, but which is useful and even desirable in many cases. The chapter argues that the maze pattern of 10 PRINT is entwined with a complex history of aesthetic and utilitarian coin flips and other calculations of chance.

Since a random occurrence is "hap," the root of happy, it might seem that "random" would have a happy etymology. But this is not so. In centuries past, before the philosophers and mathematicians in the Age of Enlightenment sought to rationalize chance, randomness was a nightmare. Likely ancestors of the word "random" are found in Anglo-Norman, Old French, and Middle French and include *randoun, raundun, raundoun, randon, randun,* and *rendon*—words signifying speed, impulsiveness, and violence. These early forms are found beginning around the twelfth century and probably derive from *randir,* to run fast or gallop ("random, n., adv., and adj." 2011). Bumper stickers implore drivers to "practice random acts of kindness," but only because people in our culture fear random acts of violence so much that this phrase has become ingrained and can be punned upon—and at a deeper level, perhaps, because the speed and violence of other vehicles are to be feared. While in recent days it might be harmless to encounter "a random" sitting in the computer lab exploring a system at random, a "random encounter" centuries ago was more likely to resemble a random encounter in *Dungeons & Dragons*: a figure hurtling on horseback through a village, delivering death and destruction.

Only recently have the meanings of the word "random" coalesced around science and statistics. The history of this word is strewn with obsolete meanings: the degree of elevation of a gun that maximizes its range; the direction of a metallic vein in a mine; the sloping board on the top of a compositor's frame where newly arranged pages are stored before printing. These particular randoms kill opponents, create wealth, or help assemble texts. The RND command in 10 PRINT selects one of two graphical characters—a kind of textual composition that recalls the last of these meanings of random. 10 PRINT's random is a flip or flop, a symbol like a slash forward or backward (but fortunately less fearsome than the horseman's random slash). The program splays each random figure across the screen using the PRINT command, another echo of the printing press and a legacy of the early days of BASIC, when PRINT literally meant putting ink on paper. Although RND on the Commodore 64 may seem remote from these early meanings of "random," there are, beneath the surface, connections to speed, violence, devastation, and even printing.

## GAMES OF CHANCE

Life itself is full of randomness and the inexplicable, and it is no small wonder that children and adults alike consciously incorporate chance into their daily lives, as if to tame it. Games of chance are one of the four fundamental categories of games that all humans play, according to the French cultural historian Roger Caillois. Whereas *agon* are competitive games dependent upon skill, games of *mimicry* are imaginative, and *ilinx* are games causing disorder and loss of control, the *alea* are games of chance. Craps, roulette, the lottery—these are some of the games in this category, ones with unpredictable outcomes. Taken from the Latin name for dice games, *alea* "negates work, patience, experience, and qualifications" (Caillois 2003, 17) so that everything depends on luck. In Latin, the *āleātor* is a gambler; in French, *aléatoire* is the mathematical term for random.

### The Appeal of the Random

In his *Arcades Project* on nineteenth-century Paris, Walter Benjamin devotes an entire section to dice games and gambling, a curious assemblage of notes and excerpts from sources ranging from Casanova to Friedrich Engels. "Gambling," Anatole France is quoted as saying, "is a hand-to-hand encounter with Fate" (Benjamin 1999, 498 [O4A]). Every spin of the roulette wheel is an opportunity to show that fate smiles upon the player.

Fortunes rise and fall in the blink of an eye, the roll of the die, or the cut of the cards. Every gambler knows this, accepts it, and even relishes it.

The allure of gambling—and more generally, the allure of chance in all games—rests on uncertainty. Uncertainty is so compelling that even otherwise skill-based games usually incorporate formal elements of chance, such as the coin toss at the beginning of a football game. As Katie Salen and Eric Zimmerman put it, uncertainty "is a key component of meaningful play" (2004, 174). Once the outcome of a game is known, the game becomes meaningless. Incorporating chance into the game helps delay the moment when the outcome will become obvious.

Consider the case of George Hurstwood in Theodore Dreiser's *Sister Carrie,* first published in 1900. Driven by "visions of a big stake," Hurstwood visits a poker room:

> Hurstwood watched awhile, and then, seeing an interesting game, joined in. As before, it went easy for awhile, he winning a few times and cheering up, losing a few pots and growing more interested and determined on that account. At last the fascinating game took a strong hold on him. He enjoyed its risks and ventured on a trifling hand to bluff the company and secure a fair stake. (Dreiser 1981, 374)

What is intriguing about Dreiser's account is that it is only when Hurstwood's good fortune wavers that his interest in the game grows and he begins to enjoy it. Losing a few hands makes a winning streak that much more thrilling. "A series of lucky rolls gives me more pleasure than a man who does not gamble can have over a period of several years," Edouard Gourdon avers in one sexually charged extract in the *The Arcades Project.* "These joys," he continues, "vivid and scorching as lightning, are too rapid-fire to become distasteful, and too diverse to become boring. I live a hundred lives in one" (Benjamin 1999, 498 [O4A]).

Unlike the early, purely malevolent associations of randomness described in the beginning of this chapter, randomness here involves the masochistic interplay between pleasure and pain. There is also a monumental compression of time: a hundred lives in one. Anatole France calls gambling "the art of producing in a second the changes that Destiny ordinarily effects only in the course of many hours or even many years" (Benjamin 1999, 498 [O4A]). Benjamin himself declares that "the greater the component of chance in a game, the more speedily it elapses" (512 [O12A,2]). Waiting, boredom, monotony—these frustrations disappear as "time spills from his [the gambler's] every pore" (107 [D3,4]).

## Forms of Randomness

Perhaps Benjamin describes games of chance with a bit more whimsy than is useful for critical discussion of the role of randomness in culture. Although words like randomness, chance, and uncertainty may be casually interchanged, not all forms of chance are actually the same. To highlight distinctions between various forms of chance, consider the anthropologist Thomas Malaby's account of gambling in a small Greek city on the island of Crete—an appropriate site of exploration, given *alea*'s Greek etymology. Malaby's goal is to use gambling as a "lens through which to explore how social actors confront uncertainty in . . . key areas of their lives" (2003, 7). How do people account for the unaccountable? How do we deal with the unpredictable? And what are the sources of indeterminacy in our lives?

Malaby presents a useful framework for understanding indeterminacy based on four categories. The first category is *formal indeterminacy*, or what is commonly referred to as chance. This is any form of random allotment, which often can be understood and modeled through statistical methods. Malaby argues that the ascendancy of statistical thinking in the social sciences has so skewed our conception of indeterminacy in gambling (in particular) and in our lives (in general) that formal indeterminacy has become a stand-in for other types of indeterminacies. The second category is *social indeterminacy*, the impossibility of knowing or understanding someone else's point of view or intentions. A bluff is a type of social indeterminacy. The third category is *performative indeterminacy*, that is, the unreliability of one's own or of another's actions, say a fumble in football game or misreading the information in plain view on a chessboard. Finally, the fourth category Malaby describes, *cosmological indeterminacy,* refers to skepticism about the fairness and legitimacy of the rules of the game in the first place at a local, institutional, or cosmological level. Suspicion that a game is rigged, for example, is concern about cosmological indeterminacy (Malaby 2003, 15–17).

Privileging of the stochastic principles of formal determinacy means that players, scholars, and even programmers dismiss social and performative indeterminacies altogether. In the case of 10 PRINT, thinking about social indeterminacy can reveal several new layers of randomness, such as the idiosyncratic line numbers in the 1982 and 1984 versions of the program. Likewise, understanding performative indeterminacies may account for the textual variants of the program, for example, the version that appeared in the online publication *Commodore Free* that will not actually execute as printed (Lord Ronin 2008).

Cosmological indeterminacy is perhaps the most difficult form of indeterminacy to apply to 10 PRINT. The rise of the scientific method can be seen as one enduring struggle to impose a more rational view upon the world and to abolish cosmological indeterminacy. From Aristotle to Galileo to Newton, classical mechanics defined the universe as an organized system without random actions. Einstein declared that "God does not play dice with the universe." Yet, as a closer examination of randomness on the Commodore 64 will reveal, there is evidence that randomness on this computer—and indeed, on any computer—is fundamentally "rigged" in a way that echoes Malaby's idea of cosmological indeterminacy. Randomness and chance operations are so necessary to daily life, well beyond the realm of games, that randomness itself is framed as fixed, repeatable, and knowable.

## RANDOMNESS BEFORE COMPUTING

Just as the different categories of indeterminacy in games are often grouped together and called "chance," so too in the visual arts, music, and other aesthetic practices is the word "chance" used instead of "randomness." In his chapbook *Chance Imagery*, the conceptual artist George Brecht (1966) describes two distinct types of chance operations by which an artist might create a work: "one where the origin of images is unknown because it lies in deeper-than-conscious levels of the mind" and a second "where images derive from mechanical processes not under the artist's control." The first definition describes the work of the Surrealists and Abstract Expressionists, who sought to allow subconscious processes to dictate their work. The second definition is reminiscent of Dada and closer to the typical concept of randomness in computing; it describes the mechanical operations of the artists most directly connected to 10 PRINT. These two senses are worth noting because it is difficult to pull on one of the two senses of "chance" without the other one—the unconscious, in this case—at least feeling a tug.

The tension between these two chance operations is captured in William Burroughs's story about a Surrealist rally in the 1920s. Tristan Tzara suggested writing a poem "on the spot by pulling words out of a hat," and as Burroughs tells it, "a riot ensued" and "wrecked the theater." In his version of events, André Breton, the leading Surrealist, expelled Tzara from the group, his purely mechanistic chance operation being an affront to the power and vagaries of the Freudian unconscious (Burroughs 2003). Burroughs is most certainly conflating several events, and the break between Surrealism and Dada had as much to do with a personality clash between Breton and Tzara as with their approaches to art (Brandon 1999, 127). Burroughs himself clearly preferred the anarchic mode of Tzara and famously described a similarly unpredictable mode of composition, the cut-up method, also proposed by Tzara in his 1920 "To Make a Dadaist Poem." Burroughs explains that "one way to do it" is to cut a page in four quarters and then rearrange the sections: "you will find that it says something and something quite definite" (90). Tzara suggests pulling words blindly from a bag. The generative possibilities of this cut-up technique resemble the collage in art and the montage in film, and have become far more mainstream today than Tzara might have imagined in 1920. For instance, Thom Yorke, the lead singer for the band Radiohead, wrote the lyrics to "Kid A" in 1999 by pulling fragments of text out of a top hat.

## Chance Operations

Though Yorke employed a type of cut-up method to address severe writer's block, artistic experimentation with randomness in the early part of the twentieth century can be seen as a response to the sterile functionality of rationality and empiricism wrought by the Industrial Age and as a deliberate reaction against World War I. Consider Marcel Duchamp's *Three Standard Stoppages* (1913–1914). According to his description of the piece, Duchamp dropped three meter-long pieces of string from the height of one meter and let gravity and chance dictate the paths of the twisting string downward. Then he adhered the twisted string onto canvas, the shape and length of which he preserved in 1918 in wooden cutouts, creating three new "stoppages" that parodied the supposed rationality of the meter. When Duchamp described his method in 1914, he observed that the falling thread distorts "itself as it pleases" and the final result becomes "the meter diminished," subverting both the straightness and the length of what commonly goes unquestioned (Duchamp 1975, 141–142). On his use of randomness, Duchamp said, "Pure chance interested me as a way of going against logical reality" (Cabanne 1971, 46).

Duchamp, like the other Dada artists with whom he associated, saw "logical reality" as a failure, epitomized by the horrors of World War I. Satire, absurdity, and the embrace of indeterminacy seemed to the Dadaists to be the most "reasonable" response to modernity. In the words of the Dada artist Jean (Hans) Arp, "Dada wished to destroy the reasonable frauds of men and recover the natural, unreasonable order. Dada wished to replace the logical nonsense of the men of today with an illogical nonsense." To Arp, individual authorship was synonymous with authoritarianism and random elements were used to liberate the work (Motherwell 1989, 266).

The major twentieth-century composer to explore randomness was certainly John Cage, who was strongly influenced by Duchamp. From Cage's point of view, random elements remove individual bias from creation; they may be used to reach beyond the limitations of taste and bias through "chance operations." Cage influenced generations of artists through his compositions as well as through his writing, lectures, and classes. In his text "Experimental Music," Cage wrote, "Those involved with the composition of experimental music find ways and means to remove themselves from the activities of the sounds they make. Some employ chance operations, derived from sources as ancient as the Chinese *Book of Changes*, or as modern as the tables of random numbers used also by physicists in research" (1966, 10).

Cage's method of random composition was to create a system of parameters and then leave the results to circumstance. Cage explained, "This means that each performance of such a piece of music is unique, as interesting to its composer as to others listening. It is easy to see again the parallel with nature, for even with leaves of the same tree, no two are exactly alike" (1996, 11). Random components are used to transform a single composition into a space of potential compositions. Over the decades, Cage used an array of techniques to insert unexpected elements into his compositions. He defines the range of techniques he and his contemporaries used in the 1958 lectures "Composition as Process." There are generally two methods for using random values in music: to define the work at the time of composition or to allow for variation when the work is performed. The most obvious use of randomness in 10 PRINT is in the second category as random decisions are made during the program's execution—that is, while the BASIC instructions are performed by the Commodore 64.

Within two-dimensional visual art, artists also explored mechanical random processes for reasons championed by Cage. The eminent contemporary painter Gerhard Richter provided a simple answer to this method's benefits when he said, "I'm often astonished to find how much better chance is than I am." There are precedents for chance used within visual works dating back to collage works by Arp from 1916, but the two early works most relevant in the discussion of 10 PRINT are the *Spectrum of Colors Arranged by Chance* collage series (1951) by Ellsworth Kelly and *Random Distribution of 40,000 Squares Using the Odd and Even Numbers of a Telephone Directory* (1961) by François Morellet. These works start with an even grid and fill the grid carefully with elements based on the algorithms developed by the artists. Kelly uses squares of colored paper, placed according to a system he designed. He assigned a number to each color and plotted the numbers on the grid systematically (Malone 2009, 133). Morellet employed a stricter system, reading a series of numbers from the telephone book. He made a grid of 200 vertical and horizontal lines, painting a square blue if its assigned number is even, painting it red if it is odd. In both of these artworks and in 10 PRINT, the structure of the grid is what makes it possible to focus on the variability created through the random operations.

### A Million Random Digits

The need for large batches of random numbers is so acute that there are standardized collections of them. In Deborah Bennett's history of humans' quest for randomness—which she suggests goes as far back as ancient Babylonia (1998, 17)—she highlights one of the earliest and largest sets of random numbers, *A Million Random Digits with 100,000 Normal Deviates* (135). This series of numbers (figure 40.1) was generated in 1947 from "random frequency pulses of an electronic roulette wheel" by the RAND Project, a research and development think tank that would eventually become the RAND Corporation. The 1955 publication of the series in book form was an important contribution to any study of probability; the book is still in use today. As the forward to the undated online edition of the table notes:

> The tables of random numbers in the book have become a standard reference in engineering and econometrics textbooks and have been widely used in gaming and simulations that employ Monte Carlo trials. Still the largest known source of random digits and normal deviates, the work is routinely used by statisticians, physicists, polltakers, market analysts, lottery administrators, and quality control engineers. (RAND Corporation 1955)

Considering its sophisticated origins and uses, *A Million Random Digits* proposes a surprisingly unscientific method of using the book: "In any use of the table, one should first find a random starting position. A common procedure for doing this is to open the book to an unselected page of the digit table and blindly choose a five-digit number." The RAND report goes on to somewhat ominously explain that its one million random numbers were originally "prepared in connection with analyses done for the United States Air Force." Like so many other advances in computing, randomness, it turns out, is intimately linked to Cold War military strategies. In fact, most of the early work on computer-based random number generation was performed under the auspices of the U.S. Atomic Energy Commission see, for example, Rotenberg's [1960] work in the late 1950s) or the U.S military (see Green, Smith, and Klem's [1959] work at MIT, done with joint support of the U.S. Army, Navy, and Air Force).

## RANDOMNESS COMES TO COMPUTING

The RND command acts as the algorithmic heart of `10 PRINT`, its flip-flopping beat powering the construction of the maze. The RND function is as fully specified as any BASIC keyword, but its output is, by that definition, unpredictable. Mathematicians and computer scientists don't think in terms of predictability, though; rather, the standard mathematical treatment of randomness defines randomness in terms of probability. A random process generates a sequence of values selected from a set of possible values ac-

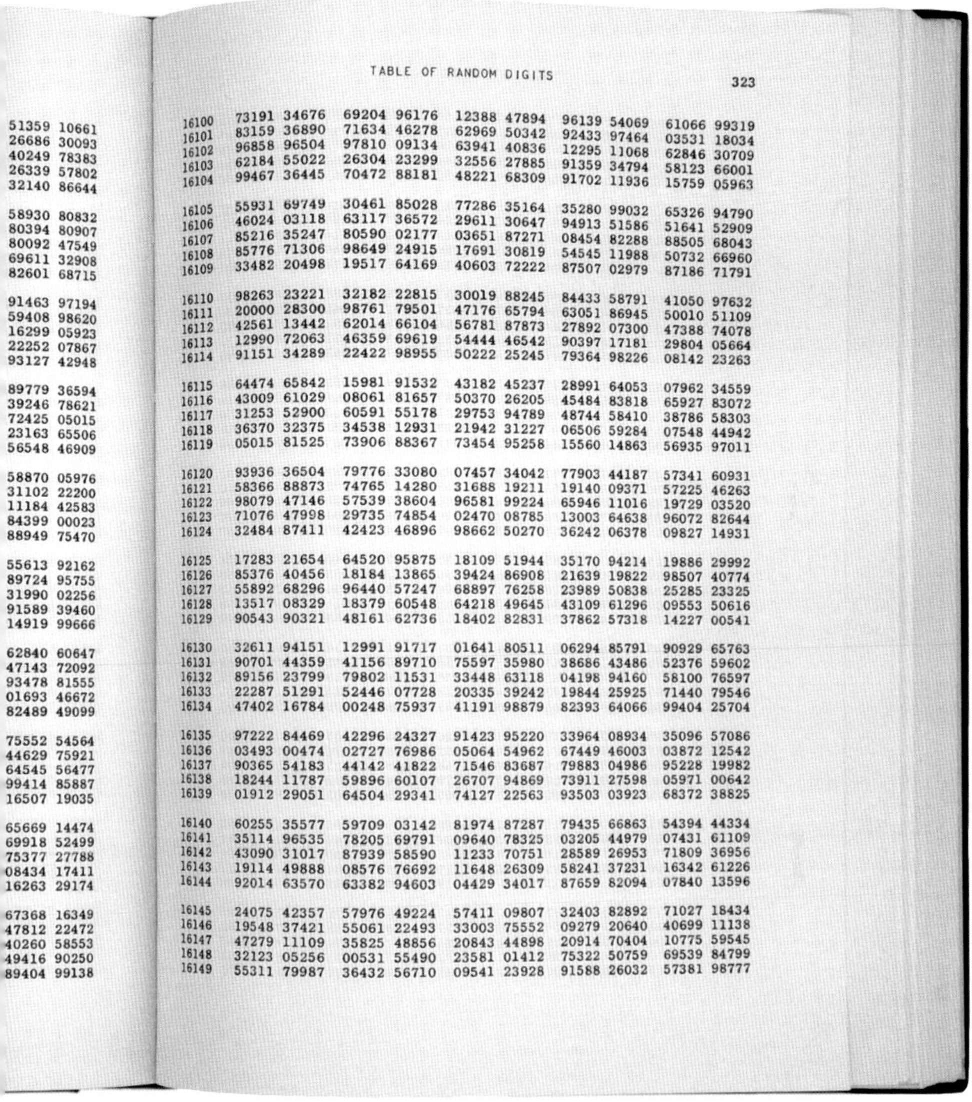

| | |
|---|---|
| 51359 | 10661 |
| 26686 | 30093 |
| 40249 | 78383 |
| 26339 | 57802 |
| 32140 | 86644 |
| 58930 | 80832 |
| 80394 | 80907 |
| 80092 | 47549 |
| 69611 | 32908 |
| 82601 | 68715 |
| 91463 | 97194 |
| 59408 | 98620 |
| 16299 | 05923 |
| 22252 | 07867 |
| 93127 | 42948 |
| 89779 | 36594 |
| 39246 | 78621 |
| 72425 | 05015 |
| 23163 | 65506 |
| 56548 | 46909 |
| 58870 | 05976 |
| 31102 | 22200 |
| 11184 | 42583 |
| 84399 | 00023 |
| 88949 | 75470 |
| 55613 | 92162 |
| 89724 | 95755 |
| 31990 | 02256 |
| 91589 | 39460 |
| 14919 | 99666 |
| 62840 | 60647 |
| 47143 | 72092 |
| 93478 | 81555 |
| 01693 | 46672 |
| 82489 | 49099 |
| 75552 | 54564 |
| 44629 | 75921 |
| 64545 | 56477 |
| 99414 | 85887 |
| 16507 | 19035 |
| 65669 | 14474 |
| 69918 | 52499 |
| 75377 | 27788 |
| 08434 | 17411 |
| 16263 | 29174 |
| 67368 | 16349 |
| 47812 | 22472 |
| 40260 | 58553 |
| 49416 | 90250 |
| 89404 | 99138 |

TABLE OF RANDOM DIGITS 323

| | | | | | | | | | | |
|---|---|---|---|---|---|---|---|---|---|---|
| 16100 | 73191 | 34676 | 69204 | 96176 | 12388 | 47894 | 96139 | 54069 | 61066 | 99319 |
| 16101 | 83159 | 36890 | 71634 | 46278 | 62969 | 50342 | 92433 | 97464 | 03531 | 18034 |
| 16102 | 96858 | 96504 | 97810 | 09134 | 63941 | 40836 | 12295 | 11068 | 62846 | 30709 |
| 16103 | 62184 | 55022 | 26304 | 23299 | 32556 | 27885 | 91359 | 34794 | 58123 | 66001 |
| 16104 | 99467 | 36445 | 70472 | 88181 | 48221 | 68309 | 91702 | 11936 | 15759 | 05963 |
| 16105 | 55931 | 69749 | 30461 | 85028 | 77286 | 35164 | 35280 | 99032 | 65326 | 94790 |
| 16106 | 46024 | 03118 | 63117 | 36572 | 29611 | 30647 | 94913 | 51586 | 51641 | 52909 |
| 16107 | 85216 | 35247 | 80590 | 02177 | 03651 | 87271 | 08454 | 82288 | 88505 | 68043 |
| 16108 | 85776 | 71306 | 98649 | 24915 | 17691 | 30819 | 54545 | 11988 | 50732 | 66960 |
| 16109 | 33482 | 20498 | 19517 | 64169 | 40603 | 72222 | 87507 | 02979 | 87186 | 71791 |
| 16110 | 98263 | 23221 | 32182 | 22815 | 30019 | 88245 | 84433 | 58791 | 41050 | 97632 |
| 16111 | 20000 | 28300 | 98761 | 79501 | 47176 | 65794 | 63051 | 86945 | 50010 | 51109 |
| 16112 | 42561 | 13442 | 62014 | 66104 | 56781 | 87873 | 27892 | 07300 | 47388 | 74078 |
| 16113 | 12990 | 72063 | 46359 | 69619 | 54444 | 46542 | 90397 | 17181 | 29804 | 05664 |
| 16114 | 91151 | 34289 | 22422 | 98955 | 50222 | 25245 | 79364 | 98226 | 08142 | 23263 |
| 16115 | 64474 | 65842 | 15981 | 91532 | 43182 | 45237 | 28991 | 64053 | 07962 | 34559 |
| 16116 | 43009 | 61029 | 08061 | 81657 | 50370 | 26205 | 45484 | 83818 | 65927 | 83072 |
| 16117 | 31253 | 52900 | 60591 | 55178 | 29753 | 94789 | 48744 | 58410 | 38786 | 58303 |
| 16118 | 36370 | 32375 | 34538 | 12931 | 21942 | 31227 | 06506 | 59284 | 07548 | 44942 |
| 16119 | 05015 | 81525 | 73906 | 88367 | 73454 | 95258 | 15560 | 14863 | 56935 | 97011 |
| 16120 | 93936 | 36504 | 79776 | 33080 | 07457 | 34042 | 77903 | 44187 | 57341 | 60931 |
| 16121 | 58366 | 88873 | 74765 | 14280 | 31688 | 19211 | 19140 | 09371 | 57225 | 46263 |
| 16122 | 98079 | 47146 | 57539 | 38604 | 96581 | 99224 | 65946 | 11016 | 19729 | 03520 |
| 16123 | 71076 | 47998 | 29735 | 74854 | 02470 | 08785 | 13003 | 64638 | 96072 | 82644 |
| 16124 | 32484 | 87411 | 42423 | 46896 | 98662 | 50270 | 36242 | 06378 | 09827 | 14931 |
| 16125 | 17283 | 21654 | 64520 | 95875 | 18109 | 51944 | 35170 | 94214 | 19886 | 29992 |
| 16126 | 85376 | 40456 | 18184 | 13865 | 39424 | 86908 | 21639 | 19822 | 98507 | 40774 |
| 16127 | 55892 | 68296 | 96440 | 57247 | 68897 | 76258 | 23989 | 50838 | 25285 | 23325 |
| 16128 | 13517 | 08329 | 18379 | 60548 | 64218 | 49645 | 43109 | 61296 | 09553 | 50616 |
| 16129 | 90543 | 90321 | 48161 | 62736 | 18402 | 82831 | 37862 | 57318 | 14227 | 00541 |
| 16130 | 32611 | 94151 | 12991 | 91717 | 01641 | 80511 | 06294 | 85791 | 90929 | 65763 |
| 16131 | 90701 | 44359 | 41156 | 89710 | 75597 | 35980 | 38686 | 43486 | 52376 | 59602 |
| 16132 | 89156 | 23799 | 79802 | 11531 | 33448 | 63118 | 04198 | 94160 | 58100 | 76597 |
| 16133 | 22287 | 51291 | 52446 | 07728 | 20335 | 39242 | 19844 | 25925 | 71440 | 79546 |
| 16134 | 47402 | 16784 | 00248 | 75937 | 41191 | 98879 | 82393 | 64066 | 99404 | 25704 |
| 16135 | 97222 | 84469 | 42296 | 24327 | 91423 | 95220 | 33964 | 08934 | 35096 | 57086 |
| 16136 | 03493 | 00474 | 02727 | 76986 | 05064 | 54962 | 67449 | 46003 | 03872 | 12542 |
| 16137 | 90365 | 54183 | 44142 | 41822 | 71546 | 83687 | 79883 | 04986 | 95228 | 19982 |
| 16138 | 18244 | 11787 | 59896 | 60107 | 26707 | 94869 | 73911 | 27598 | 05971 | 00642 |
| 16139 | 01912 | 29051 | 64504 | 29341 | 74127 | 22563 | 93503 | 03923 | 68372 | 38825 |
| 16140 | 60255 | 35577 | 59709 | 03142 | 81974 | 87287 | 79435 | 66863 | 54394 | 44334 |
| 16141 | 35114 | 96535 | 78205 | 69791 | 09640 | 78325 | 03205 | 44979 | 07431 | 61109 |
| 16142 | 43090 | 31017 | 87939 | 58590 | 11233 | 70751 | 28589 | 26953 | 71809 | 36956 |
| 16143 | 19114 | 49888 | 08576 | 76692 | 11648 | 26309 | 58241 | 37231 | 16342 | 61226 |
| 16144 | 92014 | 63570 | 63382 | 94603 | 04429 | 34017 | 87659 | 82094 | 07840 | 13596 |
| 16145 | 24075 | 42357 | 57976 | 49224 | 57411 | 09807 | 32403 | 82892 | 71027 | 18434 |
| 16146 | 19548 | 37421 | 55061 | 22493 | 33003 | 75552 | 09279 | 20640 | 40699 | 11138 |
| 16147 | 47279 | 11109 | 35825 | 48856 | 20843 | 44898 | 20914 | 70404 | 10775 | 59545 |
| 16148 | 32123 | 05256 | 00531 | 55490 | 23581 | 01412 | 75322 | 50759 | 69539 | 84799 |
| 16149 | 55311 | 79987 | 36432 | 56710 | 09541 | 23928 | 91588 | 26032 | 57381 | 98777 |

Figure 40.1

*A Million Random Digits with 100,000 Normal Deviates* was published in 1955 by the RAND Corporation and was the largest list of random values yet published. It was necessary for RAND to execute their research without repeating values from previously published, smaller number tables.

cording to a probability distribution. In the case of a discrete distribution (heads or tails, for instance), the distribution explains how much weight is on each possible outcome—how likely that value is to appear.

If, for example, one draws a single card from a thoroughly shuffled deck, the probability distribution from which this draw is done is uniform: it is equally likely that any particular card will be chosen. Similarly, random numbers are typically defined as numbers drawn from a uniform distribution over all possible numbers in some range. A difficulty with this definition is that the randomness of a number is defined in terms of that range. Given a number such as 42, it is impossible to tell how random a selection it was. To determine randomness without knowing the means of generation, one must consider a sequence of numbers; knowing the range in which the numbers are supposed to lie or, more generally, the distribution from which they are supposed to be drawn, is also essential.

Digital computers are deterministic devices—the next state of the machine is determined entirely by the current state of the machine. Thus, computer-based random number generators are more technically described as pseudorandom number generators. The somewhat dismissive-sounding "pseudo" refers to the fact that a deterministic process (a computer program) is being used to generate sequences of numbers that appear to be uniformly distributed. This works well in practice for sequences that aren't astronomically long. But eventually, for long enough sequences, the deterministic nature of a pseudorandom number generator will be unmasked, in that eventually statistical properties of the generated sequence will start diverging from those of a true random process. In an extremely long sequence, for example, a true random process will generate the same number many times in a row. A version of `10 PRINT` running using a true random process will eventually generate the regular image in figure 40.4 (and the image in figure 40.5, and every other possible pattern), while the pseudorandom number generator in the Commodore 64 will not. Tests for long runs are one of the many statistical tests used to judge the quality of pseudorandom number generators.

An obvious question to ask about randomness is why a computer would need to implement it in any form. Chance might produce stunning poetry, breathtaking art, uncanny music, and compelling games, but what is its role in the sciences? Why provide a calculating machine with the ability to generate random numbers in the first place? Certainly, one stereotype of computing is that it is done exactly, repeatedly, with perfect precision and accuracy. Computers are commonly thought to order the world, to sift through reams of data and then model possible outcomes, possible futures, providing certain—and deterministic—answers. Yet a function to generate random numbers was present in the first Dartmouth BASIC. Every version of BASIC since then has had one or more ways to create random numbers. Nearly every contemporary programming language, including Python, Perl, Java, JavaScript and C++, has a built-in way to generate randomness.

Quite simply, the answer to this puzzle is that randomness is necessary for any statistical endeavor, any simulation that involves unknown variables. Practically *everything* involves unknown variables: the meteorological conditions at a rocket launch site, the flow of air under a bomber's wings, and the spread of an infectious disease. Additionally, there is the movement and halting of traffic, the cost of bread, and the drip of water from the kitchen faucet. Forecasting any of these phenomena requires reckoning with uncertainty, which in turn requires a pool of random numbers. Furthermore, one or two random numbers are not enough. Large-scale statistical calculations or simulations require large batches of random numbers.

John von Neumann was the first to propose the idea of harnessing a computer to generate random numbers (Knuth 1969, 3). It was around 1946 and von Neumann was fresh off the Manhattan Project and soon to begin his lead work on the hydrogen bomb. Seeking a way to statistically model each stage of the fission process, von Neumann and his colleague Stanislaw Ulam first relied on the Monte Carlo method to generate tables of random numbers. These tables, however, soon grew too large to be stored on computers (Bennett 1998, 138–139). Von Neumann's solution was to design a computer program to produce random numbers on the fly, using the middle-square method. It worked by squaring an initial number, called the seed, and extracting the middle digits; this number was then squared again, and the middle digits provided a new random number (von Neumann 1961). Because each number is a function of the one before it, the sequence, as Donald Knuth explains, "isn't random, but it appears to be" (3)—that is, it is "pseudorandom."

## GRAPHING RANDOM MAZES

Randomness has enabled the construction of mazes for decades. These mazes are not grown in a careful arrangement of hedgerows, or built amid the mossy walls of Cretan dungeons. Instead, they are typically graphs, mathematical objects consisting of a set of nodes (also called vertices), pairs of which may be connected with a link (also called an edge). Graphs, or networks, don't need to have any particular geometry. They are simply nodes linked to other nodes, and they can be drawn on paper in many different ways that are correct representations.

Consider, however, a piece of graph paper, blank white except for a regular grid of pale blue lines. Each point where two lines cross can be taken to represent a node, while the lines between these points can define links. This construction, based on a lattice, is a special kind of graph called a grid graph. Using a pencil and tracing only along the pale blue demarcations, how does one draw a maze whose links (hallways) connect all of the nodes (rooms) to each other?

Graph theory, a field of mathematics, offers a number of methods for producing random mazes of this kind. The most well-known approaches are algorithms for calculating a minimal spanning tree, a graph in which all links are connected and with only one simple path between any two points. (Minimum spanning trees are found to solve problems in various domains, from phone networks to demographic analysis.) Because they lack cycles—there is exactly one path between any two nodes—the mazes produced by such trees are called "perfect mazes." Spanning solutions are not always mazes in the multicursal sense; they don't need to have forking paths. For example, on a grid graph, it's possible to create a minimal spanning tree using a single line, winding back and forth on a labyrinthine path until the page is filled. Of the myriad spanning solutions to a piece of graph paper, however, the vast majority of them *are* branching mazes. Thus, selecting a solution at random can be a good way to produce different mazes. A straightforward maze-generation technique involves adding random values (or weights) to all the links in the grid graph, then employing an algorithm to find a minimum spanning tree and thus generate a maze. Depending on the algorithm used, the resulting mazes may reflect different aesthetics, for instance, having different proportions of shorter and longer paths.

Significant minimum spanning tree algorithms were pioneered by Czech mathematicians in the early twentieth century (Otakar Borůvka in 1926; Vojtěch Jarník in 1930) and independently rediscovered many times thereafter, including decades later by computer scientists writing in English (e.g., Sollin in 1965). Two of the most well-known maze-generating algorithms in graph theory today are Joseph Kruskal's and Robert Clay Prim's. Both algorithms were published in 1957—although Prim's was a rediscovery of Jarník's and was in turn rediscovered by Dutch computer scientist Edsger W. Dijkstra, famous opponent of GOTO, in 1959 (Foltin 2011, 15). Both are greedy algorithms, which means that they choose the best link to take at every turn. Kruskal's algorithm chooses across the entire graph, while Prim's algorithm builds up a connected path. These algorithms can be modeled with paper and pencil, but computational randomization allows them to rapidly generate a plethora of maze forms, thanks to the interaction of the regularity of the grid, the deterministic algorithm, and the random weighting of links.

## COMPUTATIONAL RANDOMNESS IN THE ARTS

To those interested in randomness and expressive culture, perhaps the most intriguing element of Donald Knuth's magisterial discussion of random numbers appears in a footnote. Knuth recalls a CBS television documentary in 1960 called "The Thinking Machine" which featured "two Western-style playlets" written by a computer (Knuth 1969, 158–160). In fact, three playlets were acted out on national television that day in October 1960, generated by a TX-0 computer housed at MIT's Electronics Systems Laboratory. SAGA II, the script-writing program behind the mini Westerns, took programmers Douglas Ross and Harrison Morse two months to develop and consisted of 5,500 instructions (Pfeiffer 1962, 130–138). The key to SAGA II was its thirty "switches," which made "various alternative or branching paths" possible (136). "Among other things," Pfeiffer observed, "the robber may go to the window and look out and then go to the table, or he may go to the table directly. You cannot tell in advance which one of these alternatives the program will select, because it does the equivalent of rolling a pair of dice" (136).

Even before the SAGA II playlets, there were other literary experiments with randomness and computers. Noah Wardrip-Fruin identifies the

British computer scientist Christopher Strachey as the creator of the first work of electronic literature, a series of "love letters" generated by the Ferranti Mark I computer at Manchester University in 1952 (Wardrip-Fruin 2005). Affectionately known as M.U.C., the Manchester University Computer could produce the evocative love letters at a pace of one per minute, for hours on end, without producing a duplicate. The "trick" is, as Strachey put it, the two model sentences (e.g., "My *adjective noun adverb verb* your *adjective noun*" and "You are my *adjective noun*") in which the nouns, adjectives, and adverbs are randomly selected from a list of words Strachey had culled from Roget's *Thesaurus*. Adverbs and adjectives randomly drop out of the sentence as well, and the computer randomly alternates the two sentences. On the whole, Strachey is dismissive of his foray into the literary use of computers, using the example of the love letters simply to illustrate his point that simple rules can generate diverse and unexpected results (Strachey 1954, 29–30). Nonetheless, a decade before Raymond Queneau's landmark combinatory work *One Hundred Thousand Billion Poems,* Strachey had unwittingly laid the foundation for the combinatory method of composition by computer, a use of randomness that would grow more central to literature and the arts in the following decades.

Other significant early works involving random recombination had more visible connection to literary tradition and artistic movements. The 1959 "Stochastic Texts" of Theo Lutz combined texts from Franz Kafka with logical operations to produce "EVERY CASTLE IS FREE. NOT EVERY FARMER IS LARGE" among other statements (Lutz 1959/2005). In the next decade, Fluxus artist Alison Knowles and James Tenney, a programmer who worked in FORTRAN, devised *A House of Dust.* The program's output combines a regular stanza form and repetition with random variation in vocabulary, and was printed on a scroll of line printer paper for a 1968 chapbook publication (Pearson 2011, 194–203). More than a decade later, Jackson Mac Low made use of the venerable book *A Million Random Digits* to devise "Converging Stanzas," which were randomly populated with words from the 1930 850-word *Basic English Word List* (Mac Low 2009, 236). This poet's "Sade Suit" similarly used playing cards and *A Million Random Digits* to rewrite the work of Marquis de Sade (46).

## Early Experiments in Computational Art

The 1960s were a time of radical experimentation with randomness in the visual arts. Even though computers were available at that point for the exploration of chance operations, they were used in a very limited way because it was difficult to gain access to the machines, and there was a general distrust of computer technology in the arts. The `10 PRINT` program is remarkable because it was created later, when these barriers were far fewer. The Commodore 64 was relatively inexpensive and accessible. The public image of the computer was changing from a machine that supported technocracies to a tool for self-empowerment and creativity. Before personal computers, calculating machines could only be found in universities and research labs and, because of their cost and perceived purpose, they were typically used exclusively for what seemed more serious work, not for creating aesthetic images. When artists did gain access to these machines, it was typically through artists-in-residence programs at companies such as Bell Labs and IBM, and through infrastructures such as Experiments in Art and Technology (E.A.T.) based in New York or the Los Angeles County Museum of Art's Art and Technology initiative. Many of the first aesthetic computer graphics were made not by artists, but by mathematicians and engineers who were curious about other uses to which the machines at their labs could be put.

Within the first years that computer images were made, random processes were explored thoroughly. The first two exhibitions of computer-generated graphics appeared in art galleries in 1965; both shows included pieces that were created using random values. In New York, the works of A. Michael Noll and Bela Julesz, both researchers at Bell Labs, were exhibited at the Howard Wise gallery from April 6–24, 1965, under the title "Computer-Generated Pictures." In Stuttgart, the works of Georg Nees and Frieder Nake were exhibited at the Wendelin Niedlich Gallery from November 5–26, 1965, under the title "Computer-Grafik Programme."

In 1962, Noll published a technical memorandum at Bell Labs entitled "Patterns by 7090," the number referring to the IBM 7090 digital computer. He explained a series of mathematical and programming techniques that use random values to draw "haphazard patterns" to a Carlson 4020 Microfilm Printer. The eight patterns documented in the memo are the basis for his Gaussian Quadratic image that was exhibited in the 1965 exhibition. Noll used existing subroutines of the printer to draw a sequence of lines to connect a series of x- and y-coordinates that he calculated and stored inside an array. The x-coordinates in the array were generated by a custom subroutine he wrote called WNG (White Noise Generator), which produced random values within the range of its parameters, and the y-coordinates were set using a quadratic equation. Through this series of patterns, Noll explored a tension between order and disorder, regularity and random values.

In 1965, Nake created his *Fields of Rectangular Cross Hatchings* series, which succeeds through pairing ordered patterns with random placement (figure 40.2). Nake explained the way random values are used in the images:

> Within a given (arbitrarily chosen) image size, a random number of hatchings were generated. Each one of them was determined by the following random variables: location (x, y), size (a, b), orientation of lines within rectangle (horizontal or vertical), number of lines, pen. So for each rectangle there were seven random numbers determining its details. (Nake 2008)

After the first wave of visual images were created on plotters and microfilm at universities and research labs, a few professional artists independently started to gain access to computers and use them in their practice. The artists with the most success integrating a computer into their work had previously created drawings using formal systems. These artists continue to use computers in their work to this day. Artists who worked seriously with computers in the late 1960s, either individually or with technical collaborators, include Edward Zajec, Lillian Schwartz, Colette Bangert, Stan Vanderbeek, Harold Cohen, Manfred Mohr, and Charles Csuri. All of them employed random numbers in their early works created with software.

Manfred Mohr, for example, started as a jazz musician and later studied art in Paris; he began writing software to create drawings in 1969, at the Meteorological Institute of Paris, during the night after researchers had left for the day. In 1971, Mohr's work was featured in "Une Esthétique Programmée" at the Musée d'Art Moderne de la Ville de Paris (see figure 40.3), the first solo exhibit of artworks created with a computer at a museum. Random values are used extensively in the creation of the work shown.

Figure 40.2

Frieder Nake, *Fields of Rectangular Cross Hatchings, Overlaid by Vertical Lines. 22/10/65 Nr. 2.* Computer drawing, ink on paper, 50 × 44 cm. Collection Etzold, Museum Abteiberg Mönchengladbach. Courtesy of Frieder Nake.

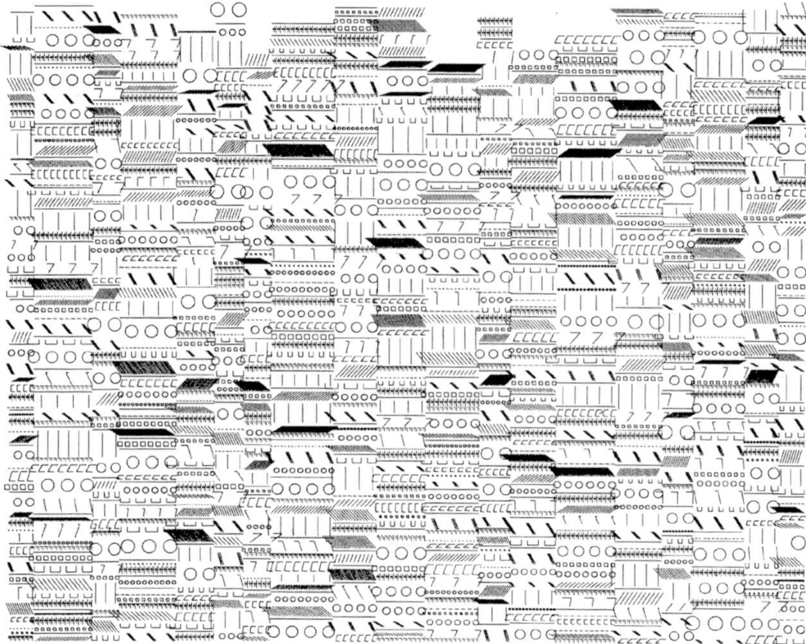

Figure 40.3

Manfred Mohr, *P-071*, 1970. Plotter drawing, ink on paper, 13.75 x 16.5" / 35 x 42 cm. Courtesy of bitforms gallery nyc.

Charles Csuri's *Random War* (1967) is an early notable work of computer art to use random values. Like much of Csuri's early computer work and unique in relation to his contemporaries, *Random War* is figurative rather than abstract. This plotter drawing comprises outlined military figures, patterned off of the toy figures of little green army men that were popular at the time. Each figure, named after a real person, is placed randomly on the page and randomly given a status: dead, wounded, or missing. The soldiers of one army are drawn in red, of the other army in black; the name and status of each soldier appear at the top of the drawing. In general terms, Csuri's work comments on the often arbitrary nature of war through both its form and its content; more specifically, with his reliance on random number generation, Csuri gestures toward the days of computers, random numbers, and their inextricable link to the Cold War.

## Acceptance and Resistance

While the first decade of computer-generated art was well documented in magazines, books, and exhibition catalogues, there are fewer source materials from the 1970s, when public interest veered and the energy needed to publish and exhibit waned. Later in the decade, computer graphics started to make their way into advertising and films. The 1982 film *Tron* is a landmark in the history of computation and aesthetics that pushed graphics to a new aesthetic level and therefore revealed the limitations of computer imagery at that time. *Tron*'s images are purely geometric and cold; they lack the organic qualities of our natural world. Ken Perlin, one of the programmers for the graphics in *Tron*, expressed frustration with the clean look. Later, in 1983, he developed a technique called Perlin Noise to generate organic textures that have a random appearance even though they are fully controllable to allow for careful design. Perlin Noise makes it possible for computer graphics models to have the subtle irregularities of real objects; it is used to create hard surfaces such as rocks and mountains and softer systems like fire and clouds. By the 1990s, it was being used extensively in Hollywood special-effects films and had been incorporated into most off-the-shelf modeling software.

Today the most widely known artists to use random values still do so without computers. For example, 2002 Turner Prize winner Keith Tyson designed sculptures not by using a computer to produce random numbers, but by rolling dice. One reason for this sort of reluctance to use computers, certainly, is the stigma surrounding computers in art. As Manfred Mohr remarked in an interview, "I called my work generative art, or occasionally also algorithmic works. The problem was that no-one understood either of these terms, and I was forced—so to speak—to declare my drawings as art from the computer . . . people accused me of degrading art, because I was employing capitalistic instruments of war—computer was a word non grata!" (Mohr 2007, 35). While Mohr was referring to the situation in the 1970s, the aversion to computers in art remains strong today.

More recently, however, as a new generation of visual artists have started to program their work, computed random numbers are playing an increasing role in the visual landscape. The most prominent programming languages used by visual artists have functions for generating random numbers and noise values, as well as for setting the random seed value to allow

## RANDOMNESS IN CONTEMPORARY COMPUTING

In the many examples of randomness given here, the random element of the process—whether computational, literary, or aesthetic—is often foregrounded, or at least made very obvious. Randomness is not always visible, however, even though it is often used in ordinary computing tasks. Randomness plays an essential role in the security of networked computers, for instance, and is also a part of popular computer games. Other uses of randomness lie beyond the everyday computing experience, but security, networking, and gaming are a few of the ones that are closest at hand.

When a computer needs to generate a new password for a user, a URL that will let someone reset a password, or a CAPTCHA to keep automated spammers at bay, randomness is invoked. A nonrandom password could easily be predicted, but a random password, URL, or distorted word is much harder to crack through guessing or brute force. Randomness also plays a behind-the-scenes role in protocols such as SSH (Secure Shell) and SSL (Secure Sockets Layer) in a few ways, including the generation of keys for encryption and padding out the rest of a block when a plain-text message is too short to complete it. Without randomness, it would not be possible to complete a secure credit card transaction on the Web, which happens over SSL. Early versions of SSL as implemented in the Netscape browser suffered from being insufficiently random: The seeds for random number generation were the current time, the process ID, and the parent process ID, which were sufficiently predictable to leave the browser vulnerable to attack. Better randomness was the solution to this problem.

Computers using Ethernet—almost all of those that are plugged into wired networks—communicate with one another thanks to randomness, too. All systems on a single local area network send information over the same wire. If two of them start sending on this single wire at the same time, what is known as a "collision" occurs; the data sent is not intelligible to the intended recipients. When a collision happens, the computer that detects the problem sends a jamming signal and tries to restart the transmission. But rather than restarting immediately, the computer chooses at random to start or wait—and the other computer that was trying to send does the same. If there is another collision, the computers either send immediately or wait for one of three intervals. The increasing number of intervals is part of the technique of exponential backoff; the selection of one of these intervals at random is an essential part of this method of avoiding network congestion.

A typical computer user of the 2010s will encounter randomness in many computer games. Randomness will shuffle the cards in poker or solitaire, for example, and will be invoked to arrange jewels and tiles in casual games. Randomness may also be used to determine the behavior of computer opponents, whether in poker, chess, or a first-person shooter. Some action, arcade-style, open-world, and other types of games incorporate randomness in other ways to determine what happens. Many early games and certain contemporary ones, however, are entirely deterministic. As those who discovered and exploited *Pac-Man* patterns know, that game is deterministic; *Ms. Pac-Man,* in contrast, uses randomness.

Though modern computers have many ways to provide initial values to seed their pseudorandom number generators, when higher levels of randomness are required one of the most reliable methods is to look beyond the computer. External entropy collection means that the random seed cannot be determined by knowing information about the computer's hardware, a common source for seeds inside the computer. In some cases the computer has to turn to a human to become more random, recording data from users mashing the keys on their keyboard or wiggling their mouse around to generate a random key or password. Even more unguessable are inputs from physical systems of sufficient complexity—anything from video of a lava lamp to atmospheric radio distortions can be used to create random numbers for computation. These levels of randomness are now required for demanding applications like high-level cryptography and scientific simulations. With continual increases in processing power, attacks on encryption are becoming easier, and the goal of making random numbers *more* random will be critical for securing society's constant digital transactions.

for the repetition of sequences. With the perspective of time, it seems that aesthetic computational work and random values are intertwined. Writing in 1970, Noll highlights randomness as an essential feature of the computer in relation to the arts:

> The computer is a unique device for the arts since it can function solely as an obedient tool with vast capabilities for controlling complicated and involved processes, but then again, full exploitation of its unique talents for controlled randomness and detailed algorithms could result in an entirely new medium—a creative artistic medium. (Noll 1970, 10)

## THE COMMODORE 64 RND FUNCTION

The way that 10 PRINT invokes the randomness provided by the Commodore 64 is of interest for reasons that will each be explored in turn. First, using randomness is aesthetically necessary in this program; there is no other way to achieve a similar effect. Second, the methods used in Commodore 64 BASIC are historically quite typical of computational approaches to pseudorandomness since the 1950s. Finally, out of several common approaches to randomness available on the Commodore 64, 10 PRINT uses a very standard method that is well suited to experimentation, debugging, and the production of canonical results, although this method is not without its deficiencies.

10 PRINT produces a wrapping series of diagonal lines that alternate between left and right unpredictably. This unpredictability is crucial to producing the impression of a maze. Looking at variations of 10 PRINT that have regular or no alternation demonstrates the significance of randomness in the program. It's possible to write an even simpler program than 10 PRINT to draw only the left diagonal to the screen in a regular pattern (figure 40.4):

```
10 PRINT CHR$(205); : GOTO 10
```

This program can be extended by writing the other diagonal character to the right to form a chevron that repeats (figure 40.5):

Figure 40.4

Screen capture from `10 PRINT CHR$(205); : GOTO 10`, a regular repetition of the ╲ character.

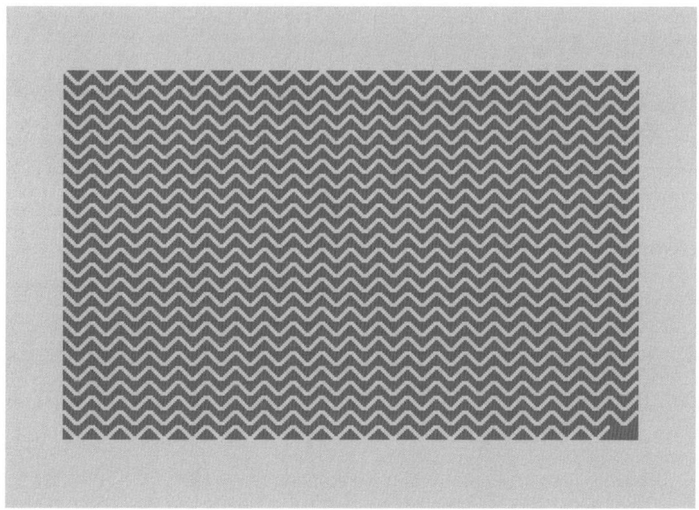

Figure 40.5

Screen capture from `10 PRINT CHR$(205)CHR$(206); : GOTO 10`, a regular repetition of the ╲ character followed by ╱.

```
10 PRINT CHR$(205)CHR$(206); : GOTO 10
```

The next step in this elaboration is the canonical **10 PRINT**, which draws either the left or right diagonal to the screen based on the result of the random number (figure 40.6):

```
10 PRINT CHR$(205.5+RND(1)); : GOTO 10
```

In **10 PRINT**, random numbers are provided through RND, one of ten mathematical functions available in BASIC since the earliest version of the language. As described the original Dartmouth BASIC manual (1964), RND produces a "new and different random number" between 0 and 1 "each time it is used in a program" (39). These numbers can then be used to drive unpredictable processes, as in fact they do drive the coin-toss decision between diagonal lines in **10 PRINT** output. A similar process might also determine the direction changes of ghosts in *Ms. Pac-Man* or the way other game elements appear or behave.

RND is, like most computational sources of randomness, a pseudorandom number generator. While there may be no apparent pattern between any two numbers, each number is generated based on the previous one using a deterministic process. When the first number is the same, the entire sequence will always be the same. In the case of the Commodore 64, this is particularly important because the same seed, and thus the same first number, is set at startup. So when RND(1) is invoked immediately after startup, or before any other invocation of RND, it will always produce the same result: 0.185564016. The next invocation will also be the same, no matter what Commodore 64 is used or how long the system has been on. The next invocation—and all others—will also be the same. Since the sequence is deterministic, the pattern produced by the **10 PRINT** program typed in and run as the first program is always the same, on every computer or well-functioning emulator.

When called on *any* positive number, as when RND(1) is invoked in **10 PRINT**, RND produces the next number in this sequence. RND(8), RND(128), and RND(.333) do exactly the same as RND(1). RND, however, has two other modes besides the one used in **10 PRINT**. The second is stopwatch-based: when RND(0) is called, the clock time since the computer was powered on is used in generating a new seed, meaning

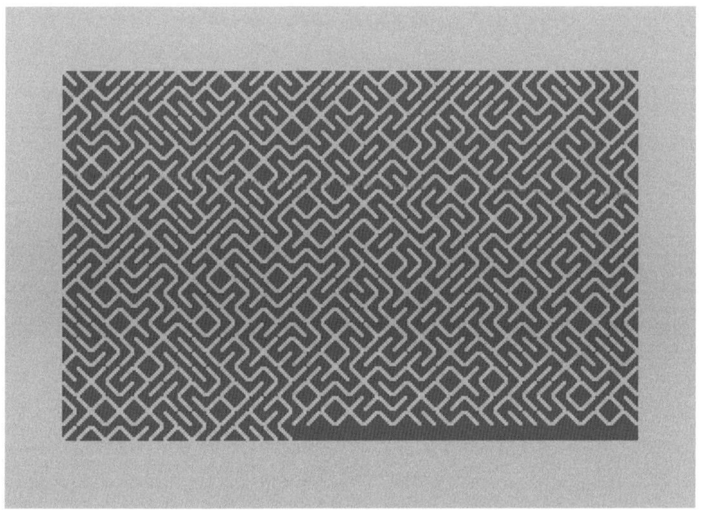

Figure 40.6
Screen capture from `10 PRINT CHR$(205.5+RND(1)); : GOTO 10`, which has a 50/50 chance of writing a ╲ or ╱ at each loop.

that if `RND(0)` replaces `RND(1)`, each run of `10 PRINT` at a different second should generate a different output. After a single call to `RND(0)`, subsequent calls to `RND(1)` will continue generating numbers in that new sequence.

The third mode for RND applies when any negative number is called. A call to `RND(-17)` stores −17 as the seed value for the random number generator, directly, and produces a new number. This negative seeding must be followed by positive calls to the function, such as `RND(1)`, in order to provide a useful sequence. Because negative calls simply set the seed, calling `RND(-1)` repeatedly will always return 0.544630526. For this reason, `10 PRINT` could not be a single-line loop that calls a negative `RND` value; that program would output the same diagonal again and again. A single call to `RND`, however, with any negative number, followed by the rest of the `10 PRINT` program, will generate a unique (and repeatable) `10 PRINT` pattern.

Pseudorandomness, however lacking it may sound, is generally acceptable and in many situations desirable. Engineers running a computer simulation, for example, often have many random variables, but every run of the simulation needs those variables to have the same values; otherwise the program cannot be tested or the experiment repeated. Pseudorandom number generators are also highly useful in hashing, since they allow data to be distributed widely but also placed in known locations. Similarly, they are useful in cryptography, where it is vital that sequences be repeatable if (and only if) the initial conditions are known.

The *Commodore 64 User's Guide* introduces the concept of randomness using an example that sidesteps the origins of randomness in computing. There is no mention of the hydrogen bomb, computer-generated literature, or prime numbers. Randomness comes into play in the shape of a game when it is necessary to, as the manual puts it, "simulate the throw of dice" (Commodore 1982, 48). This example takes the reader back to preindustrial notions of randomness. Yet, centuries ago, long before Mallarmé provided his assurance that a throw of the dice would not abolish chance, Sir Walter Raleigh wrote of this event as apocalyptic:

> Dead bones shall then be tumbled up and down,
> In every city and in every town.

Fortune's wheel and what Paul Auster called *The Music of Chance* have long been considered a matter of life and death. As `10 PRINT` scrolls its playful, pleasing maze pattern upon the screen, there may be the faintest echo of the dead bones of the dice and the random simulation of the hydrogen bomb. And perhaps, as well, there is the transformation of this grim, military use of randomness into a thing of beauty.

# 45
# REM
# ONE-LINERS

One-liners, as single-line programs such as `10 PRINT` are known, predate home computing, the exchange of BASIC code in magazines, and even the BASIC programming language itself. These concise little programs were written at least as early as the beginning of the 1960s. The language that was most famous for writing such programs was APL, designed by Kenneth Iverson using special (non-ASCII) notation. APL was first described in his 1957 book *A Programming Language* and was first implemented at IBM beginning in 1960.

In APL there is no limit on the length of a line; anything that a programmer can express as a single statement counts. A report shows that "all 'practically' computable functions" can be written as APL one-liners (Lipton and Snyder 1977, 2), so perhaps one-liners in this language should not be particularly impressive. Programmers have nevertheless been impressed by them. APL one-liners have been published that solve the problem of placing N queens on an N × N chessboard (Selfridge 1977, 243) and that completely encode John Conway's Game of Life (McDonnell 1988, 6). The final Game of Life APL function presented is only nine tokens long. While not everyone involved with computing shares an enthusiasm for one-liners, or for APL, the exchange and academic publication of APL one-liners does demonstrate that interest in this form of program was not limited to amateurs or newcomers to computing.

In the early 1980s, magazines published one-line programs, sometimes regularly, to fascinate and intrigue home computer users and to help them explore programming. In the Commodore-specific magazine *RUN*, they appeared in a section near the front of the magazine entitled "Magic," which contained "Hints and tricks that will let you perform computing wizardry." Some of their one-liners and tips were clearly for amusement and educational purposes. Others were practical programming aids. Many were quite expressive and produced interesting visual effects.

Here is the first trick, numbered zero in hexadecimal, in the very first "Magic" section from the inaugural issue of *RUN*:

> **Trick $00.** This month's "one line special" is an antiquity—from the far-off days of 1978, when an 8K Commodore PET cost $795, and readable documentation was unheard of. There weren't any books, and the only magazines were newsletters produced by amateurs.
>
> *The PET Gazette* was one of them, and here is one of its early

offerings, called "BURROW":

```
1A$="[up][down][left][right]":PRINTMID$(A$,RND(.5)*4+1,1)"
*[left]";:FORI=1TO30:NEXT:PRINT"[rvs on][space][left]";:GOTO1
```

It fits on one 40-column line, and it *does* get exciting. We'd like to see *your* one-line programs, and we want to print at least one good one each month. Programs can be fun, funny, useful or useless, as long as they fit in 40 columns or less. What do you have? (Sander 1984)

The program featured here (see figure 45.1) moves the cursor randomly either up, down, left, or right, prints an asterisk, moves left over it, turns on reverse video, prints a space, and moves left over that—and then repeats. This means that it will "dig" a reverse-video hole (green, not black, on a PET computer) haphazardly, although orthogonally, from its starting point to wherever it ends up around the screen. Its mazelike path involves both regularity (each move is directly along an axis) and randomness (which of the four directions it moves in is chosen at random), producing the promised excitement. The program has some affinity with **10 PRINT**, although **10 PRINT** creates a different sort of scrolling pattern and suggests a structure rather than traversing the screen a character at a time.

This printing of the "BURROW" program, already declared an antique, also shows an awareness of computing history and a willingness to rediscover older programs so they can be enjoyed by a new generation of programmers and users.

Here is another intriguing one-liner from *RUN* (Rapp 1985):

When he's not looking, run this on a friend's VIC or C-64. Then get him to type a line or two, and watch the fun as he scrambles for his warranty.

```
10 POKE207,0:POKE204,0:WAIT198,1:GETA$: PRINT"{CTRL RVS OFF}"
CHR$(ASC(A$)+1.1*RND(0));:GOTO 10
```

This program is similar to **10 PRINT** in a few ways. It runs in an infinite loop; it also makes use of the RND function. These are true of "BURROW" as well. An additional similarity between this April Fool's program and **10 PRINT** is the use of CHR$. There is a significant difference, too. Rapp's program doesn't do anything obvious when run. After running it, the cursor sits blinking as if one were in the BASIC interpreter. Once run, this one-liner is actually in control of keyboard input and screen output and effectively

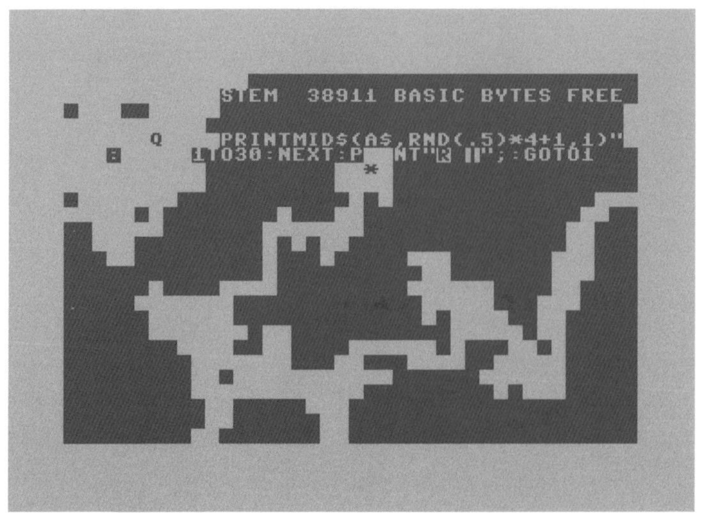


Figure 45.1

Screen capture from one-line "BURROW" program.

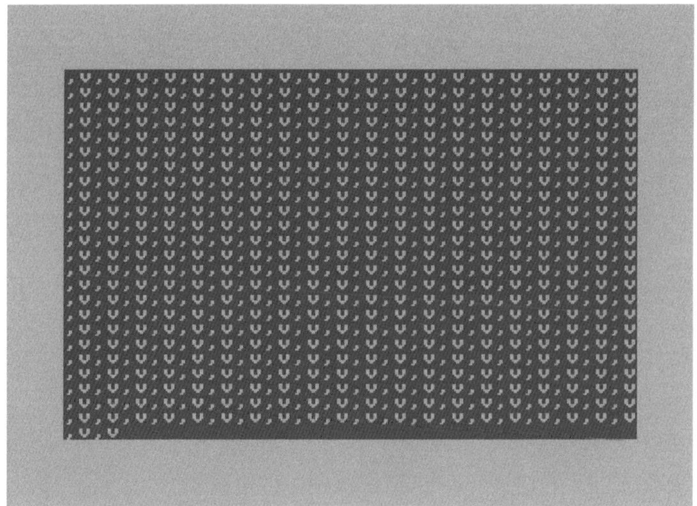

Figure 45.2

Screen capture from one-line program featured in *RUN* magazine to check monitor resolution.

intercepts input from BASIC and the Commodore 64's operating system, the KERNAL, running atop them. Typing something will (often) cause the typed characters to appear on the screen as they usually would, but about one time in eleven, the next character in the PETSCII sequence will appear instead, possibly transforming the user's typed `10 PRINT "HELLO"` to the puzzling and frustrating `10 PRJNT "HFLLO"`.

`10 PRINT` uses `RND` differently, to draw from an even distribution of two characters. As the *Commodore 64 User's Manual* explains, this distribution can be skewed, as it is in the first variant of the program presented in the first remark, written in BASIC. Even with a somewhat unbalanced distribution, the larger impression is still mazelike. The "essential frustration" of the maze, on the one hand, is one that is evident and stems from its interlocking, larger structure to which the randomness contributes. Rapp's prank is tricky, on the other hand, because it is biased toward intermittent unpredictability and operates invisibly.

By the late 1980s, although the "Magic" section continued in *RUN* (through the magazine's last issue), it was handed off to other editors and filled with utility programs, in BASIC and assembly, that were significantly longer—often around twenty lines. This late one-liner from *RUN* (Hubbard 1987) offers help for the Commodore user looking for a new monitor and shows the utilitarian turn that programs took in later years (see figure 45.2):

```
10 PRINT CHR$(14):FOR A=1TO40*23:PRINT",V";:NEXT
```

> Enter the program and run it. The screen will fill with 23 lines of commas and lowercase V's. To check the resolution, look at the single pixel that forms the point of the center of the v or the tail of the comma. On a monochrome monitor the pixels should be a single round point of light.

Some one-line utilities were compatible across BASIC machines such as the Commodore, Apple, and Atari home computers and might also run on the original Dartmouth BASIC—but many of the fun and exciting ones were specific to particular platforms. The numerous versions of BASIC included some which included commands such as `PLOT` and `SOUND` to facilitate making graphics and music. Of course, a one-liner in a BASIC of this variety could take advantage of these special commands. In these cases, one-liners were often teaching tools: programs that helpfully introduced commands needed to perform higher-level tasks.

This practice continues in the contemporary practice of programming tutorials; one example is Peteris Krumins's "Perl One-Liners Explained" (Krumins 2009–2011). It introduces more than a hundred single-line pieces of code such as:

```
perl -MPOSIX -le'@now = localtime; $now[0] -= 7;
$now[4] -= 14; $now[7] -= 9; print scalar localtime
mktime @now'
```

Each of Krumins's examples includes a description—often a somewhat mysterious one, such as this program's: "Print date 14 months, 9 days and 7 seconds ago." The first question a non-coder might consider is "Why that? What was 14 months ago?" This sort of arbitrary program construction is not valuable as a utility in its given form. Rather, it is useful to try out because of what the programmer can accomplish by daring to change it and by inserting the code into a more complex program. That code snippet could be useful, for example, in a vacation scheduling or beer fermentation system. It resembles `10 PRINT` in that it unlocks the workings of higher-level functions (such as `localtime` and `mktime`). `10 PRINT` arouses interest not only from its visually active display with minimum code but because that code reveals an elegant means of accessing the higher-level video terminal system, which is an entry point vital to writing a diverse area of types of programs.

Many programmers of one-liners took advantage of the BASIC commands for high- and low-resolution graphics on computers contemporaneous with the Commodore 64, such as the Apple II. Apple II users enjoyed a rich culture of one-line graphics display programming as well as a tradition of "two-step" programs, which consisted of two lines instead of one. Apple II users also benefited from having a longer maximum line size than on the Commodore.

The two-line format came about because often one line was reserved to initialize the graphics display hardware and other variables. It did not and should not have run multiple times. The second line was a loop that, like `10 PRINT`, produced animated graphical output. In `10 PRINT`, an initialization line was unnecessary, because the default state of the Commodore 64 was a pseudo-graphics terminal: at power-up not only was the computer in a state to immediately begin accepting and executing BASIC commands, it could also draw graphics characters from a set which was printed on the keyboard. Computers, such as those in the Atari and Apple series, had BASIC multimedia commands (**COLOR**, **GR**, **PLOT**, **HLIN**, **PSET**, to name a few) to access their platform hardware, and could be said to have led to more impressive one-liners that were not possible on the Commodore computers—something that only increased the value of the most impressive Commodore one-liners, including **10 PRINT**.

By way of example, consider the one-liner "Icicle Storm," developed for this book to demonstrate how the use of one-liners can communicate valuable details about a computer system. The program generates a simple multimedia display that looks like the sky filling with icicles, drawn using one of the diagonal graphics characters used in 10 PRINT (see figure 45.3):

```
10 POKE 1024+RND(1)*1000,78: GOTO 10
```

Although it is a minimal simulation, the code highlights several useful details about the Commodore 64 platform. First, the repeated calls to **POKE** the distribution **1024+RND(1)*1000** indicate setting values in a section of memory. This is the "direct route" or memory-mapped access to the text/graphics terminal on the platform. To experienced programmers of other computers, this one-liner communicates "This computer has a screen memory just like many others. This particular one begins at 1024 and is 1000 bytes long." The transfer of knowledge from platform to platform is a key part of the practice of programming; another key part is learning the differences among platforms. Sometimes knowing just a few details about a new system enables one to leverage a great deal of previous experience into competency of the new system.

While such addresses were not secret—they could be obtained simply by buying the *Commodore 64 Programmer's Reference Guide* that Commodore published (1982)—they held a certain value when printed material about programming was still sparse, in the early days of home computing. While commercial software empowered users within the realm of their applications, short programs in books and magazines illustrated how to make the computer do impressive things and empowered readers to program. They associated brief BASIC texts with sufficiently compelling title and graphical output or other effects to allow one to build up a catalogue of

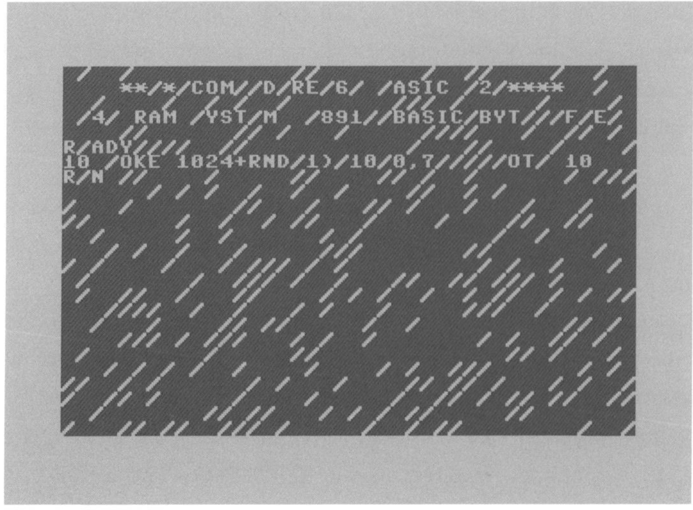

Figure 45.3
Screen capture from the "Icicle Storm" one-liner. Characters are drawn at random positions on screen one at a time.

appropriately useful code segments. Thus "Icicle Storm," like `10 PRINT`, is not an effort to tell a story about weather. It is a cartoon that presents the physics of the virtual world it runs in, the text/graphics terminal, through the speed of the screen update and the properties of its regular grid.

The slow, ruthless instantiation of icicles mimics the dynamics of a mounting storm because the computer cannot draw them fast enough to fill the screen instantly. The pace of that experience is CPU-limited. It would be possible to *slow down* the drawing, but not to speed it up without resorting to something other than changes in BASIC code. Understanding the general pace or speed at which a platform executes code is useful information to programmers.

The kinetic movement of the storm, determined by the update rate of the screen, fulfills the purpose of the illusion sufficiently that the impression is uniquely identifiable and memorable. It thus invites and aids the programmer to remember the useful numbers in the program. As part of the cartoon illusion that the program conjures, the evoked scene also assumes the default foreground and background colors of the computer, producing blue ice crystals against an azure sky. This may even be a more appropriate and specific play on the default colors than 10 PRINT provides.

A similar one-line program developed for this book, "Windy Day in Chicago," illustrates another feature of the VIC-II that is useful to programmers, smooth horizontal scrolling:

```
10 POKE 53248+22,INT(192+4+3*SIN((TIME*3.456+RND(1)
*.5))): GOTO 10
```

The program doesn't change any of the characters or colors on the screen; it simply causes everything on the screen to move back and forth semi-regularly as if the display were being blown around. This program demonstrates the relative simplicity of working with the side-scrolling register in the video chip, an advanced topic which is never taught explicitly in the Commodore 64 manuals.

Finally, another way to go about probing the capabilities of complex chips, including the Commodore 64's sound chip, the SID, is to simply write random values to their registers and attend to the result. Here is such a program for the SID, one which produces random sounds:

```
10 POKE 54272 + (0*TI+(RND(1)*25)),(RND(1)*256)
AND255:GOTO 10
```

Computers no longer power on to the READY prompt and the BASIC programming language, but, as the discussion of Perl one-liners shows, short, impressive, inviting programs live on in other languages and environments. There is more on the way that some Perl one-liners are apprehended and remembered in the next chapter, in the section "BASIC in Human Memory."

# 50
# BASIC

PROGRAMMING AND THE BEGINNING OF BASIC
BASIC COMES TO THE HOME
COMMODORE BASIC
THE CIRCULATION OF BASIC PROGRAMS
LATE BASIC

The character graphics themselves, the way they line up in rows and then in columns, and even the speed at which they appear—these characteristics all contribute to the aesthetic of `10 PRINT`'s output. However, `10 PRINT` functions the way it does, in part, because it is written in a specific programming language with particular affordances and attributes: BASIC.

This "Beginner's All-purpose Symbolic Instruction Code" has a fabled cultural and technical history. BASIC was developed by John Kemeny and Thomas Kurtz, two professors at Dartmouth College. In 1964 its creators freely shared a working version of the language, leading to its widespread adoption at the high school and college level. By that time, general-purpose computers had existed for about two decades. Many were still programmed in low-level machine languages, but high-level languages, abstracted from the idiosyncrasies of an individual machine, had also been in widespread use for a decade. BASIC continued the evolution of high-level languages, building on some of what FORTRAN, Algol, and other languages had accomplished: greater portability across platforms along with keywords and syntax that facilitated understanding the language and writing programs.

The language was developed for an early time-sharing environment, the Dartmouth Time-Sharing System (DTSS). This revolutionary configuration allowed multiple programmers to use a single system at the same time. A system of this sort—with many terminals connected to a mainframe or minicomputer—differs considerably from the personally owned, relatively inexpensive, single-user computers of the microcomputer era. But in the early 1960s, the DTSS also distinguished itself from earlier systems that required the batch processing of stacks of punched cards. Time-sharing allowed people to engage with and explore computation in significant new ways, with what felt like "real time" processing; BASIC was an important part of this computing revolution. Given the educational purpose of DTSS and BASIC, ease of use was paramount. Being easy to use helped BASIC's massive popularity and success.

BASIC became even more influential as microcomputers entered people's homes. In 1975 the MITS Altair 8800 computer, widely acclaimed as the first home computer, became available. Perhaps the most significant piece of software for this system was Altair BASIC, a version of BASIC that was the first product of a young company called Microsoft. Following its success with the Altair 8800, Microsoft wrote versions of BASIC for many popular microcomputers. Thanks in large part to Microsoft, BASIC became the lingua franca of home computing. BASIC resided in the ROM of these computers, meaning a user could turn on the computer and immediately begin programming. From the late 1970s through the early 1980s, BASIC reigned supreme on home computers, with `10 PRINT` and thousands of other programs circulating through books, magazines, and computer club newsletters. BASIC was so canonical that some books of BASIC programs did not even bother to mention "BASIC" on their covers.

Despite or because of its ubiquity, BASIC has become a target of derision for many modern programmers. Inextricably associated with Microsoft and that bane of structured programmers, `GOTO`, the language has been said to encourage tangled, unmanageable code, to be unbearably slow, and to be suitable only for children and amateurs. Yet BASIC has not completely disappeared, and many programmers in the early twenty-first century remember BASIC fondly. The language was a popular success, worked well for small programs that let home users explore computing, and fostered creativity and innovation in several generations of computer users and programmers.

## PROGRAMMING AND THE BEGINNING OF BASIC

While there is some dispute over who should rightly be called the first computer programmer, many have awarded this designation to Ada Byron, the Countess of Lovelace (1815–1852). She was raised by her mother and educated extensively in mathematics and logic specifically so that she might follow a different path from that of her father, Lord Byron. Such a stark separation in Ada's upbringing offers a very early example of the perceived incompatibility between computation and poetics.

Ada Lovelace's contributions as an early programmer are most evident in her translation of and notes to an Italian article by Louis Menabrea about Charles Babbage's Analytical Engine (Menabrea 1842). In this work, completed in 1843, she envisioned the Analytical Engine as a general-purpose computer and described an algorithm that could be used to output Bernoulli numbers. Although the computer to execute Lovelace's program was never built, her project made an important contribution to the modern idea of computing (Fuegi and Francis 2003). Lovelace's "program" was an algorithm described in mathematical notation.

The computer programs that followed in the electromechanical and early electronic age of computing were less intelligible than Lovelace's algorithm, bearing little relationship to any kind of written word. For example, the ENIAC, a fully electronic computer built at the University of Pennsylvania from 1943 to 1945, was programmed initially by plugging in an elaborate set of cables (da Cruz 2011). To run particular calculations, constants were then set using dials. Though the notion of punch cards dates back at least to Babbage in the nineteenth century and Falcon and his loom from the eighteenth century, programming the ENIAC was a matter of direct physical interaction with hardware rather than the manipulation of symbols. The operators of the ENIAC, who were primarily women, "played an important role in converting the ENIAC into a stored-program computer and in determining the trade-off between storing values and instruction" (Chun 2011, 31). Historically, even as programming continued to expand away from direct hardware manipulation and into progressively higher levels of abstraction, these operators were inventing both computation and the act of programming as embodied, materially engaged activities and vocations.

### Machine Language and Assembly Language

The move beyond cables and dials was accomplished with machine language. A program in machine language is simply a sequence of numbers that causes the computer to operate but can be understood by humans. On the ENIAC, the numbers that formed a machine language program were decimal (base 10), but different bases were used on other early systems. The EDVAC used binary; the ORDVAC, octal; and the BRLESC, sexadecimal (Bergin 2000, 62). The numbers specify what operations the computer is to carry out and consist of *opcodes* (indicating low-level commands) that may be followed by *operands* (giving one or more parameters to those commands). For instance, the opcode to add a value to the accumulator has to have one operand after it, specifying what value is to be added, while the opcode to increment the x register does not have any operands at all, since that opcode by itself specifies everything that is to be done.

To jump unconditionally to a particular absolute address, an opcode such as "76" (in base 10) is used, followed by two bytes specifying the address. In fact, this is the opcode used for an unconditional branch to an absolute address on the Commodore 64. While the sequence of numbers in a machine language program is unambiguous to the computer, it is far from obvious at a glance even which numbers represent opcodes and which operands. An expert in machine language could pick out some patterns, but would often have to start at the beginning, recognizing each opcode, knowing how many operands correspond to those opcodes, and continuing through as if simulating the calculations and memory storage operations as the program executes. Writing a machine language program requires similar low-level expertise. Working at this level is clearly something that computers do better than people, as was acknowledged when programming took the next step.

A more legible form of code arose in the second generation of programming languages, called assembly languages. Assembly allows mnemonics for operators such as `lda` (load accumulator), `jmp` (jump), and `inc` (increment memory) to stand in for the more esoteric numerical codes. On the Commodore 64, the letters `jmp` followed by an absolute address are converted by the assembler to 76, translating the human-legible mnemonic into machine language. The first assembler ran on Cambridge University's EDSAC in 1949. EDSAC was, incidentally, the first computer capable of storing programs, a feature modern computer users have taken for granted for decades (Campbell-Kelly and Aspray 1996, 184). Although cryptic compared to a high-level language such as BASIC, an assembler program is nevertheless more comprehensible to a human than a machine language program. While assembly is still used today in, for instance, programming firmware and in the demoscene, there are usually significant disadvantages to programming at this level. While programming in assembly highlights technical details of platforms and the transfer of values between memory locations and registers, higher-level languages allow the programmer to concentrate on other matters, such as solving mathematical and scientific problems or modeling financial processes.

### High-Level Languages

During the first decade of electronic computing, programming was still crawling toward the ideal of Lovelace's "program" that specified an algorithm in high-level, human-readable form. To reach a level of programming more appropriate for mathematical and scientific tasks, FORTRAN (FORmula TRANslation) was outlined in 1954 and first implemented in 1957. This language, and particularly the next version of it (FORTRAN II, which appeared in 1958), had a very strong influence on BASIC. Just as FORTRAN was designed with mathematics in mind, COBOL (COmmon Business-Oriented Language) was introduced in 1960 to address business uses.

FORTRAN and COBOL both allowed for more intelligible code, improving on assembly. But both were also developed in the context of batch processing, for use with stacks of punched cards that would be processed by the machine one at a time. Punch cards were first used in the eighteenth century to define patterns in mechanical textile looms, as discussed in the chapter Regularity, but the concept was adopted in computing in the twentieth century. The paragon of the punched card became known as simply "the IBM card," the eighty-column punched card introduced by that company in 1928. The Commodore 64's eighty-column logical line, which appears as two forty-column lines on the screen, is one legacy of this early material medium for computing.

Programs written in early versions of COBOL and FORTRAN were specific to the punched card in definite ways. COBOL reserved columns 1–6 for the line number and column 7 for a continuation mark if the card's code ran on from the previous one. FORTRAN was similar, with columns 1–5 indicating the statement number. "Comments" (usually the program name) went in columns 73–80 in both languages; a "C" in the first column indicated that the whole FORTRAN card was to be considered a comment. Unless a programmer wrote a one-liner—which in this case means writing a program that fits on a single card—a COBOL or FORTRAN program would take the form of a stack, often a massive stack, of punched cards. These had to be punched on a keypunch machine and fed into a card reader by an operator. Line numbers were essential in one particular case: if someone dropped a stack of cards and they needed to be sorted back into order.

FORTRAN's `GOTO` command was the basis for the `GOTO` in the original BASIC (Kurtz 2009, 86), which was carried over into Commodore 64 BASIC. `GOTO` functions in the same way the assembly language `jmp` does, shifting the interpreter to a specific location within the program. If one were simply interested in easily writing `jmp` statements, BASIC offers little advantage. The benefits of BASIC can be seen in commands such as `PRINT`. What takes many steps in machine language is efficiently accomplished by this single command that employs a clear, natural language metaphor.

BASIC was a language specifically designed for the next computing revolution, one that would go beyond punched cards and batch processing to allow numerous users interactive access to a system simultaneously. This revolution was time-sharing.

## Dartmouth BASIC and Time-Sharing Minicomputers

In 1962, change was sweeping through Dartmouth. Late that year, in an article that declared the isolated college was coming "out of the woods," *Time* noted that the school had built a major new arts center and that John Kemeny, who had made full professor at age twenty-seven, had built "the best college math department in the country." Also in 1962, Kemeny and his colleague Thomas Kurtz had begun developing a time-sharing computer system and a new programming language to be used by all students at Dartmouth—not just those studying math, science, or engineering. Kemeny and Kurtz aimed for nothing less than a computing revolution, radically increasing access to computers and to computer programming. "While the availability of FORTRAN extended computer usage from a handful of experts to thousands of scientific users," Kemeny wrote, "we at Dartmouth envisaged the possibility of millions of people writing their own computer programs" (Kemeny 1972, 30).

To reach millions, Kemeny and Kurtz would have to lower the existing barriers to programming, barriers that were related not only to the esoteric aspects of programming languages, but also to the physical limits and material nature of computing at the time. The two began working with a team of undergraduates to develop the Dartmouth Time-Sharing System and, with it, the BASIC programming language (figure 50.1). They considered developing a subset of FORTRAN or Algol, but found these options unsuitable (Kurtz 2009, 79). As Kurtz told an interviewer, "we wanted . . . to get away from the requirements that punched cards imposed on users, which was that things had to be on certain columns on the card" (81). They saw the value of an interactive, time-sharing system for allowing users to correct minor errors quickly rather than coming back twenty-four hours later with a new stack of punched cards for their next scheduled batch job. They also relaxed some of the specific requirements that were tied to using keypunch machines and cards. Oddly enough, BASIC was so relaxed

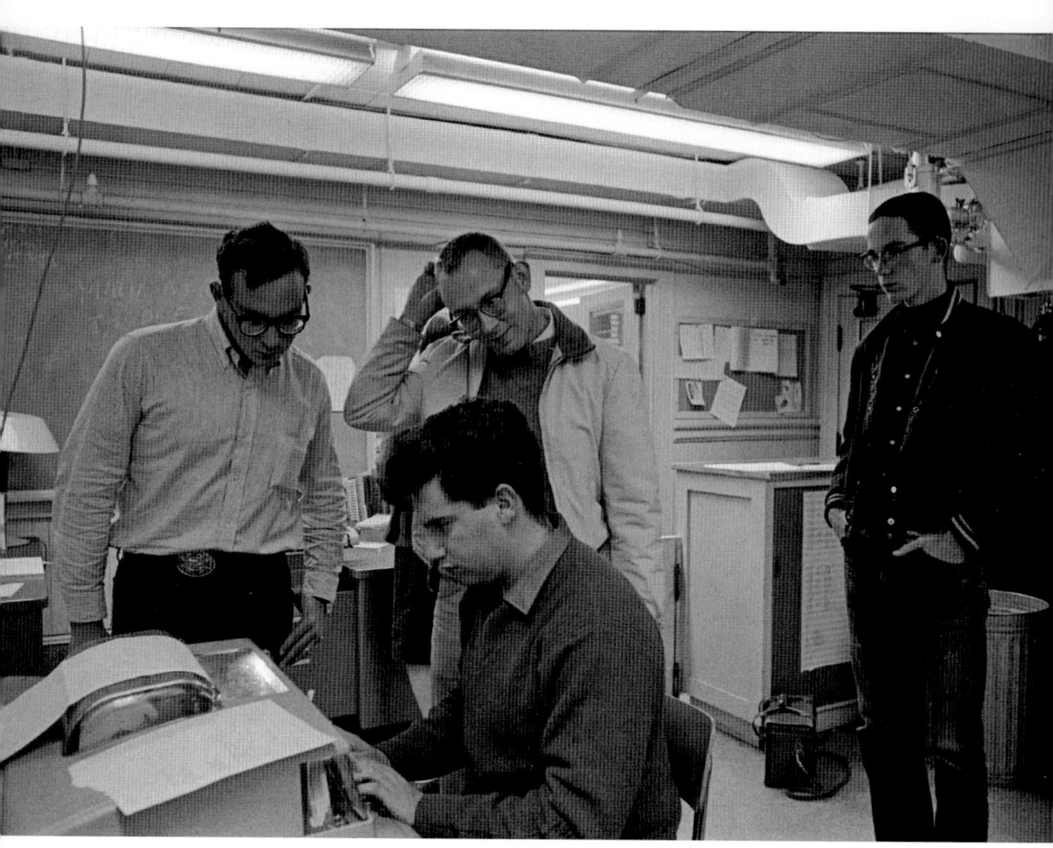

Figure 50.1
This image illustrated John Kemeny and Thomas Kurtz's essay "Bringing Up BASIC" with the caption "Students at Dartmouth working with the first version of BASIC." Photo by Adrian N. Bouchard, courtesy of Dartmouth College Library.

that spaces between tokens were optional in Dartmouth's versions of the language. Spaces were ignored, as Kurtz explains, because "some people, especially faculty members, couldn't type very well" (81). This aspect of Dartmouth BASIC was carried over onto the Commodore 64.

BASIC was designed in other ways to help new programmers, with "error messages that were clear and friendly" and default options that would satisfy most users' needs (Kemeny and Kurtz 1985, 9). "If the expert needs something fancier," the creators of the language declared, "let the expert do the extra work!" (11). Kemeny and Kurtz envisioned BASIC as a true high-level language, allowing programmers to operate without any detailed knowledge of the specific hardware they were using. The initial idea, at least, was that programmers need only pay attention to BASIC instead of the computer that BASIC happened to be running on.

DTSS and the versions of BASIC that ran on it served almost all of the students at Dartmouth; by 1971, 90 percent of the seven most recent classes of freshmen had received computer training. Dartmouth extended access to its system to other campuses and also inspired the creation of other time-sharing systems with BASIC. By 1965, General Electric, on whose computers DTSS and the original BASIC ran, was offering a commercial time-sharing service that included BASIC (Waldrop 2001, 292). Well before the microcomputer revolution of the late 1970s, other college and university students were taking required courses in computing using BASIC—at NYU's business school, for instance. Even before the arrival of home computers with built-in BASIC, the language was very widely used. The permissive attitude of Kemeny and Kurtz led to many different implementations of BASIC for different systems. Writing in 1975, one observer noted that "BASIC systems differ among themselves in much the same way that the English language as we know it differs among the English-speaking nations around the globe" (Mullish 1976, 6). There was a downside to this, however: the very permissiveness that led to BASIC's widespread adoption and adaptation meant that the language, as actually implemented, wasn't as independent of particular hardware as Kemeny and Kurtz had planned.

In addition to BASIC and the DTSS, there is yet another legacy from Dartmouth that has powerfully swayed the direction of modern computing: the almost evangelical mission to foster a more productive and creative relationship to computing. In his 1972 book *Man and the Computer,* Kemeny defends programming and playing games and other "recreational" uses of the computer as important, writing that such activities are relaxing and help people to overcome their fear of computers (35). Kemeny also describes some of the context in which BASIC programming was done at Dartmouth: "The computation center is run in a manner analogous to Dartmouth's million-volume open-stack library. Just as any student may go in and browse the library or check out any book he wishes without asking for permission or explaining why he wants that particular book, he may use the computation center without asking permission or explaining why he is running a particular program" (33). Computers were for everyone (at

## CHR$ AND THE DOLLAR SIGN IN BASIC

In designing BASIC, Kemeny and Kurtz wanted to distinguish between variables that held numeric values and variables that held strings of text. They chose to have string variables and string functions end with a "$," so that a string variable might be named A$ and the function that produced one-character strings based on ASCII values was called CHR$. They selected the dollar sign because there "were not so many keys on a Teletype, and we needed to find one that had not yet been used for BASIC. Of the few remaining ones, none seemed very appropriate. Then one of us observed that $ looks like S for string" (Kemeny and Kurtz 1985, 28).

Computers are fundamentally machines that add and multiply, so it is a curious circumstance that the Commodore 64 keyboard, like modern North American keyboards, has a dollar sign on it but does not have a multiplication sign. Instead, the asterisk (*), the typographical mark once used to indicate a footnote, is pressed into service as the symbol for multiplication.

Why would a keyboard have a dollar sign but not a multiplication sign? Even though interactive processing (as opposed to batch processing with punched cards) was a novelty, teletypewriters had been used as interfaces to computers long before the 1960s. Various sorts of TTYs, teleprinters, or "printing telegraphs" were used commercially as a means of textual communication beginning in the 1910s. These

least within the campus community) and for any purpose. BASIC was the embodiment of this openness, which allowed for programs with no obvious military, business, or scientific purpose—programs such as `10 PRINT`—to come about.

It's not surprising that Kemeny's liberal ideas about computers and education played some part in his achievements as the president of Dartmouth College, a position he served in from 1970 to 1981. Kemeny presided over Dartmouth's conversion to a coeducational campus, removed the "Indian" as the college's mascot, and encouraged the recruitment of minority students. On his final day as president, he gave a commencement address that warned students, including those involved in the recently founded conservative *Dartmouth Review*, against the impulse that "tries to divide us by setting whites against blacks, by setting Christians against systems were based on pre-ASCII character codes that came from telegraphy, and were used to transmit dollar amounts much more frequently than they were used for sending mathematical equations. Murray Code, the 1901 revision of the standard 1870 telegraph code, included two characters that allowed "shifting" into alternate sets. A shifted "D" would become a "$" in Murray Code.

Interestingly, the original, North American Commodore 64 keyboard sported a pound sterling sign (£), a glyph absent from other US computers of the time. The presence of this key no doubt pointed to Commodore's plans to sell its computers in the United Kingdom, although that key had a precedent in Murray Code, which also features a pound sterling sign.

The dollar sign is still used in some of today's workhorse programming languages, such as Perl and PHP. In both of these, it is used to indicate a variable by being placed at the beginning, rather than the end, of the variable name. In Perl it specifically indicates a *scalar* variable, since $ looks like S for "scalar." Despite these varying uses, the impact of BASIC's role as an entry-level language in the 1970s and 1980s was such that some modern programmers, including one of this book's authors, still pronounce "$" as "string" when reading code aloud regardless of the character's meaning in the language under discussion.

Jews, by setting men against women. And if it succeeds in dividing us from our fellow beings, it will impose its evil will upon a fragmented society" (Faison 1992). After leaving the presidency of Dartmouth, he returned to full-time teaching. Kemeny died in 1992. Thomas Kurtz continued to teach at Dartmouth long after he worked on BASIC, directing the Computer and Information Systems program there from 1980 to 1988.

## BASIC COMES TO THE HOME

The computer had already become more welcoming and accessible thanks to innovations on university and college campuses, but it wasn't until the computer moved into the home that the true revolution began. In popular lore that revolution started with a single photograph of a panel of switches and LEDs on the cover of the January 1975 issue of *Popular Electronics*—the first public look at the Altair 8800 minicomputer (figure 50.2). While the history of BASIC at Dartmouth shows that personal computing did not suddenly spring to life fully developed in 1974, that year does mark an inflection point for home computing.

Proclaiming in a headline that "THE HOME COMPUTER IS HERE," that issue of *Popular Electronics* gushes about the possibilities of the $395 Altair 8800 ($495 assembled, $1812 and $2271 in 2012 dollars, respectively). The magazine claims that the computer can be used as a "sophisticated intrusion alarm system," an "automatic IC tester," an "autopilot for planes, boats, etc.," a "time-share computer system," a "brain for a robot," and a "printed matter-to-Braille converter for the blind," among other things, noting that "many of these applications can be performed simultaneously" (Roberts and Yates 1975, 38). As it happened, even the applications that were within the capabilities of the device were rather difficult to realize, since the system by default could only be programmed in machine language. Furthermore, unless one happened to have a Teletype or other terminal lying around, the programming had to be done using the toggle switches on the front panel. The home computer may have arrived, but most hobbyists would have no effective way of programming it. From the outset, it was clear to many that the Altair 8800 needed a programming language that facilitated experimentation. *Popular Electronics* mentions four programming languages by way of explaining the distinction between hardware and software (34); one of these languages was BASIC, the language that showed the most promise to early Altair 8800 enthusiasts.

### Altair BASIC and Microsoft

There were two successful efforts to develop a BASIC interpreter for the Altair. Their varied histories have had a lasting impact on modern computing and modern culture. While this tale of two BASICs is not about the best of BASIC and the worst of BASIC, it does highlight two extremes in software development: one commercial, closely coordinated with hardware manufacturers and highly tied to licensing and cost structures; the other community based, nonprofit, and "copyleft." The BASICs that led in these directions were Microsoft's Altair BASIC, the official BASIC for the platform, licensed to MITS, the Altair's manufacturer; and Tiny BASIC, which originated at the People's Computer Company or PCC. The Commodore 64's BASIC is directly descended from Altair BASIC, by the company whose name was later standardized as "Microsoft." The BASIC for this system is—although this is not visible on the startup screen—a Microsoft product. At the same time, the `10 PRINT` program participated in a context of BASIC sharing and exploration that was strongly influenced by the People's Computer Company.

The story of Microsoft BASIC, and of Microsoft, begins with Paul Allen catching sight of the now-famous January 1975 issue of *Popular Electronics* just after it hit the stands. Allen read the Altair 8800 article and raced to show it to his friend and business partner Bill Gates, telling him, "Well here's our opportunity to do something with BASIC" (Wallace and Erikson 1992, 67). The two had already had some limited business success when Gates was still in high school, with a venture called Traf-O-Data that produced hardware and software to count cars. They programmed the Intel 8008 microprocessor that powered Traf-O-Data using a simulator running on a Washington State University mainframe.

By 1975, Gates was at Harvard University, and he and Allen were ready for a project with broader reach. Seeing *Popular Electronics,* they came up with the idea of writing BASIC for the Altair and called Ed Roberts at MITS, asking if he would be interested in having their BASIC for his system. Roberts said he would buy the first version that worked (Wallace and Erikson 1992, 74). As Gates and Allen had done when developing their Traf-O-Data system, they initially programmed on a university's computer system. They used a simulator to program the Altair 8800, a computer Gates and Allen had never seen in person. What they were programming at this point was, of course, a modified and minimized version of the original 1964 BASIC. Given how often the success of personal computing is attributed to entrepreneurial and business advances and to Microsoft in particular, it's remarkable that Microsoft's first product was developed by borrowing time on Harvard's computer and was (as Microsoft always acknowledged) an implementation of a freely available programming language from Dartmouth.

Gates and Allen devised the Altair BASIC project and did most of the programming, but there was a third Altair BASIC programmer, a sort of legendary "fifth Beatle." This was Monte Davidoff, who wrote the floating point routines. Gates and Allen were discussing how they needed to code

JANUARY, 1975

**EXCLUSIVE!**

# ALTAIR 8800 The most powerful minicomputer project ever presented—can be built for under $400

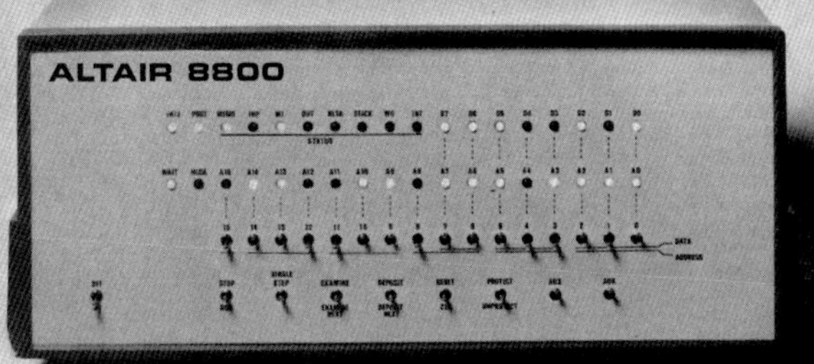


BY H. EDWARD ROBERTS AND WILLIAM YATES

THE era of the computer in every home—a favorite topic among science-fiction writers—has arrived! It's made possible by the POPULAR ELECTRONICS/MITS Altair 8800, a full-blown computer that can hold its own against sophisticated minicomputers now on the market. And it doesn't cost several thousand dollars. In fact, it's in a color TV-receiver's price class—under $400 for a complete kit.

The Altair 8800 is not a "demonstrator" or souped-up calculator. It is the most powerful computer ever presented as a construction project in any electronics magazine. In many ways, it represents a revolutionary development in electronic design and thinking.

The Altair 8800 is a parallel 8-bit word/16-bit address computer with an instruction cycle time of 2 μs. Its central processing unit is a new LSI chip that is many times more powerful than previous IC processors. It can accommodate 256 inputs and 256 outputs, all directly addressable, and has 78 basic machine instructions (as compared with 40 in the usual minicomputer). This means that you can write an extensive and detailed program. The basic computer has 256 words of memory, but it can be economically expanded for 65,000 words. Thus, with full expansion, up to 65,000 subroutines can all be going at the same time.

The basic computer is a complete system. The program can be entered via switches located on the front panel, providing a LED readout in binary format. The very-low-cost terminal presented in POPULAR ELECTRONICS last month can also be used.

**PROCESSOR DESCRIPTION**

Processor: 8 bit parallel
Max. memory: 65,000 words (all directly addressable)
Instruction cycle time: 2 μs (min.)
Inputs and outputs: 256 (all directly addressable)
Number of basic machine instructions: 78 (181 with variants)
Add/substract time: 2 μs
Number of subroutine levels: 65,000
Interrupt structure: 8 hardwire vectored levels plus software levels
Number of auxiliary registers: 8 plus stack pointer, program counter and accumulator
Memory type: semiconductor (dynamic or static RAM, ROM, PROM)
Memory access time: 850 ns static RAM; 420 or 150 ns dynamic Ram

JANUARY 1975 33

Figure 50.2

The January 1975 issue of *Popular Electronics* featured the Altair 8800, which inspired the creation of Microsoft BASIC.

these when Davidoff, a student sitting with them at the table, spoke up and said he could write them. After talking it over with him, they enlisted him to contribute them (Wallace and Erikson 76–77). The code of this first Microsoft project is mainly by Gates and Allen, though, with Gates listed as first author. Comments at the beginning of the code declare, "BILL GATES WROTE THE RUNTIME STUFF," which he did over a period of eight weeks at Harvard. Gates would say years later that this 4 KB BASIC interpreter "was the coolest program I ever wrote" (76–77).

Allen flew to visit MITS in Albuquerque, taking along a paper tape with Altair BASIC on it. During the plane's descent he realized that he did not have a way to get the Altair to read the tape and run it—a bootloader. So he wrote one in machine language as the plane was landing. He then went to see an actual Altair 8800 for the first time. The demo of BASIC, written on a simulator, was a success on the machine itself, and the interpreter was licensed by MITS. Gates and Allen moved to New Mexico to create new versions of BASIC for the Altair and to maintain the original code. Microsoft was booted and running.

Altair BASIC included alterations to Dartmouth BASIC, many of which would have made no sense on earlier time-sharing systems but which were helpful, even crucial, on home computers. While none of Microsoft's changes to BASIC were critical to the functioning of `10 PRINT`, Gates and Allen did create the `POKE` and `PEEK` statements, which have been widely used in microcomputer BASIC and in programs found throughout this book.

`POKE` allows a programmer to write a value to a specific memory location. For example, `POKE 53272,23` places the value 23 into address 53272, a location in memory that is mapped to a register of the VIC-II graphics chip. In this case, `POKE 53272,23` switches the Commodore 64 into lowercase mode. `PEEK` is `POKE`'s complementary statement; instead of writing a value to memory, `PEEK` reads the value of a given location.

Both statements are extremely powerful. Altair BASIC—and later, the Microsoft BASIC used on the Commodore 64—sets no restriction on which memory addresses can be changed with `POKE`. This means, as the *Altair BASIC Reference Manual* warns, "Careless use of the `POKE` statement will probably cause you to 'poke' BASIC to death; that is, the machine will hang, and you will have to reload BASIC and will lose any program you had typed in" (1975, 35). This process would have been particularly painful on microcomputers on which BASIC was bootloaded rather than being provided a part of the system's ROM. It's clear why earlier versions of BASIC did not include POKE or PEEK equivalents. A user on a time-sharing minicomputer should not have been able to write values directly to the microprocessor or memory; such a privilege would have threatened the stability of the entire shared system.

From a technical and business standpoint, Altair BASIC was not an early oddity, but rather, a Microsoft product with a strong relationship to the company's later flagship products. To see the connection, it's important to understand the nature of computing platforms and their relationship to markets of different sorts.

In *Invisible Engines*, Evans, Hagiu, and Schmalensee (2006) introduce a theory of two-sided software platforms. In a predominantly one-sided market—for example, a swap meet with people trading comics—there is only one class of participant, a person interested in exchanging goods with other people. A classic land-line telephone company also participates in a one-sided market, because every customer is more or less the same sort of participant, one who wants to make and receive calls. However, a credit card company has two different classes of customer: merchants, who receive payments and need terminals; and cardholders, who have a line of credit and make purchases.

When Atari released the Atari VCS in 1977, it was initially a one-sided platform. Atari made the system as well as all the games and controllers. The only participants in the market, and users of the platform, were the players. By the early 1980s, when Activision, Imagic, and other third-party companies had entered the market, there was another class of participant—one that was not paying royalties to Atari for the privilege of making games for their console.

Microsoft Windows is another example of a platform with at least two sides. On one side, computers need an operating system and desktop environment to function. This leads hardware manufacturers such as Dell to purchase licenses to Windows and to include the software with their systems. On the other side, computers are only valuable if there are applications written for them. Microsoft writes some of the applications for Windows, but third-party developers write many others. The abundance of software has a network effect that is positive for Microsoft: it encourages users to stay with Windows. And, since Windows is pre-installed on many computers, companies want to write applications for it.

Of course, Windows was not the first two-sided platform, or even Microsoft's first. By retaining the rights to what IBM called PC-DOS, Microsoft had previously been able to license MS-DOS to other companies, much as it would later sell OEM copies of Windows to them. And before that, there are continuities with the company's first product line, Microsoft BASIC. BASIC was a programming language, not an operating system, but the presence of BASIC allowed programs to be written on a computer and sometimes sold. There were at least two sides to BASIC as a software platform: the computer companies, beginning with MITS, who wanted it on their machines; and the computer hobbyists who wanted to write (and in many cases sell) BASIC programs. At Gates and Allen's young company, the success of BASIC and the essential business plan used with that family of software products formed the basis of Microsoft's later success licensing MS-DOS and Windows.

## Tiny BASIC and Copyleft

Even as Microsoft was securing its future as a multisided company, addressing both manufacturer and computer user demand, a different version of BASIC—indeed, a different philosophy of software altogether—was brewing in the San Francisco Bay area. In 1975, volunteer programmers and the nonprofit People's Computer Company (PCC) developed an alternative BASIC for the Altair 8800. Bob Albrecht, who had founded "probably the world's first completely free, walk-in, public computer center—People's Computer Center—in a storefront in Menlo Park, California" (Swaine 2006) was one of many, along with Paul Allen, who had seen the *Popular Electronics* cover story on the MITS Altair. He discussed it with Dennis Allison, who taught at Stanford, and Allison began to develop a specification for a limited BASIC interpreter called Tiny BASIC. In a collaborative hobbyist spirit, Allison's documents were published in three parts by Albrecht in issues of the PCC newsletter, a serial that had been running since October 1972. At the conclusion of this series of specifications, Allison called for programmers to send in their implementations and offered to circulate them to anyone who sent a self-addressed, stamped envelope.

The first interpreter written in response to this call was by Dick Whipple and John Arnold and was developed in December 1975. To disseminate it, Albrecht and Allison started a new serial, initially photocopied and originally intended to just run for a few issues. This was *Dr. Dobb's Journal of Tiny BASIC Calisthenics and Orthodontia;* it printed the code for the interpreter in octal machine language, ready for hobbyists to toggle in or, even better, key in on their Teletypes. It is an understatement to call this publication a success. By January of 1976 the journal title was made more general by removing the explicit mention of Tiny BASIC, an editor was hired, and *Dr. Dobb's* was launched as a newsletter offering code and articles on computing topics. In 1985, *Dr. Dobb's* further participated in the culture of sharing and openness by publishing Richard Stallman's "GNU Manifesto," a foundational document of the free software movement. The journal ran as a print periodical until 2009, with a circulation of 120,000 shortly before that. It still exists as an online publication.

The development of Tiny BASICs continued after Allison's first version. The fourth Tiny BASIC, written by Li-Chen Wang, was called Palo Alto Tiny BASIC. It, too, was published initially in *Dr. Dobb's.* The source listing for this BASIC interpreter began:

```
;**************************************************************
;*
;*                 TINY BASIC FOR INTEL 8080
;*                       VERSION 1.0
;*                     BY LI-CHEN WANG
;*                      10 JUNE, 1976
;*                        @COPYLEFT
;*                  ALL WRONGS RESERVED
;*
;**************************************************************
```

While this header does not use "copyleft" in the same sense that free software licenses would beginning in the late 1980s, this anticopyright notice was a jab at the closed culture of locked-up, proprietary code. Because Wang chose to disclaim copyright and reserve only the "wrongs" of the program, Palo Alto Tiny BASIC was able to serve as the basis for a commercial BASIC: Level I BASIC for the TRS-80, the influential microcomputer that came on the market in late 1978.

## The Ethic vs. The Corporation

In *Hackers: Heroes of the Computer Revolution,* Steven Levy describes the early history of home computing and the development of BASICs for the Altair and its immediate successors as a battle between an ethic of openness and the sort of corporate powers who were "a foe of the Hacker Ethic" (1984, 227).

This portrayal has helped to set up what is often remembered as the first major clash between free software and the corporate will of Microsoft: Bill Gates's "Open Letter to Hobbyists" (Gates 1976a). Published at the beginning of 1976 in numerous newsletters, including the *Altair Users' Newsletter* and that of the Homebrew Computer Club, this confrontational letter gave Gates the opportunity to scold home computer users for the same kind of sharing that the original BASIC at Dartmouth encouraged. In the letter, Gates soundly declared, "As the majority of hobbyists must be aware, most of you steal your software." The letter spurred hundreds of responses, public and personal, causing the first major controversy in home computing. Many see it as the start of Microsoft's history of unfair dealing—and of embracing and extending, a practice in which the company takes existing tools and ideas and creates its own version for competitive advantage. Decades later, in the antitrust case against Microsoft, Judge Thomas Penfield Jackson would write that "Microsoft is a company with an institutional disdain for both the truth and for rules of law that lesser entities must respect." He was hardly the only one with this view by that point. Did Microsoft's rise to the height of corporate ruthlessness begin with this letter to hobbyists?

There are a few complications to the most popular version of this early clash, just as there would be complications in considering Altair BASIC as completely wrongheaded and Tiny BASIC as perfect in every way. To begin with, neither Microsoft, nor Gates, nor Allen was the party fingered in Levy's book as the "foe" of the hacker ethic. That distinction belongs to Ed Roberts, the head of MITS, who was running a business with dozens of employees, many of whom would be furiously working at any given hour to fulfill computer hobbyists' orders (and their dreams of computer ownership). At the beginning of 1976, "Micro-Soft" (the spelling had not been regularized by the time of the first letter) was simply two partners, both recent college dropouts, one a teenager and the other only slightly older.

## LINE NUMBERS AND COLONS: RESPONSES TO CHANGING HARDWARE

Microsoft has used its position as the major implementor of microcomputer BASIC to make many changes to the language, adding and removing components that became necessary or obsolete as hardware progressed. For example, to allow programs to be written more compactly—an important feature given the Altair's switch and toggle interface, which could literally be painful to programmers—Microsoft's Altair BASIC introduced the colon (:) to place separate statements on the same line. Used this way, the colon allowed lines such as:

```
160 R=16:PRINT"HOW MANY DECKS (1-4)";
```

Multiple statements on the same line were not possible with minicomputer BASICs and the ANSI standard; Kemeny and Kurtz saw the compression of statements as potentially confusing rather than helpful. When they released their much-revised True BASIC for home computers in 1983, they still did not allow multistatement lines. The colon is, however, important in `10 PRINT`; this program could not be written as a concise one-liner without it.

Another prominent feature of `10 PRINT` is also an artifact of the hardware underlying the language. Unlike its punch card-derived predecessors, BASIC didn't require programmers to put anything in certain columns; yet there was a requirement that a number such as 10 appear at the beginning of each line. While line numbers made branching possible by allowing `GOTO` and `GOSUB`, BASIC did not technically need line numbers for this purpose. Labels, such as those used in preexisting languages like assembly, would have sufficed. The line number's real value is seen on a Teletype or other print terminal, or in any environment where full-screen, nonlinear editing is not an option. Line numbers make it easy in those cases to delete existing lines: simply type the line number without any further instructions, and the line disappears. To correct a single existing line, just retype a line with the same line number. To see what code is currently on a particular line, `LIST 50` will do the trick—although if one had written the line recently, one could also look up or literally "scroll" back to where the line had been printed out.

The practice of numbering program statements by multiples of five or ten is not merely rhythmic or aesthetic (as it is in this book's table of contents); the insertion of new lines in a program requires that, as an early manual puts it, "the original line numbers not be consecutive numbers" (Dartmouth College Computation Center 1964, 22). Numbering a program 10, 20, 30, and so on ensured that, between every existing program statement, there was room for nine more. It was an acknowledgment that a program is dynamic, rather than fixed and perfect. The *Commodore 64 User's Guide* also advises that "it is good programming practice to number lines in increments of 10—in case you need to insert some statements later on" (33). While line numbers became an iconic feature of BASIC early in the personal computing era, they also contributed to a perception among programmers that the language is limited to simple tasks. Leaving space to add nine new lines of code between every original line may initially seem like plenty of flexibility, but sometimes, when programmers have a complex problem to solve, it is not enough. BASIC can still accommodate this situation by allowing the programmer to use `GOTO` and `GOSUB` in order to jump to as-of-yet unused numbers for a separate routine and then return to the original program flow when complete. Unfortunately, too many subroutines can result in "spaghetti code"—so named because the flow chart of a program becomes so confused and self-referential that all the lines look like a plate of spaghetti, making the program nearly unintelligible.

In 1991 Microsoft realized that the perception of BASIC as limited to simple programs was holding the language back, and that this perception was largely due to a feature of the language that was no longer even necessary. Text editors that could display and allow access to screenfuls, or windowfuls, of lines had long been available, and line numbers were now doing more damage than good. In QBasic, released in 1991, the company dispensed with line numbers, replacing them with the assembly-like text labels.

That `10 PRINT` includes both the colon and the line number—features that have been added and removed from BASIC in response to hardware changes—signals that `10 PRINT` is from a particular time and related to a specific era of computing caught between competing input mechanisms. Its heritage and provenance are written right into its code.

The company had paid other people, such as BASIC contributor Davidoff, but would not get its first official employee until April 1976.

Furthermore, copyright protection for computer programs, on which Gates based his argument, was well established by 1976. While sharing of programs certainly happened in users' groups and other contexts, today's concept of free software had not been articulated at that time. Richard Stallman started the GNU project in 1983; he published the GNU Manifesto and founded the Free Software Foundation in 1985, a decade after Altair BASIC. An argument has been made that, even though the discussions of this period have been overlooked, some of the ideas important to the free software movement were first publicly stated in the columns of magazines and newsletters in response to Gates's letter (Driscoll 2011). But many hobbyists were not interested in free (as in freedom) software as it is conceptualized today; rather, they were interested in (as the editorial in the first issue of *Dr. Dobbs* explained) "free and very inexpensive" software.

In the aftermath of his first letter, Gates wrote a "Second and Final Letter," replying to objections raised by his readers. In it, he conceded that, at least for certain types of programs, the free sharing of code was likely to become the norm. He also suggested that good "compilers and interpreters" (such as Microsoft's Altair BASIC) would enable such shared software:

> In discussing software, I don't want to leave out the most important aspect, vis., the exchange of those programs less complex than interpreters or compilers that can be written by hobbyists and shared at little or no cost. I think in the foreseeable future, literally thousands of such programs will be available through user libraries. The availability of standardized compilers and interpreters will have a major impact on how quickly these libraries develop and how useful they are. (Gates 1976b)

Gates certainly had a concept of software that would allow for it to be sold and tightly controlled by a corporation, but he was hardly seeking to eliminate hobbyist programming and the sharing of code. The company's policies did run counter to the ethic of the Homebrew Computer Club and the People's Computer Company in significant ways; yet Microsoft facilitated not only the creation of new software with its version of BASIC, but also the exchange of programs that Gates mentioned. Through licensing deals with computer companies, Microsoft did a great deal to bring BASIC out of the minicomputer time-sharing environment and onto microcomputers and beyond, to early adopters and enthusiast programmers. Microsoft signaled it was not completely at odds with the PCC in Appendix M of the original Altair BASIC manual. It lists "a few of the many texts that may be helpful in learning BASIC," all but one of which can be ordered from the PCC, whose address is also provided. Five of the six books are about BASIC specifically, but the manual also lists the radical and countercultural *Computer Lib/Dream Machines* by Theodore H. Nelson (1974), an edition of which Microsoft would itself publish in 1987.

Ultimately, BASIC became what it was in 1982 thanks to the institution of higher education where it was first developed, the corporation that implemented and licensed it for use on home computers (including the Commodore 64), and, significantly, the hacker ethic of code sharing that allowed BASIC programs—such as `10 PRINT`—to circulate freely.

## COMMODORE BASIC

The ability to program a computer—to use its general power in customized ways—was a core selling point for many home computers including the Commodore 64. Home computers were often positioned against videogame systems in advertisements. Implicitly, this comparison reminded the prospective buyer that a computer could be used to play video games; explicitly, it pointed out that computers could be used with business and educational software—and that they could be programmed to do much more. This point was driven home in the many Commodore TV ads that compared the VIC-20 to game systems, including one in which William Shatner says "unlike games, it has a real computer keyboard" (Commodore Computer Club 2010).

That computers were programmable and that they specifically could be programmed in BASIC were hardly afterthoughts in their development or marketing. A Commodore 64 advertisement that was aired in Australia in 1985 provides evidence that BASIC was a central selling point (Holmes3000 2006). After the television spot showed bikini-clad women descending a waterslide ("♪ In a world of fun and fantasy . . . ♪") and cut to a woman happily using a Commodore 64 in a retail store ("♪ . . . and ever-changing views . . . ♪"), it cut once again: to a screenful of BASIC, and then to depict a boy programming in BASIC ("♪ . . . and computer terminology . . . Commodore and you! ♪"). The commercial suggests that computer programming was an obvious, important, and fun use of a home computer.

An early print ad for the Apple II that ran in *Scientific American* among other publications boasted, "It's the first personal computer with a fast version of BASIC—the English-like programming language—permanently built in. That means you can begin running your Apple II the first evening, entering your own instructions and watching them work, even if you've had no previous computer experience." It was very easy for home computers users to type in or modify a BASIC program, and the fact that the manufacturers encouraged such behavior in mass media advertising primed users to partake of programming once they'd purchased a machine.

At the opposite extreme were programs fixed in the ROM of cartridges, such as the cartridges of videogame systems. They were convenient, and they showed that such game systems had the flexibility to work in many different ways, but hacking cartridge code or writing one's own programs on a cartridge-based system was far from easy in the early 1980s. The Commodore 64 provided the flexibility of BASIC out of the box, but—like the TI-99/4A, among other computers—it also had a cartridge slot. By offering BASIC along with the ability to plug in cartridges (many of which were games), the Commodore 64 turned one of its Janus-like faces to the generality and power of home computing and another to the convenience and modularity of gaming.

The Commodore 64 BASIC on which `10 PRINT` runs is a Microsoft product and a descendant of Altair BASIC. The first step for achieving this BASIC was creating a version for the Commodore 64's chip, the MOS 6502 processor. The Altair had used the Intel 8080, which had a different instruction set. The task of developing a version of Microsoft BASIC to work with the MOS 6502 was undertaken in 1976 and fell mainly to Richard Weiland. When a user types "A" in response to the startup question "MEMORY SIZE?", the version of Microsoft 6520 BASIC licensed to Ohio Scientific replies "WRITTEN BY RICHARD W. WEILAND," while version 1.1 for the KIM declares "WRITTEN BY WEILAND & GATES." The first version of Microsoft's 6502 BASIC that made its way into the ROM of a shipping system, in 1977, was a version for Commodore—not for the Commodore 64, but for the company's first computer, the Personal Electronic Transactor or PET.

The BASIC included with the Commodore PET was very similar to

Commodore BASIC 2 for the Commodore CBM and the BASICs included on the VIC-20 and Commodore 64. (The version history of Commodore BASIC is a bit complicated, as the "COMMODORE 64 BASIC V2" that appears on the top of the screen indicates the second release of BASIC V2.0; this version was originally provided with a model of the PET 2001.) Other aspects of Commodore computers, such as the PETSCII character set, are similar across models as well. For these reasons, **10 PRINT** will run without modification on a Commodore PET or a VIC-20. What mainly suggests that the program should be identified with the Commodore 64 is the presence of **10 PRINT** variants in a Commodore 64 manual, a later magazine, and other contexts specific to the Commodore 64.

Versions of Microsoft's 6502 BASIC were used not only on the PET and Commodore 64 but also on competing computers: the Apple II series and Atari's eight-bit computers, the Atari 400 and Atari 800. Microsoft certainly benefited from selling the same product to multiple computer manufacturers but didn't manage to make the usual licensing deal with Commodore. As the founder of Commodore, Jack Tramiel, explained at the Computer History Museum at a twenty-fifth anniversary event honoring the Commodore 64, Bill Gates "came to see me. He tried to sell me BASIC. And he told me that I don't have to give him any money. I only have to give him $3 per unit. And I told him that I'm already married." Tramiel told Gates he would pay no more than a $25,000 flat fee for BASIC—an offer that Microsoft ultimately accepted. This was a very good deal for Commodore, since about 12.5 million Commodore 64s were ultimately sold (Steil).

Features of BASIC highlighted by **10 PRINT** and which are fairly specific to the Commodore 64 version are seen in the RND command, discussed in the Randomness chapter, and in the PETSCII character set that CHR$ refers to, discussed in the Commodore 64 chapter.

Before turning to the way Commodore 64 BASIC programs circulated, it's worth noting what the creators of Commodore 64 BASIC went on to do. Bill Gates's career trajectory is, of course, well known. It is indeed the case that one of the programmers of Commodore 64 BASIC became the richest person in the world. Paul Allen is not far behind in wealth; he left full-time work at Microsoft in 1982. Gates and Allen are notable philanthropists today. The other coder who contributed to the original Altair BASIC, Monte Davidoff, did not strike it nearly as rich but, according to an interview, was still active as a programmer in 2001, running Linux and preferring to program in Python (Orlowski 2001).

The programmer of Microsoft's 6502 BASIC, Richard Weiland, a grade-school classmate of Gates and Allen, joined Microsoft when the company was based in Albuquerque. He worked for Microsoft until 1988 and devoted much of his time and money from then until his death in 2006 to philanthropy. He supported the Pride Foundation (with the largest-ever donation to LBGT rights), Stanford University (with the largest donation that university had ever received), the Audubon Society, and the Nature Conservancy (Heim 2008). While the dichotomy between profit-driven corporations and people-powered programming is not artificial, the generosity of the people behind Commodore 64 BASIC shows that those on the corporate side aren't without altruistic, community concerns.

## THE CIRCULATION OF BASIC PROGRAMS

From the first years of the language, BASIC programs circulated as ink on paper. In 1964 and for many years afterward, there was no Web or even Internet to allow for the digital exchange of programs, and it was often impractical to distribute software on computer-readable media such as paper tape. From the mid-1970s through the early 1980s, BASIC was known in print not only through manuals and textbooks that explicitly taught programming, but also through collections of programs that appeared in magazines and computer club newsletters. The printed materials that remain today reveal insights into the practices of BASIC users and the culture that developed among them.

### Programs in Print

Computer magazines often featured BASIC programs a home user could easily key in to his or her home computer. There was the previously mentioned *Dr. Dobb's,* but also many others. For instance, *Creative Computing* was a significant early magazine for microcomputer hobbyists. Launched in 1974 before the debut of the Altair 8800, *Creative Computing* was published until 1985 and spanned the era of BASIC's greatest growth and popularity.

As *Creative Computing* was nearing the end of its run, other magazines, many of them platform-specific, were just getting started. One was the previously-mentioned *RUN* (1984–1992), a monthly magazine published by IDG Communications, focused on the Commodore 64 and VIC-20. *RUN* is particularly noteworthy in the current discussion because a one-line variant of `10 PRINT` appeared in its pages in 1984. A German edition of *RUN* was published as well, and *ReRUN* disks made programs in the magazine available for purchase in machine-readable format. Another home computer magazine of this era was *Compute!* (1979–1994), which began as *Pet Gazette*, a 1978 magazine put together by Len Lindsay about the Commodore PET computer. In July 1983, *Compute!* launched a spinoff publication, *Compute!'s Gazette*, for Commodore 64 and VIC-20 owners. In the UK there were several magazines for Commodore users, including *Zzap! 64*, *Commodore User*, and *Commodore Format*—suggesting that putting the pound sterling symbol on the Commodore keyboard was a good move after all. Interestingly, the last of these UK magazines did not start publishing until October 1990, well into the twilight of the Commodore 64. *Commodore Format* was not about BASIC or learning to program, however, instead focusing on what was by 1990 nearly retro-gaming. The magazine came with a "Powerpack" tape, offering full games and demos for subscribers to load and run.

While magazines were ready and regular sources of BASIC programs, many enthusiasts also discovered code in long-form books. David H. Ahl's influential compilation, *101 Basic Computer Games*, was first published in 1973 by the Digital Equipment Corporation (DEC). This was the first book to collect only games in BASIC. It includes a sample run of each game and acknowledges the programmers who contributed them. Each program's "computer limitations" are described so that users understand the specific BASIC dialects and hardware that are supported, evidence that even as early as 1973 BASIC had drifted from its creators' goal of a platform-agnostic high-level language. Hand-drawn illustrations punctuate *101 Basic Computer Games*—a rather playful presentation for a corporate publication. The game's titles are all abbreviated so they can serve as filenames, which at the time were limited, on some systems, to six characters. The abbreviations are humorously cryptic, with ACEYDU standing for "Acey Deucy Card Game"; AMAZIN for "Draw a Maze"; or POET for "Random Poetry (Haiku)." In the preface, the educational value of playing and creating games and the need for "unguided learning" are emphasized, echoing

Kemeny's own thoughts about the value of play on computers.

A new edition of this book, *Basic Computer Games, Microcomputer Edition,* appeared in January 1978—reflecting BASIC's move from time-sharing minicomputers to microcomputers. This edition's preface begins with a dictionary definition (from an unnamed dictionary) of the word "game." It then provides a cursory history of sports and games from ancient times to the modern age, emphasizing that games offer recreational breaks from the "realities of life" and have other "important redeeming virtues." The programs in this book are meant to run on the gold standard of microcomputer BASICs: MITS Altair 8K BASIC, Rev. 4.0 (ix). The games, no longer referred to by cryptic six-character tags, are organized by category—e.g., Educational, Number and Letter Guessing, Sports Simulation, Gambling Casino, Card and Board, and so on. While none of these categories would easily accommodate `10 PRINT`, it is notable that so many of them rely upon a key feature of that program: randomness.

Later in 1978, this compilation was published again by Workman Publishing under the lengthy title *Basic Computer Games, Microcomputer Edition. 101 Great Games to Play on Your Home Computer. By Yourself or with Others. Each Complete with Programming and Sample Run.* Its translation into German in 1982 (reprinted in German in 1983) shows how BASIC games, thanks in this case to a book's large trade publisher, made their way abroad.

The People's Computer Company not only published a newsletter (figure 50.3) but also offered a book collecting BASIC games: Bob Albrecht's large-format *What to Do after You Hit Return* came out originally in 1975. This popular book underwent several printings from different publishers. Not once did the acronym BASIC appear on the front or back cover, perhaps indicating that the language was so prevalent for recreational programming that it need not be named.

Given the growing popularity of BASIC and computers among hobbyists, it is not surprising to see books of BASIC that go beyond games. Promising to teach a BASIC that would work with all the various "dialects," the 1977 *Illustrating BASIC (A Simple Programming Language),* was published by no less a scholarly authority than Cambridge University Press. In 1978 came *The Little Book of BASIC Style: How to Write a Program You Can Read,* by John M. Nevison. With its allusion to the *Elements of Style* by Strunk and White, this book insists that programs have human readers and can be written with them in mind. Similar titles include the 1978 *BASIC*

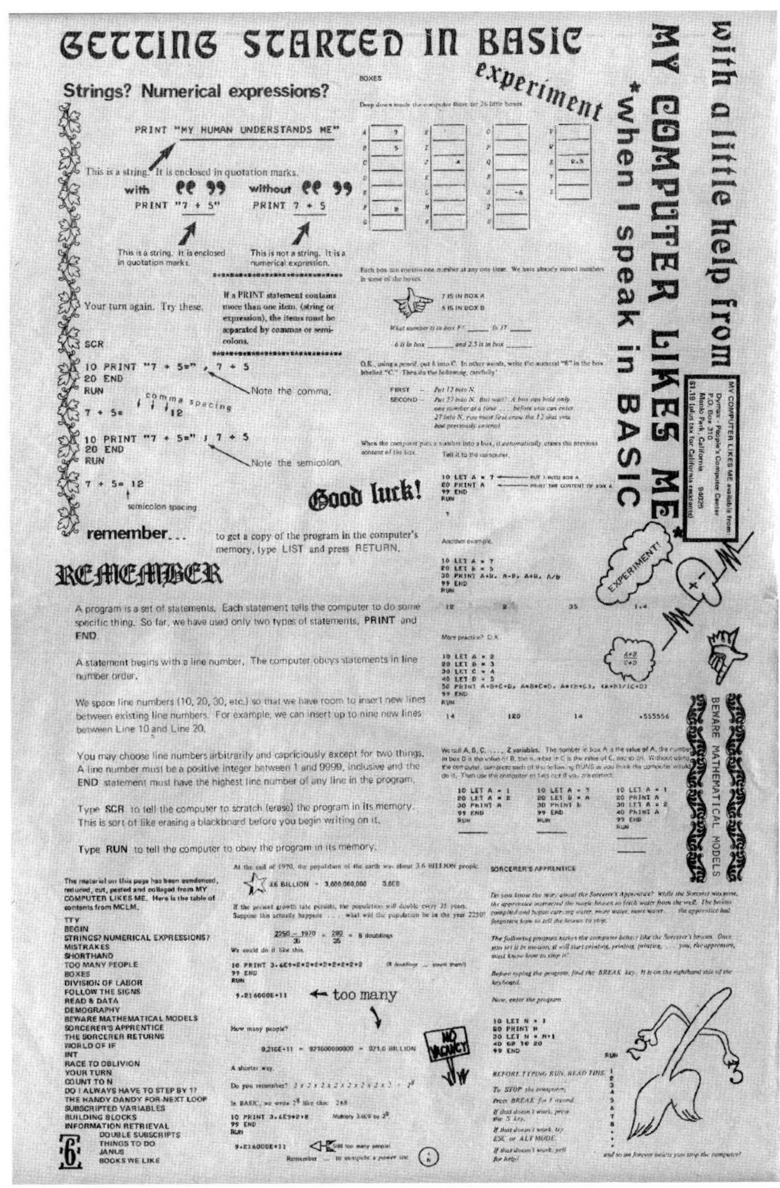

# GETTING STARTED IN BASIC

with a little help from MY COMPUTER LIKES ME *when I speak in BASIC

## Strings? Numerical expressions?

```
PRINT "MY HUMAN UNDERSTANDS ME"
```

This is a string. It is enclosed in quotation marks.

with " " — `PRINT "7 + 5"` — This is a string. It is enclosed in quotation marks.

without " " — `PRINT 7 + 5` — This is not a string. It is a numerical expression.

**If a PRINT statement contains more than one item, (string or expression), the items must be separated by commas or semicolons.**

Your turn again. Try these.

```
SCR

10 PRINT "7 + 5=" , 7 + 5
20 END
RUN

7 + 5=          12
```

Note the comma. (comma spacing)

```
10 PRINT "7 + 5=" ; 7 + 5
20 END
RUN

7 + 5= 12
```

Note the semicolon. (semicolon spacing)

**remember...** to get a copy of the program in the computer's memory, type LIST and press RETURN.

**Good luck!**

## REMEMBER

A program is a set of statements. Each statement tells the computer to do some specific thing. So far, we have used only two types of statements, **PRINT** and **END**.

A statement begins with a line number. The computer obeys statements in line number order.

We space line numbers (10, 20, 30, etc.) so that we have room to insert new lines between existing line numbers. For example, we can insert up to nine new lines between Line 10 and Line 20.

You may choose line numbers arbitrarily and capriciously except for two things. A line number must be a positive integer between 1 and 9999, inclusive and the **END** statement must have the highest line number of any line in the program.

Type **SCR** to tell the computer to scratch (erase) the program in its memory. This is sort of like erasing a blackboard before you begin writing on it.

Type **RUN** to tell the computer to obey the program in its memory.

## experiment

BOXES

Deep down inside the computer there are 26 little boxes.

Each box can contain one number at any one time. We have already stored numbers in some of the boxes.

7 IS IN BOX A
5 IS IN BOX B

*What number is in box F? _____ In J? _____*

*6 is in box _____ and 2.5 is in box _____*

O.K., using a *pencil*, put 6 into C. In other words, write the numeral "6" in the box labelled "C." Then do the following, carefully!

FIRST — *Put 12 into N.*
SECOND — *Put 27 into N. But wait! A box can hold only one number at a time . . . before you can enter 27 into N, you must first erase the 12 that you had previously entered.*

When the computer puts a number into a box, it *automatically* erases the previous content of the box.

Tell it to the computer.

```
10 LET A = 7      <-- PUT 7 INTO BOX A
20 PRINT A        <-- PRINT THE CONTENT OF BOX A
99 END
RUN

 7
```

Another example.

```
10 LET A = 7
20 LET B = 5
30 PRINT A+B, A-B, A*B, A/B
99 END
RUN

 12        2         35        1.4
```

More practice? O.K.

```
10 LET A = 2
20 LET B = 3
30 LET C = 4
40 LET D = 5
50 PRINT A+B+C+D, A*B*C*D, A*(B+C), (A+B)/(C+D)
99 END
RUN

 14        120       14        .555556
```

We call A, B, C, . . . , Z **variables.** The number in box A is the value of A, the number in box B is the value of B, the number in C is the value of C, and so on. Without using the computer, complete each of the following RUNS as you think the computer would do it. Then use the computer to find out if you are correct.

```
10 LET A = 1        10 LET A = 7        10 LET A = 1
20 LET A = 2        20 LET B = A        20 PRINT A
30 PRINT A          30 PRINT B          30 LET A = 2
99 END              99 END              40 PRINT A
RUN                 RUN                 99 END
                                        RUN
```

BEWARE MATHEMATICAL MODELS

At the end of 1970, the population of the earth was about 3.6 BILLION people.

3.6 BILLION = 3,600,000,000 = 3.6E9

If the present growth rate persists, the population will double every 35 years. Suppose this actually happens . . . what will the population be in the year 2250?

$$\frac{2250-1970}{35} = \frac{280}{35} = 8 \text{ doublings}$$

We could do it like this.

```
10 PRINT 3.6E9*2*2*2*2*2*2*2*2
99 END
RUN

 9.216000E+11
```

(8 doublings ... count them!) ← too many

How many people?

9.216E+11 = 921600000000 = 921.6 BILLION

NO VACANCY

A shorter way.

Do you remember? $2 \times 2 \times 2 \times 2 \times 2 \times 2 \times 2 \times 2 = 2^8$

In BASIC, we write $2^8$ like this: 2↑8

```
10 PRINT 3.6E9*2↑8
99 END
RUN

 9.216000E+11
```

Multiply 3.6E9 by $2^8$. Still too many people!

Remember ... to compute a *power* use ↑

SORCERER'S APPRENTICE

*Do you know the story about the Sorcerer's Apprentice? While the Sorcerer was gone, the apprentice instructed the magic broom to fetch water from the well. The broom complied and began carrying water, more water, more water . . . the apprentice had forgotten how to tell the broom to stop.*

*The following program makes the computer behave like the Sorcerer's broom. Once you set it in motion, it will start printing, printing, printing, . . . you, the apprentice, must know how to stop it!*

*Before typing the program, find the BREAK key. It is on the righthand side of the keyboard.*

*Now, enter the program.*

```
10 LET N = 1
20 PRINT N
30 LET N = N+1
40 GO TO 20
99 END
RUN
 1
 2
 3
 4
 5
 6
 7
 8
 .
 .
```

*BEFORE TYPING RUN, READ THIS.*

*To STOP the computer,*
*Press BREAK for 1 second.*
*If that doesn't work, press the S key.*
*If that doesn't work, try ESC or ALT MODE.*
*If that doesn't work, yell for help!*

*and so on forever unless you stop the computer!*

The material on this page has been condensed, reduced, cut, pasted and collaged from MY COMPUTER LIKES ME. Here is the table of contents from MCLM.

TTY
BEGIN
STRINGS? NUMERICAL EXPRESSIONS?
MISTRAKES
SHORTHAND
TOO MANY PEOPLE
BOXES
DIVISION OF LABOR
FOLLOW THE SIGNS
READ & DATA
DEMOGRAPHY
BEWARE MATHEMATICAL MODELS
SORCERER'S APPRENTICE
THE SORCERER RETURNS
WORLD OF IF
INT
RACE TO OBLIVION
YOUR TURN
COUNT TO N
DO I ALWAYS HAVE TO STEP BY 1?
THE HANDY DANDY FOR-NEXT LOOP
SUBSCRIPTED VARIABLES
BUILDING BLOCKS
INFORMATION RETRIEVAL
DOUBLE SUBSCRIPTS
THINGS TO DO
JANUS
BOOKS WE LIKE

MY COMPUTER LIKES ME available from:
Dymax - People's Computer Center
P.O. Box 310
Menlo Park, California 94025
$1.19 (plus tax for California residents)



Figure 50.3

The People's Computer Company (PCC) Newsletter #1 in October 1972 featured a selection of BASIC programs from *My Computer Likes Me.* Courtesy DigiBarn Computer Museum via the Creative Commons Attribution-Noncommercial 3.0 License.

*with Style. Programming Proverbs* and the 1979 *Programming for Poets. A Gentle Introduction Using BASIC*. Lest the utilitarian function of computers become overshadowed by these more aesthetically oriented books, there is Charles D. Sternberg's *BASIC Computer Programs for the Home* (1980), filled with programs specifically designed to satisfy "the practical requirements of the home." Should one of these programs not work on the reader's own machine, Sternberg encouraged their "modification."

This quick survey of BASIC books from the 1970s and early 1980s highlights the extent to which BASIC facilitated exploration, play, modification, and learning. It also reveals the nature of the home computing movement at the time, which emphasized sharing and learning from others, often through the medium of print. While programs in machine language occasionally circulated in print, published BASIC programs such as `10 PRINT` were a different beast altogether. BASIC was legible code. It could be read straight from the page and some sense of the program's nature was evident before the program was ever even executed. Furthermore, as a user typed in a program, he or she could easily alter it, sometimes mistakenly, yet often with purpose. Sometimes the magazines and books had typos themselves or didn't work with a particular reader's dialect of BASIC, and modifying the program—debugging it—became essential. The transmission of BASIC programs in print wasn't a flawless, smooth system, but it did encourage engagement with code, an awareness of how code functioned, and a realization that code could be revised and reworked, the raw material of a programmer's vision.

## BASIC in Human Memory

Not so long ago, software was primarily transmitted on physical media, such as cassette tapes, floppy disks, and CD-ROMs. The notion that programs would routinely be published in print and typed in by users seems alien now. But there is an even stranger way that programs, particularly short ones such as BASIC one-liners could make their way from computer to computer and from person to person: as memorized pieces of code, like a software virus whose host is a human rather than a machine.

The dream of total recall of a computer program appears in science fiction. In Cory Doctorow's short story "0wnz0red," a programmer named Murray spirals downward in terms of his life and his code quality after the apparent death of his only friend (Doctorow 2002). When this friend returns, having actually hacked his own body and mind into near-perfection, Murray attains similarly superhuman capabilities. Among these is the ability to precisely remember large amounts of text, including technical documentation of code, which "he closed his eyes and recalled, with perfect clarity." Murray's powers of recall even extend beyond human language. As the story ends, Murray "had the laptop open and began to rekey the entire codebase, the eidetic rush of perfect memory dispelled all his nervousness, leaving him cool and calm as the sun set over the Mission."

In Doctorow's story, the ability to memorize a large program is a superpower. At the same time, the story's treatment of the human body and mind as machines that can be mastered by a programmer and owned (or even 0wnz0red) by an adversary is consistent with the idea that memorizing code is enslaving one mind's to the machine, treating it as a storage peripheral. For many programmers, however, memorizing one-liners (not an entire massive codebase) is both possible and useful—and pleasing, much as memorizing a poem might be. Such memorization would hardly seem strange in the context of what N. Katherine Hayles (2005) calls the "legacy systems," speech and writing, out of which code evolves (as developed in her chapter "Speech, Writing Code: Three Worldviews").

In the case of home computing in the early 1980s, it could be advantageous for someone to memorize a one-liner or a handful of short programs. A memorized one-liner could be typed into a friend's computer, initiating a kind of two-way cultural economy; in exchange for sharing a particularly interesting or visually affecting program, one earned prestige, or street cred, a currency a teenager in the early 1980s would surely appreciate. In the late 1970s and early 1980s, many of these short programs worth memorizing were of course in BASIC. (See the remark One-Liners for several examples.) And because programmers typically had to memorize certain BASIC statements anyway, such as `? CHR$(147)`(which clears the screen), it was not much of a leap to memorize a program that contained two statements in that language, such as `10 PRINT CHR$(205.5+RND(1)); : GOTO 10`.

In addition to being able to show off and seem elite, there are some strictly utilitarian reasons to memorize a short program. For example, Perl is used for a wide variety of text-processing tasks; many who program in it find it useful to write, recall, or adapt one-line programs that work on the command line. For instance, to convert a file `dosfile.txt` with DOS-

## STUDIES OF PROGRAM MEMORIZATION

In Doctorow's story, Murray finds it easier to remember pages of code than a string of random characters, an idea supported by experimental research. In an effort to better understand how people comprehend computer programs—which has ramifications for programmer efficiency—scientists began studying program memorization in the mid-1970s. In 1976 Ben Shneiderman, referring to the cognitive science literature on remembering sentences, reported a statistically significant difference between subjects of different ability levels attempting to memorize a FORTRAN program and a series of valid statements in scrambled order, "leading us to the conclusion that the structure of a program facilitates comprehension and memorization" (1976, 127).

Ruven Brooks published a more elaborate theory of program comprehension in 1983; `10 PRINT` shows some ways in which this theory is not generally applicable. In Brooks's theory, a programmer reconstructs knowledge about the real-world domains that the program models, developing an initially underspecified hypothesis and refining and elaborating it "based on information extracted from the program text and other documentation" (1983, 543). Brooks posited the useful idea that certain lines were "beacons," indicating key program structures and operations (548). But his theory is otherwise difficult to apply to `10 PRINT`. Brooks lists seven internal and five external "indicators for the meaning of a program," including "Indentation or pretty-printing" and "Flowcharts" (551). None are present in `10 PRINT.` More fundamentally, Brooks's model is meant for programs that simulate recognizable business processes, not computer programs in general. In fact, Brooks's model cannot directly apply to any creative program that lacks a real-world domain.

Brooks's concept of beacons was revisited in another memorization study by Susan Widenbeck. In this 1986 study, Widenbeck found that beacon lines were recalled more often by experienced programmers, presumably because they know what to look for. Widenbeck also noted, "Memorizing a program is a very unusual programming task, and it is possible that it changed the subjects' normal program comprehension strategies and procedures" (1986, 705). Interestingly, given the contemporary mantra that "code is poetry," Widenbeck found that program memorization was not at all like the memorization of text: "If subjects were taking a strictly linear, or text-reading, approach to understanding the program, we would expect the lines near the beginning of the program to be better remembered . . . this was not the case" (707). At the same time, Widenbeck made analogies to the reading of texts in describing how her subjects read programs: "Using beacons to understand a program seems to be something like skimming an English text. They help to figure out the general, high-level function, but they do not contribute to a detailed understanding of the code" (708).

Shneiderman's early acknowledgement that programs can be memorized is significant; his result, furthermore, shows that the memorization of programs relates to the memorization of language in some important ways (Shneiderman 1976). But there are differences between this study's perspective and the consideration of how BASIC one-liners are memorized. Memorization was used as a barometer of comprehension, the real focus of this research. Although it seems evident from these studies that memorization and comprehension are deeply connected, memorization is nevertheless being considered along the way to understanding something else. Shneiderman's study is about the short-term memorization of programs of about twenty lines, assigned as a task. Because short-term memory is the concern, Shneiderman cites Miller's famous paper on the topic, "The magical Number Seven, Plus or Minus Two" (Miller 1996) and discusses how his results may be consistent with the ones in that paper.

`10 PRINT` represents a category of programs that were historically memorized but that existing theories of program memorization, formulated for longer programs that model business processes, do not cover. The memorization of BASIC one-liners was rather long-term, done for fun, and of course involved very short programs. This type of memorization has certain things in common with the tasks done in these memorization studies, but it may also relate to the way people memorize jokes, proverbs, and other oral texts. These studies do at least show how people can remember key statements (beacons) and the high-level workings of a program without memorizing it character by character. Also, the appearance of program variants that work identically but are written differently is consistent with studies on and theories of program memorization.

style line endings to Unix format, a common task for many programmers, the carriage returns (indicated `\r`) must be removed. This can be accomplished with the command `perl -p -i -e's/\r\n/\n/g' dosfile.txt` which includes a very short program (between quotes) to perform the needed substitution. With a few changes, this code can be adapted to replace one word with another, for instance, substituting "Commodore" for every occurrence of "Atari": `perl -p -i -e's/Atari/Commodore/g' manuscript.txt`.

Programmers who use such Perl one-liners do not seem to remember them in exactly the way one memorizes lines from a play or a song. They would generally understand how the substitution operator (`s///`) functions and how command-line flags to Perl work. In other words it is knowing Perl, not just the memorization of a string of symbols, that is important to most uses of Perl one-liners. But the phrase "Perl pie" (a mnemonic for `perl -p -i -e`) does help some to quickly recall which command-line flags are needed in this case, and one-liners are at times as much recalled as figured out and programmed. Many common one-liners are not programmed "from scratch" each time they are used.

This type of non-rote memorization is the sort that BASIC programmers also employed in bringing `10 PRINT` from one computer to another as they showed off its output. Remembering code, like having it printed with the occasional typo, was a "lossy" way to transmit programs. This didn't have purely negative effects, though. Instead of the perfect but opaque way of transferring files via disk or download, the recall and reading of programs left a space for the programmer to work and play. If the recalled version of the program didn't work correctly, the programmer could think about how to change it. If it did work well, the programmer still might think to change it, to see what else the program could do. The wiring of these printed and memorized programs was sometimes messed up, but they were not sealed from view in a closed black box.

## LATE BASIC

The Commodore 64, Apple II, TRS-80, and other microcomputers of the late 1970s and early 1980s featured BASIC in its heyday. Even though Kemeny and Kurtz focused on minicomputer BASIC, it was during this phase of BASIC's run that the language truly fulfilled many of their goals: ease of use, distribution to millions of users, and availability on a wide variety of platforms. Since that time, the use of BASIC has declined thanks to changing technology, new standards, and a reputation (deserved or not) for encouraging low-quality code among programmers. Modern programming environments are indebted to BASIC in a variety of ways, however.

The most direct lineage continues Microsoft's history of building tools to support the BASIC language. Compilers and development environments supporting BASIC, including QuickBasic and QBasic, shipped with every Microsoft operating system until Windows 2000 finally broke the chain by moving away from an MS-DOS base. In 1991 Microsoft reenvisioned BASIC to produce Visual Basic, a language that was intended to fulfill the ease of use and rapid development capabilities of BASIC under the new paradigm of window-based interfaces. Visual Basic used some syntax similar to BASIC but was designed for use with graphical development tools and did not derive directly from earlier microcomputer BASICs. Visual Basic itself was followed ten years later by Visual Basic .NET, a language that again breaks from its predecessor in fundamental ways but retains the goal of being the easy-to-learn, quick-to-use introductory programming language on the Microsoft platform. As of 2012, Visual Basic is the seventh most popular programming language in the world and Visual Basic .NET is twenty-fourth (TIOBE Software BV 2012).

On the less professional end, Microsoft's most recent BASIC probably has the strongest relationship to `10 PRINT` and to how that program was used, modified, shared, and explored. This version of the language is Microsoft Small BASIC, released in 2008 and available free of charge. This is a Microsoft .NET language that is clearly aimed at students and other beginners. It incorporates turtle graphics concepts from LOGO, inviting play and exploration with graphics and GUI elements as well as text. To accompany this language, there is even a Small BASIC edition of David Ahl's *Basic Computer Games* (Kidware Software 2011).

BASIC has continued to be relevant in particular domains. There are several BASICs, or BASIC-derived languages, created specifically for game development and still in active development and use. These include Blitz BASIC (and successor languages), DarkBASIC, and GLBasic. Those interested in physical computing projects can use a microcontroller, the BASIC Stamp, versions of which have been manufactured by Parallax, Inc. since

1992. This system is powered by a nine-volt battery; hobbyists can program it in a variant language called PBASIC. A less direct descendant is the language used to program calculators from Texas Instruments in the 1990s and 2000s. It has been given the unofficial name of TI-BASIC by its programming community because, as in the heyday of BASIC, it is a relatively simple interpreted language that ships with and controls a stand-alone device.

Other successors have continued to migrate either BASIC's principles or syntax to an ever-widening array of environments. Like Microsoft's Visual Basic, True BASIC updated the BASIC language to support graphical environments. Unlike Microsoft's re-envisioning, however, True BASIC was created by Kemeny and Kurtz themselves and has remained close to both the original syntax of Dartmouth BASIC and the principle of device independence, with compilers available for several operating systems.

A more radical interpretation of BASIC's legacy might include languages that have taken over its role of inviting ordinary users to become programmers and creators. Following the release of graphical web browsers like NCSA Mosaic, Netscape Navigator, and Microsoft Internet Explorer between 1993 and 1995, that role might be assigned to HTML. Though HTML is a markup language used for formatting, not a programming language used for data processing and flow control, it copied BASIC's template of simplicity, similarity to natural language, device independence, and transparency to become many users' first introduction to manipulating code. Browsers have traditionally contained a "view source" command that shows the markup behind the page being displayed, making it as accessible as if it were printed in a magazine. This markup language also was similar to BASIC in that it led users on to more powerful languages like Javascript, Perl, and PHP as those users sought to create more interactivity than static HTML could provide.

BASIC's role as a language that introduced users to programming by necessity in the 1980s is now being fulfilled by languages designed specifically for education, some of which are so abstracted from traditional programming practices that they use entirely different metaphors. Scratch, an environment developed by the MIT Media Lab in 2006 whose creators cite 1980s-era BASIC as a predecessor (Resnick et al. 2009, 62), does not even use text as the basic unit; instead, programs are assembled by dragging and dropping puzzle-piece graphics that fit together to build functional-

## A PERSONAL MEMORY OF `10 PRINT`

When one of this book's authors, Nick Montfort, first wrote about a similarly functioning program, he presented this variant: `10 PRINT CHR$(109+RND(1)*2); : GOTO 10`. That is the program discussed very briefly in the article "Obfuscated Code" in *Software Studies: A Lexicon*, and is the same version of the program that Montfort presented to Mark Marino's online Critical Code Studies Workshop in 2010, where it sparked the discussion that led to this book.

This program is a different sequence of characters, but it does the same thing as the `10 PRINT` that forms this book's title, for two reasons: first, 205 and 206 are mapped to the same characters as 109 and 110; second, adding a random number between 0 and 2 does the same thing, due to rounding, as adding .5 and then also adding a random number between 0 and 1. The version used in the title of this book is based on (although not identical to) two early print sources for the program, the three-line program in the *Commodore 64 User's Guide* and the one-line version in *RUN* magazine. No print sources from the 1980s have been located that use `RND(1)*2` or that use character codes 109 and 110 rather than 205 and 206.

Why did Montfort initially bring up this "corrupt" version of the program? Simply because he reconstructed `10 PRINT` from memory and looked at a chart of PETSCII character values when he was doing so. Since 109 and 110 are lower numerically and closer to the values for the characters A–Z, he noticed them first on the chart and used those values.

The discussion of this program throughout this book is based on the early print versions. The version of the program that started the discussion, however, came from memory.

ity. Though the appearances and mechanisms are quite different, Scratch uses the same underlying logic and concepts as any other programming language, so that students who use it can apply what they learn to other languages.

Because BASIC was a hit at a unique time in the history of computing—when microcomputers were becoming mainstream but before executable software distribution became widespread—there may never be another language quite like it. The principles behind BASIC remain strong, though, and continue to make programming languages easier, more transparent, and more freely distributed—all of which continue to encourage new programmers to take the plunge and old programmers to experiment with new ideas.

# 55

# REM A PORT TO THE ATARI VCS

CODING THE CHARACTERS
BUILDING THE WALLS
COVERING THE SCREEN
BOUNDING THE MAZE

Alongside the general purpose home computers launched in 1977—the TRS-80, the Apple II, and the Commodore PET—was another computer, one that was hugely successful but that most people do not recognize as a computer. This was a videogame console, the Atari Video Computer System (VCS), which later came to be known as the Atari 2600. Unlike the other computers, the Atari VCS was built specifically to play videogames. It was also designed to be far less expensive: the VCS was priced at $199, while the original Apple II cost an astounding $1,298.

Due to its intended use, the requirement that the system sell for a low price, and the high costs of silicon components, the Atari VCS was designed in a very unusual way. Like the Apple II and the Commodore 64, the Atari VCS used a version of the inexpensive MOS Technology 6502 microprocessor. But in order to create moving images and sounds on an ordinary CRT television, engineers Joe Decuir and Jay Miner designed a custom graphics and sound chip called the Television Interface Adapter (TIA). The TIA supported five "high resolution" movable objects: two player sprites (movable objects that can be created once and then moved around freely), two missiles (one for each player), and a ball. These were exactly the right kind of movable graphics needed for the games first envisioned for the VCS—home versions of popular Atari arcade games including *Pong* and *Tank*. The TIA also enabled a low-resolution playfield and a changeable background color, along with a variety of methods to vary the appearance of each of these objects. To save money, the TIA was paired with a cheaper variant of the 6502 and 128 bytes of RAM, an incredibly modest amount of memory.

Unlike the Apple II and the PET, the Atari had no on-board ROM and no operating system, and only a fraction of the RAM of those other 1977 computers. As a result, Atari programmers had to write code that manipulated the TIA's registers not merely on a screen-by-screen basis, but on every single scanline of the television display. The result is one of history's most unusual methods of producing computer graphics (Montfort and Bogost 2009, 28–30). The launch titles for the Atari VCS used this system in a fairly straightforward way (see figure 55.1), while later titles exploited it to produce quite different effects.

While a number of remarkable games were designed for the Atari VCS over its lifetime, the constraints of the system make it a particularly difficult platform from the programmer's perspective. Consider the chal-

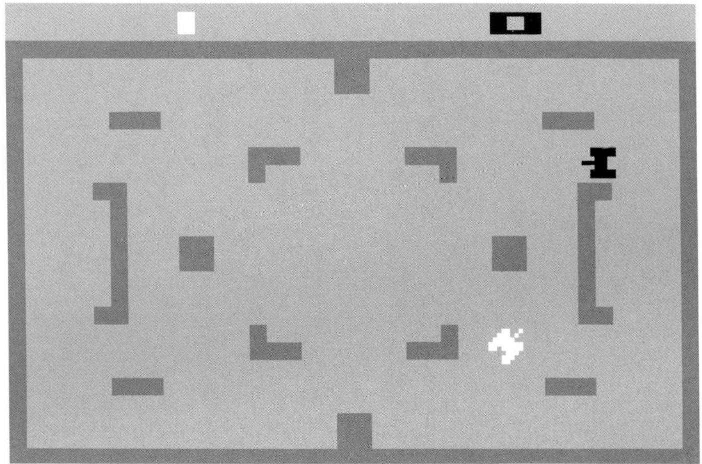

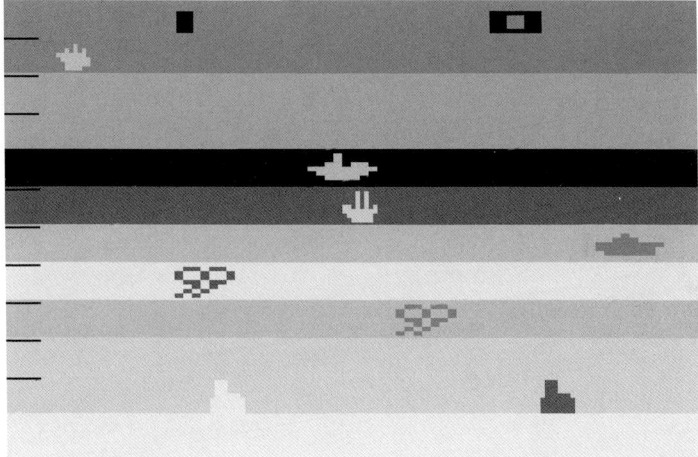

Figure 55.1

These screen captures from *Combat* (top) and *Air-Sea Battle* (below) show the visual quality of Atari VCS games.

lenges of porting 10 PRINT to the Atari VCS:

1. The Atari does not have predefined character bitmaps, grids of pixels to represent each glyph, as the Commodore 64 does, making it necessary to create the patterns corresponding to the diagonal characters from scratch.

2. The TIA supports only two high-resolution sprites for on-screen display (the missiles and ball are mere dots, a pixel each). Somehow, the Atari has to be made to produce a large, changing pattern out of just these two 8-bit graphics registers.

3. The Atari has no concept of a row-and-column screen display like those found in minicomputer terminals and PCs. It was designed to play simple videogames, not to display text and numbers. As a result, the gridded layout that 10 PRINT enjoys "for free," thanks to the Commodore 64's way of displaying text, must be laboriously simulated on the Atari VCS.

4. Once the previous hurdles are overcome, the Atari sports far less memory than the Commodore 64. The Commodore can hold all those display character references in memory because it has the room to do so, with 512 times as much storage as the Atari. Even if the Atari could be made to display enough high-resolution diagonal characters per line or per screen, the program would have to store references to those simulated characters so that each frame of the display would appear consistent with the preceding one.

Designing a port of 10 PRINT for the Atari VCS is so quixotic that it might not seem to be worth even trying. Yet just as 10 PRINT reveals much about BASIC and the Commodore 64, so too can a study of a seemingly impossible port on an incompatible platform reveal deeper levels to 10 PRINT. Figure 55.2 shows is the closest approximation of 10 PRINT that has been achieved on the Atari VCS, the output of a port written for this book.

## CODING THE CHARACTERS

The matter of simulating PETSCII characters in the Atari's eight-bit graphics registers turns out to be the least troublesome challenge of the port. With the Commodore 64, graphical patterns that produce PETSCII characters are stored in ROM, and references in BASIC like CHR$(205) look up and

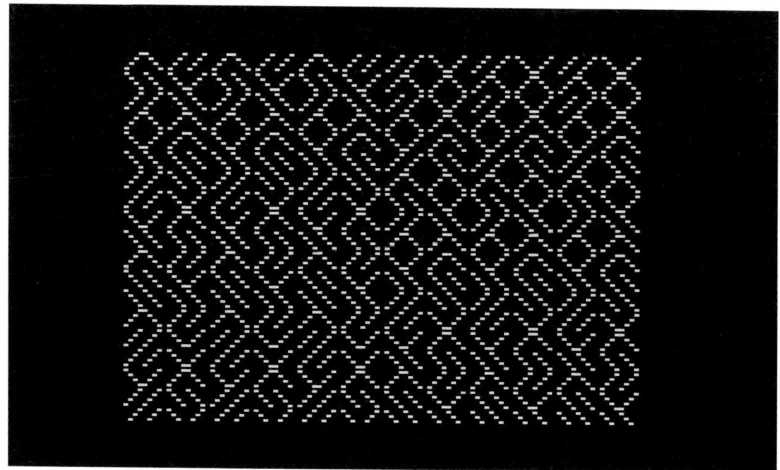

Figure 55.2
Screen capture from an Atari VCS port of 10 PRINT.

retrieve the corresponding data for on-screen display, in a process all but invisible to the BASIC user. With the Atari, which has no ROM or built-in characters, it's necessary to "draw" the needed characters by defining a data table in the Atari's cartridge-based ROM. For example, the following data could be defined:

```
Diagonal
     .byte #%11000000
     .byte #%00110000
     .byte #%00001100
     .byte #%00000011
```

This binary data describes a left-leaning diagonal line, which would appear colored on screen wherever each bit of each byte of the bitmap is on:

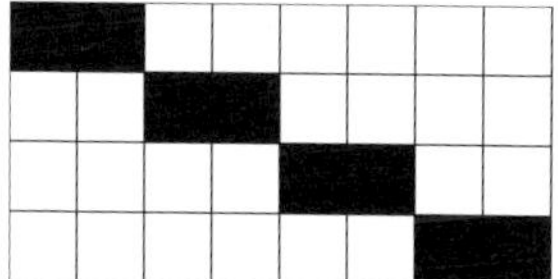

This character looks satisfactory, but changes are necessary to eke out a credible rendition of 10 PRINT on the Atari VCS. To understand why, it's important to consider the second and third challenges that were mentioned, the ones that are also the most troublesome.

The fact that TIA has only two 8-bit registers for displaying sprite graphics may come as a surprise to anyone who has played early Atari games, since many games appear to have more than two sprites on the screen at once. For example, *Air-Sea Battle*, one of the console's launch titles, depicts two antiaircraft guns at the bottom of the screen aimed up at seven rows of aeronautic enemies, each of which moves horizontally (figure 55.1). How is this possible?

The answer is strange but straightforward. It is typical to think of a computer display as a two-dimensional surface, like a painting or a photograph. Computers usually provide a block of video memory capable of storing enough information to create an entire screen's worth of display material. Typically the program resets this data during the brief moment before the 192 horizontal lines of a NTSC television screen are rescanned, a moment called the vertical blank. But the Atari has only 128 bytes of RAM total, making it impossible to set up a whole screen's worth of information at a time.

Instead, the Atari programmer sets up the display on a horizontal scanline-by-scanline basis, interfacing with the TIA to change its settings in the brief time between individual scanlines—a moment called horizontal blank. Once a particular line or group of lines is complete, the programmer can "reuse" the sprite registers later in the same screen, for a different purpose. The technique happens so fast, especially with the lingering glow of the television screen, that the reused sprites appear simultaneously, albeit with some flicker. This is exactly how the final 10 PRINT port creates more than two "diagonal" graphics on the Atari's screen.

But games like *Air-Sea Battle* still only display one or two sprites on a single line—precisely because the TIA can display at most two player sprites. 10 PRINT requires more than just two diagonals per row to look anything like a maze. The Commodore 64 screen can display forty columns of text; even half that number might be sufficient to give the sense of a maze, as evidenced by the VIC-20 version of 10 PRINT, which runs on the VIC-20's twenty-two-column display and is discussed in the next chapter.

The two-sprite limitation leads to the third challenge that was stated earlier: how to approximate the row-and-column display of the Commodore 64. Sprites may be reused on different horizontal sections of the television screen, which is helpful, but some way to display more than two columns worth of diagonals per row is needed. Three programming techniques, ranging from simple to complex, are required to produce an approximation of `10 PRINT`'s rows and columns of maze walls.

## BUILDING THE WALLS

The simplest technique involves adjusting the sprite graphics to include two diagonals in eight bits of space rather than just one, each using one nybble (half-byte, or four bits). For example, this defines two left-leaning lines that are one pixel thick:

```
Diagonals
     .byte #%10001000
     .byte #%01000100
     .byte #%00100010
     .byte #%00010001
```

In working this way, there are four necessary permutations of two-line patterns to be encoded:

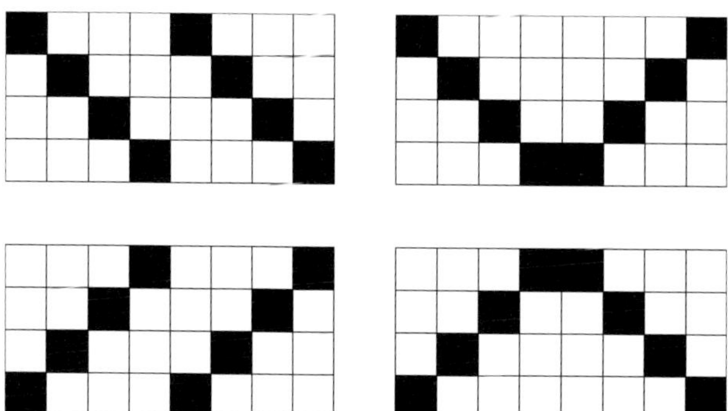

It's both easier and more efficient to store all four permutations as static data on the cartridge ROM than to try to construct them in RAM out of single diagonals, each one stores in half a byte—one-nybble diagonals.

This technique doubles the number of apparent diagonals per row, but with two sprites this still means only four diagonals—hardly a mazeworthy number. A second technique can be applied to triple that number, turning the individual diagonals into the walls of a maze.

The TIA provides a way to alter the appearance of each of the sprites automatically. These alterations include stretching the sprite to two times or four times its normal width, or doubling or tripling the sprite at different distances apart. In the VCS launch title *Combat*, many of the cartridge's plane game variants are accomplished simply by changing these settings for each player.

Stretching and multiplying the sprites is accomplished by writing specific values into special registers on the TIA chip called the Number-Size registers. By setting both registers to "three copies, closely spaced," it is possible to get six total sprites to appear on a single line of the display. Given that each sprite contains two diagonals, that's already twelve total simulated PETSCII characters per row. But, two problems remain: positioning and repetition.

## COVERING THE SCREEN

To make a computer game of the sort normally played on the Atari, a programmer might expect to be able to position a sprite on a Cartesian coordinate system at a particular (x, y) position. As described earlier, the Atari doesn't give the programmer access to such a two-dimensional memory space, meaning there's no particular location where a sprite might appear on the screen. That said, the Atari does have something like a vertical axis; the programmer can count horizontal scanlines and choose to start or continue a sprite on a particular one.

To position an object horizontally, the programmer must manually "reset" the position of the object in question by strobing a register on the TIA. When any value is written into these registers (named RESP0 and RESP1 for the two player sprites), the TIA sets the starting horizontal position of that object at that point in the scanline. To accomplish this strange task, the programmer has to count the number of microprocessor cycles that will have passed before the television's electron gun has reached the desired position on the screen. Called "racing the beam" by Atari pro-

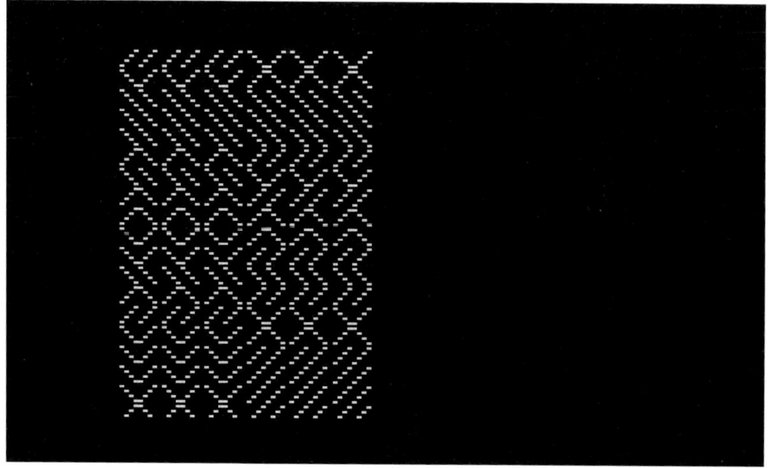

Figure 55.3

Identical copies of the diagonal pattern provide regularity rather than randomness.

grammers, this technique is relatively straightforward and can be used to position the two sprites next to one another, creating a sequence of six sets of two diagonals each.

The problem of repetition is more complex. When the TIA's number-size registers are set to triple a sprite, the result looks like three identical copies of the same pattern—whatever eight-bit value had been set in the sprite graphics register at the time the sprite was rendered to the screen. The resulting effect will be three identical copies of one diagonal pattern, followed by three identical copies of another diagonal pattern. This visual regularity (figure 55.3) is a serious problem, since the maze of `10 PRINT` is so strongly characterized by its apparent randomness. It's possible to overcome the visual repetition in the process of increasing the number of columns of sprites (and therefore diagonal lines) visible on a single row. Doing so involves taking advantage of an obscure behavior in the TIA.

When a sprite's number-size is set to double or triple, the TIA keeps an internal count of how many copies it has drawn. When the RESP0 or RESP1 is strobed, that value is reset. If that strobe occurs after the first copy is drawn but before the second has begun, the TIA's sprite counter is reset and it will start over, as if it hadn't yet drawn any copies of the sprites. By repeatedly strobing RESP0 and RESP1 in sequence, it is possible to pro-

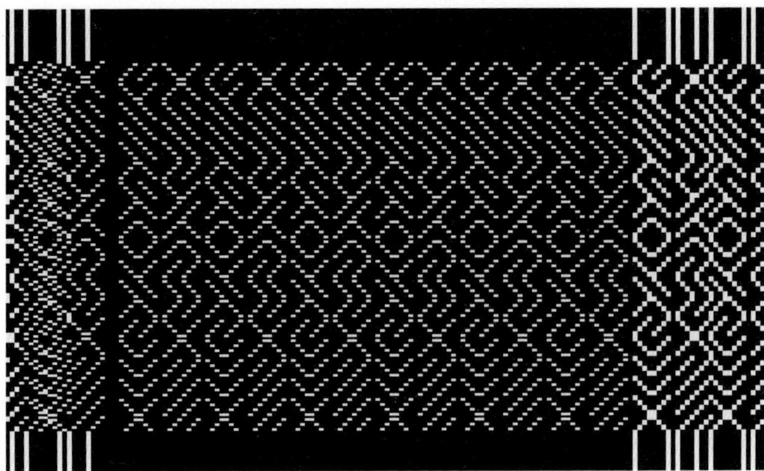

Figure 55.4

The Atari Television Interface Adapter wraps the characters around the screen. As this image shows, this is a problem for a `10 PRINT` port.

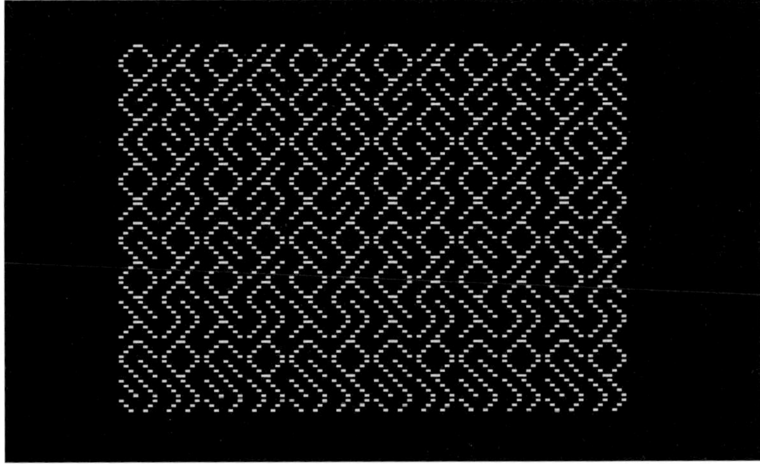

Figure 55.5

At this stage of the software development a convincing maze is generated, but the graphics are repeated and too regular in comparison to the original.

duce a tight, interleaved grid of the sprites. By performing this trick over and over again, it's possible to easily produce a grid twelve sprites across.

This technique has the additional benefit of reducing the appearance of repetition, as two different sprite patterns can be interleaved. While a repeated pattern is still visible, it's not as obvious, and there are additional techniques available to further reduce the repetition.

The obstacle at this point, however, is that the screen has been set up to render twelve columns of alternating sets of sprites, each capable of displaying one of the four patterns of diagonals. But those twelve columns don't fill the whole screen. Centering them in the middle of the screen to mimic the borders of the Commodore 64 display creates a new problem: by the time the final sprite reset strobes have taken place, the maze "characters" are so far to the right side of the screen that they begin to overlap and wrap around on the borders (figure 55.4). This happens because the TIA automatically wraps sprites around the sides of the screen, a valuable technique for single-screen games like *Asteroids* but one that is of little use for a visual pattern partially defined by its borders.

## BOUNDING THE MAZE

Luckily, low-resolution playfield graphics can hide the characters wrapping around the screen. Setting another bit on a TIA register will place the playfield in front of the sprites rather than behind it. This almost, but not quite, solves the problem. Timing the reset strobes just right leaves the twelve columns of sprites off center, so a small area of messy sprite junk is left at the right side of the pattern. The solution is the ball. Even though the name "ball" suggests a rounded image, to the TIA the "ball" is simply a square object of a single pixel that can be turned on or off. Turned on and positioned correctly, the ball will cover the offending sprite residue.

With all that work done, the fourth challenge remains: storing the diagonal pattern variation in what remains of the 128 bytes of RAM and loading the right data for each row of simulated PETSCII characters. Surprisingly, this is the least troubling task of all, although it does require more work than would be necessary on the Commodore 64. First it's necessary to write a random number-generation routine, since that function isn't provided in hardware on the machine. The next step is to write a routine that will run the random number routine and use it to choose sets of diagonal bitmap data to use in each row of the visible display. This could be a lot of data, but it's not necessary to store the bitmaps themselves, just the sixteen-bit addresses of the ROM locations where they can be found. As it turns out, the program only requires eleven bytes of RAM to run everything else, leaving enough room in RAM to store twenty-nine rows worth of bitmap data pointers for each of the two sprites.

There is an unexpected consequence to this randomization approach. The Atari's random number generator has to be seeded somehow. It could be given a fixed seed, but in order to ensure that different seeds are chosen (resulting in different mazes), the program starts with a blank screen and increments a counter each frame. The user starts the program by depressing the console's RESET switch, at which time the frame counter is put to use as a random number seed. Every subsequent flick of the Reset switch will reset the seed and the diagonal graphics pointer data, resulting in a different maze. The result looks a great deal like the output of `10 PRINT`—it's clearly identifiable as some sort of port of the program (figure 55.5). It's even possible to make the rows scroll to mimic the Commodore 64's screen buffer, using a byte of RAM to store a memory offset location for the rows of bitmap data pointers.

But notice the horizontal symmetry of the upper part of the maze—the six diamonds spaced evenly across the top. This symmetry gives lie to the supposed randomness of the maze. It occurs because the same sprite data is used across the entire line of each row of the pattern. Recycling sprite data is necessary because the sprite reset strobing technique occurs so rapidly that it's impossible to alter the sprite graphics in between them. There's yet one more programming trick invented by Atari 2600 game designers that proves helpful here: flicker. Flicker is a common technique used on the Atari to give the player the impression that more objects appear on screen than are technically possible. It's a simple solution: when more than two objects need to seem to appear on a single scanline, draw some of them on one frame and the rest on another frame. The television screen is refreshed at 60Hz, so the result appears as a light flickering effect, like a ghost image. The result can be distracting or even disorienting, particularly when (as is not the case here) the objects are also moving.

The apparent regularity of the VCS port of `10 PRINT` can be reduced by deploying the flicker technique. On odd frames, render the first six columns with one set of diagonal patterns; on even frames, render the second six with another set of patterns. To do this, it's necessary to duplicate the loop that renders the screen and send the program to the correct one. Even this seemingly simple task proves difficult, since "turning off" half the pattern is not as easy as it sounds. It requires loading the processor's accumulator with the value zero and setting the two sprite graphics registers to that value at exactly the right time, before the TIA starts to render the next one. The result is convincing, even if it still doesn't look as random as the Commodore 64 original.

The technique used here is only one possible way to reproduce 10 PRINT; other methods might allow for a more random display. For example, a common technique used in Atari games was a fairly complex routine for a six-digit score. By taking advantage of a setting called vertical delay, it's possible to push one sprite graphics value into the other by writing to the opposite register. This technique can produce six unique, closely spaced, high-resolution graphics. By combining this technique with the screen flickering approach discussed earlier, it might be possible to get a maze without any apparent repetition; but the careful cycle timing required to generate these patterns in exactly the correct place on the screen would also disrupt the evenness of the resulting maze. Violating the expected grid layout even slightly might make the "maze" look less mazelike.

The difficulty of creating the 10 PRINT pattern on the Atari VCS is a reminder that computers with similar components from similar eras were designed to do very different things. 10 PRINT depends on the Commodore 64's ability to render text in a line and screen buffer. Even though such abilities are fundamental to computers of the 1970s and 1980s, the Atari VCS was not designed with that usage in mind. The BASIC code `10 PRINT CHR$(205.5+RND(1)); : GOTO 10` is defined with text of 38 bytes; as is described in the next chapter, an assembly version of the program can be accomplished in less space. But the simplest version of the program on the Atari VCS requires 360 bytes, largely because the program has to perform "from scratch" so many functions that in the Commodore 64 are part of the ROM.

The very idea of creating a program like 10 PRINT depends on aspects of the platform and the platform's facility for such a program—the presence of BASIC and RND in ROM, the existence of PETSCII, the cultural context of shared programming techniques, and of course the ability to program the computer in the first place, something owners of an Atari 2600 did not truly have. Reimplementing the program on the Atari VCS, a platform both contemporaneous with the Commodore 64 and highly incompatible with the program that is this book's subject, helps to show all of the things the Commodore 64 programmer takes for granted. If the Commodore 64 programmer had to go to these lengths to produce the output of 10 PRINT—from writing a random number generation routine to coercing a line-buffered display with two high-resolution objects to produce a two-dimensional grid of graphics—it's possible the program would never have been written.

# 60 THE COMMODORE 64

HOME COMPUTING BEYOND THE HOBBYIST
COMMODORE BUSINESS MACHINES
PETSCII
THE VIC-II CHIP
THE KERNAL

commodore
64
!
1
BLK
"
2
WHT
#
3
RED
$
4
CYN
%
5
PUR
&
6
GRN
'
7
BLU
(
8
YEL
CTRL
Q
W
E
R
T
Y
U
I
RUN STOP
SHIFT LOCK
A
S
D
F
G
H
J
SHIFT
Z
X
C
V
B
N
M

Figure 60.1

The Commodore 64 computer was released in 1982 as a followup to the Commodore VIC-20. As the name signals, it had sixty-four kilobytes of memory. Photo by Mark Richards. Courtesy of Mark Richards.

The Commodore 64 (see figure 60.1) has been hailed by *Guinness World Records* as the best-selling single model of computer ever. People associated with Commodore have estimated, officially and unofficially, that 22 million or 17 million units were sold. A detailed study of Commodore 64 serial numbers has provided a better estimate, that 12.5 million Commodore 64s were sold (Steil 2011), which is still enough to earn the computer this distinction.

Although production ended in 1994, this computer system remains functioning and part of the popular consciousness in many ways. VICE and many other emulators allow users to start up software editions of the Commodore 64 and to run software for that system on modern computers, which is the way most people now encounter Commodore 64 software. In 2004 Jeri Ellsworth's C64 Direct-to-TV—a single-chip implementation of the Commodore 64, packed into a joystick along with thirty games—brought at least part of the Commodore experience to new users. And, in 2011, a company necro-branded with the name Commodore USA announced that they would be making new all-in-one PCs in a case (and with a keyboard) that is visually almost identical to that of the original Commodore 64 (Olivarez-Giles 2011).

The original Commodore 64 computer has particular features—the PETSCII character set (figure 60.2), built-in BASIC, and the specific appearance of the screen—that determine how 10 PRINT runs. At the same time, it was one computer among many during the early 1980s that brought forth this significant era of personal computing and, perhaps more novel, home computing.

## HOME COMPUTING BEYOND THE HOBBYIST

In the early 1980s, computers moved beyond the exclusive domain of hackers and hobbyists and into the home, a transition led by Apple, Radio Shack, and Commodore. In October 1984, 8.2 percent of all U.S. households reported owning a home computer. Of those households, 70 percent had acquired their computer quite recently, in either 1983 or 1984 (U.S. Bureau of the Census 1988, 2). By 1989—the outer boundary of the Commodore 64's mainstream popularity—computer ownership had skyrocketed to 15 percent. Households with school-aged children were nearly

Figure 60.2

The graphics characters for each key of the Commodore 64 keyboard are printed on the side. Here, the two characters used in `10 PRINT` are visible on the sides of the N and M keys. Photo by Mark Richards. Courtesy of Mark Richards.

twice as likely to own a computer (at 25.7 percent), while 45.6 percent of households earning more than $75,000 annually ($138,000 in 2012 dollars) owned computers (Kominski 1991, 1–3).

Yet even as microcomputers became *personal* computers, the prospect of computer ownership was closely tied to income (U.S. Bureau of the Census 1988, 2). This trend was exacerbated when race was factored in. Black and Hispanic families were far less likely to have a computer at home in the 1980s, and by 1997, this gap had translated into a digital divide online, in which Whites were twice as likely as Blacks and Hispanics to use the Internet (Kominski and Newburger 1999, 12).

Gender appears to have been less of a factor in computer use than race or socioeconomic status was. In 1984, boys (31.9 percent) were slightly more likely to use a computer than girls (28.4 percent), even at school, but by 1989 that small gap had closed (46.5 percent and 45.5 percent)

Figure 60.3

This 1983 advertisement for the Commodore 64 sold the system as a powerful computer within the financial reach of middle-class families.

(Kominski and Newburger 1999, table 3). The gap between adult females and males follows a similar trend: A small divide becomes smaller in the 1980s (Ibid., table 5). However, women (29 percent in 1984) were more likely to use a computer at work than men (21.2 percent in 1984), often because more women worked in data entry or administrative support positions (Ibid., table 6). A more statistically significant discrepancy appears in computer ownership by household income. Again, looking at 1984 and 1989, compare the rise in home computer ownership from 5.3 to 8 percent in households earning $15,000–$20,000 with 22.4 to 31.6 percent in households earning $50,000–$75,000 (Ibid., table 2). By 1989 the disparity appears magnified with 43.8 percent of families owning computers in the $75,000-plus range and only 3.7 percent in the $5,000–$9,000 range owning computers (table 2).

These socioeconomic, racial, and gender disparities are part of the context of `10 PRINT`, as much as the history of textured patterns or BASIC is. They can be seen playing out in one of the iconic Commodore 64 magazine advertisements of the era (figure 60.3).

Given how costly home computing was, Commodore shrewdly positioned its computers as economical yet more powerful than its competitors'. This 1983 advertisement declares, "You can't buy a better computer at twice the price" as it shames Apple, Radio Shack, and IBM for pricing their personal computers at a range only "wealthy," "whiz-kid," or "privileged" persons could possibly afford. The difference between Commodore and these other PCs is not measured solely in dollar amounts. The three costlier computers are crowded into a black and white background, almost hidden from view by the large "FOR NOBODY." The Commodore 64 occupies the bottom half of the page, bathed in warm colors. A father and mother watch their child explore the galaxy on the computer, suggesting that the Commodore is a portal to a larger universe—a universe of knowledge and opportunity. The family indicates a carefully targeted market. Parents were twice as likely to purchase a computer. It is telling, too, that this family is white and middle-class and that their child appears to be a boy. Though the statistics suggest more gender balance in access to computers, the advertisement reinforces a narrative of home computers as the realm of boys. Doug Thomas identifies the broader "hacker demographic" as predominantly "white, suburban boys" (2002, x), and contemporary programming culture, from gender imbalances in undergraduate studies to professional spaces, suggests of the force of that legacy. As would be typical of advertising of that era, "everybody" actually turned out to be an extremely specific demographic.

While the market for home computers was smaller than advertisers acknowledged, the computers themselves spanned a range of styles and forms that went far beyond the Apple-Commodore-TRS-80 trifecta. In addition to the more well-known brands, there were also Sinclair ZX Spectrums, BBC Micros, and computers from Amstrad and Acorn, all of which originated in the United Kingdom. The Texas Instruments TI-99/4A and the Coleco Adam were available, too. Among so many choices, advertisers had to build the personality of not only the brands but the individual machines as well. In the world of computing since the inundation of PC clones, it is difficult to imagine the aura produced around individual machines. Yet today's programmers can still recall their first Apple IIc, VIC-20, or TRS-80. Apple alone now clings to the marketing of "different" machines, though even their computers have Intel inside and the company tends to market product lines rather than individual model numbers. It was a very different landscape that saw the advent of a personal computer that wore its sixty-four kilobytes of memory as a badge of honor. To buy a Commodore 64 was to buy capacity itself.

This diversity meant that different manufacturers could try different types of hardware design and burn different operating systems in ROM. It fostered certain types of corporate exploration of the home computer market, while also limiting the way that software could be shared—even if that software was in the lingua franca of BASIC, given the variety of BASIC dialects. The experience of home computing was in many ways stratified by platform. The Apple Store was not the first example of a platform-specific retail establishment to sell computers. Many vendors would at least specialize in a particular company's computers; in some cases, stores were exclusively Apple, Atari, or Commodore outfits, just as Radio Shack was exclusively a seller of TRS computers (see figure 60.4).

Computer owners also created and joined user groups that were specific to platforms and that met in person. As discussed in the chapter on BASIC, they also subscribed to and read magazines that were for computers of a certain type. When Bulletin Board Systems (BBSs) came onto the scene, some hosted the users of many different types of computer and others, particularly those devoted to making software available for download,

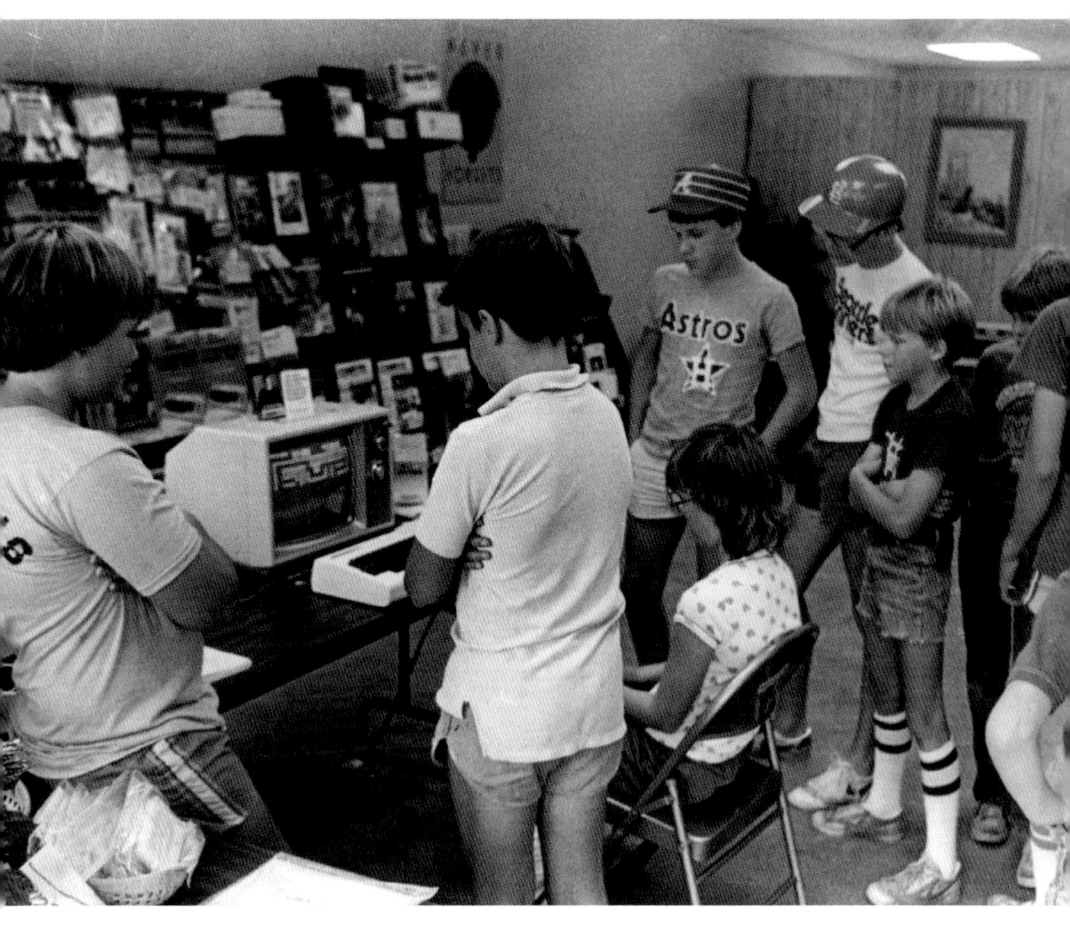


Figure 60.4

Local students at Bob West Computers in Brevard, NC, take turns with a Commodore computer. Courtesy of Bob West.

focused on a single platform.

This did not mean that every computer user was paired with a single platform. Some households had more than one computer—perhaps to keep the work computer from being occupied by a younger member of the family, the parents would decide to provide another computer more geared to games and education. Even those without a computer at home might have access to several at retail stores (which often allowed children to enjoy extended sessions with the computers available for sale), at school, and at friends' houses. Given this environment for computing, even those who were mainly Apple II users or who tooled on their Coleco Adam systems at home might have had an opportunity to play around a bit with a Commodore 64. With limited time and particularly in the context of a school or retail store, where the available software might be limited or nonexistent, it would not have been a bad idea for a visitor to the Commodore 64 to learn about and modify one-liners such as `10 PRINT`.

## COMMODORE BUSINESS MACHINES

The history of the Commodore 64 begins with the Canadian company Commodore, founded in 1958 in Toronto by Jack Tramiel. Tramiel was born Idek Tramielski, was a Polish concentration camp survivor, and changed his name after World War II, when he emigrated to the United States. After serving in Korea, Tramiel worked as a typewriter repair technician, eventually opening a repair company with a business partner. Commodore was the successor company that they formed. This new company did not repair typewriters; it manufactured them (Bagnall 2010, xiii). Once again, the history of `10 PRINT` is intertwined with earlier technologies. Personal computers were hardly a natural progression or simple next step from typewriters, but their prominent keyboards, their use as office equipment, and their use for typewriter-like word processing tasks all demonstrate they had affinities with earlier devices.

In the mid-1960s Commodore shifted its focus from manufacturing typewriters to making calculators, a move driven by strictly financial considerations. In hindsight, however, it seems to evoke the same tension between text and numbers, between poetics and algorithms, that underwrites the aesthetic and procedural dimensions of `10 PRINT`. Caught in a price war with Texas Instruments and Japanese manufacturers in the 1970s, Tramiel sought the cheapest calculator components he could find, eventually buying parts from MOS Technology, a semiconductor company where many former Motorola engineers worked. While MOS Technology earned its revenue from selling calculator chips (mostly to Commodore, its largest customer), the company was also developing a microprocessor, the 6502.

This chip, the 6502, is now legendary for its role in 1980s computing and videogaming. The 6502 became the central processing unit (CPU) for the original Apple I, the Apple II, the Atari 400 and 800, the Nintendo Entertainment System (NES), and of course, modified with an I/O port, the Commodore 64. In a lower-cost package, the chip also powered the Atari 2600. Yet MOS Technology never intended the chip to be used in computers or videogame systems. The 6502 was designed as a single chip replacement for the two- or three-chip processors found in cash registers, appliances, and industrial machines. "If we were going to do a computer," Chuck Peddle, the lead engineer on the project confessed, "we would have done something else" (Bagnall 2010, 14).

With an eye on vertical integration and the 6502 microprocessor, Jack Tramiel bought MOS Technology in September 1976, but not in the most straightforward fashion. Tramiel, widely considered a ruthless businessman, withheld payments to MOS—whether because Commodore was cash-strapped or there was a problem with an order of chips, or both, is a matter of speculation. Nevertheless, it meant that MOS was in turn facing a cash shortfall. The problem was compounded by a lawsuit from Motorola over possible intellectual property infringement (Bagnall 2010, 56). Tramiel was able to buy MOS Technology at a bargain price—about $750,000—which meant that Commodore gained its own chip design and production facility.

## The PET

Tramiel was still intent on dominating the calculator business, however, and it took Chuck Peddle and Commodore's vice-president of engineering, Andre Sousan, to persuade him that a personal computer would in fact be the next generation calculator, leapfrogging over Hewlett-Packard's successful programmable HP-65 calculator (Bagnall 2010, 62). Thus was born the project that would become the eight-bit Commodore PET (figure 60.5), the first computer under $1,000 ($3,733 in 2012 dollars) to include a monitor.

Figure 60.5

The Commodore PET computer was released in 1977. It featured four kilobytes of memory and a tape drive for storing and loading programs. Photo by Mark Richards. Courtesy of Mark Richards.

The PET was particularly successful in Europe, where Commodore already had a strong presence from its calculator business. With nearly 70 percent of its sales in Europe through the 1970s, it is no surprise that Commodore would include a pound sterling symbol on the keyboards of the VIC-20 and Commodore 64. The PET's name is a sign of the times; Sousan came up with this name to capitalize on the pet rock craze of the late 1970s, and only afterward did Peddle suggest "Personal Electronic Transactor" as a "backronym" that would explain the PET's name logically (Freiberger 1982, 13).

As discussed in the BASIC chapter, the PET was the first of Commodore's computers to include BASIC in ROM, making the PET ready for programming the moment the computer had booted up. Another legacy of the PET that made its mark on the Commodore 64 and on `10 PRINT` is its extended graphical character set, informally dubbed PETSCII. (The name "extends" ASCII, the standard character set for computers.) PETSCII was largely designed for the PET by engineer Bill Seiler and Leonard Tramiel (Jack Tramiel's son), who worked at the time as Commodore's in-house tester and debugger (Bagnall 2010, 92–93). The chief rationale for PETSCII, which included the 128 characters of ASCII plus 128 additional graphic characters, was to provide a simple way to produce graphical characters such as playing card symbols. It is commonplace to observe that innovations in computer graphics drive much innovation in computers—chip speed, bus speed, memory sizes, and so on—and here is a less obvious example. While the graphical character set of PETSCII, which features the four suits of cards, shaded patterns, and various brackets and lines, could hardly be said to be an innovation, it made possible early computer games in BASIC without the need to program sprites or other animated figures. And PETSCII made `10 PRINT` possible as well, providing programmers with the two diagonal characters found in the maze way back in 1977.

### The VIC-20

While business and education were the primary markets for the PET computers, its follow-up the VIC-20 was aimed squarely at the home computer market. Released in 1980, the outside of the VIC-20 was exactly the same physical form that the Commodore 64 would later have. (The VIC-20's plastic was lighter in color, more of an off-white instead of the Commodore

64's taupe.) Like both the PET and the Commodore 64, the VIC-20 was powered by the 6502 chip and included Microsoft's version of BASIC. The VIC-20, however, was sold with only five KB of RAM, a tiny slice of the Commodore 64's sixty-four KB. The system also had a color display that was twenty-two characters wide, powered by the forty-pin VIC chip (Video Interface Controller). The VIC 6560 chip had been designed by MOS Technology engineer Al Charpentier to be sold to other manufacturers like Apple and Atari, but none were interested (Bagnall 2010, 178). Ultimately it found its way into the VIC-20. Its shortcomings inspired the creation of a more powerful graphics chip for the Commodore 64.

Because the VIC-20 ran the same version of Microsoft BASIC and included the same PETSCII character set as the PET before it and the Commodore 64 after it, the `10 PRINT` program executes flawlessly on the VIC-20, though no published versions of the maze program intended for the VIC-20 specifically are known to exist. If users had run `10 PRINT` or a variation on the VIC-20, they would have had a different aesthetic experience than a Commodore 64 user (figure 60.6). PETSCII was designed for the forty-column PET; on the twenty-two-column VIC-20 the characters are elongated, stretched as if one were watching an old 4:3 television show on a widescreen. The maze looks almost 3D, as if seen from the isometric point of view of Sega's 1982 hit arcade game *Zaxxon*.

Despite its modest memory, the VIC-20 was seen as a dramatic improvement over the PET computers, at a price that appealed to the home market. The VIC-20 was sold in retail stores (including K-Mart) to a broader market than previous computers had reached. It was the bestselling computer of 1982 (the year when the Commodore 64 was introduced), selling 800,000 units, but then it took a back seat to the more expensive but also much more powerful Commodore 64. While the VIC-20 was discontinued in 1985, the Commodore 64 was sold through 1994.

There is much to say about the Commodore 64 as one of the most popular home computers of all time, but for the sake of clarity it is important to focus on those elements of the Commodore 64 that come into play in `10 PRINT`, namely, its unique graphical character set, the VIC-II chip that implements the computer's graphic capabilities, and the ROM-based operating system, or KERNAL.

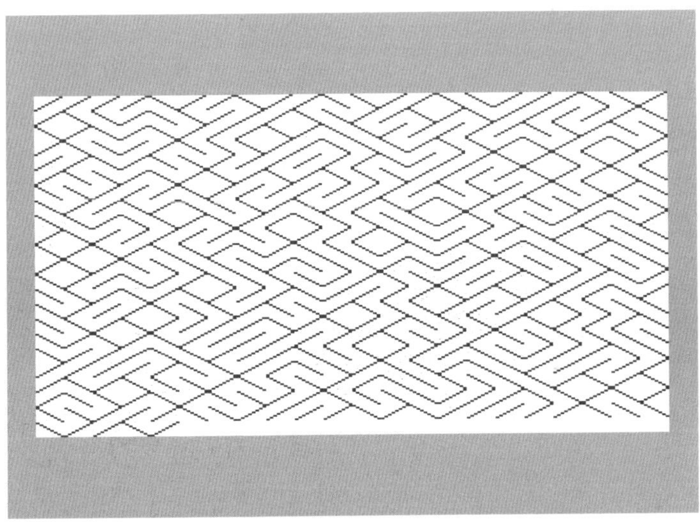

Figure 60.6

The `10 PRINT` maze on the 22 × 23 screen of the VIC-20.

## PETSCII

While the PETSCII character set was not unique to the Commodore 64, it was an idiosyncrasy of Commodore computers; neither the Apple II nor the TRS-80 line of computers, which competed with Commodore's computers, offered an extended version of ASCII. A close examination of PETSCII, and particularly its implementation on the Commodore 64, is therefore helpful in appreciating `10 PRINT`.

The facts of PETSCII are simple: it is an extension of the 128-character ASCII (American Standard Code for Information Interchange) set; in addition to letters, numbers, and punctuation, it contains color codes (to turn text white, for example), screen control codes (such as RETURN or CLR), and graphical characters (lines, curves, arrows, boxes, and shaded patterns). These graphical characters are labeled on the PET, VIC-20, and Commodore 64 keyboards, and are easily accessed with the Commodore or SHIFT keys.

These facts are well known and well documented. Less obvious are a myriad of quirks about PETSCII on the Commodore 64. To begin with, the name PETSCII is unofficial. Commodore only ever referred to its character

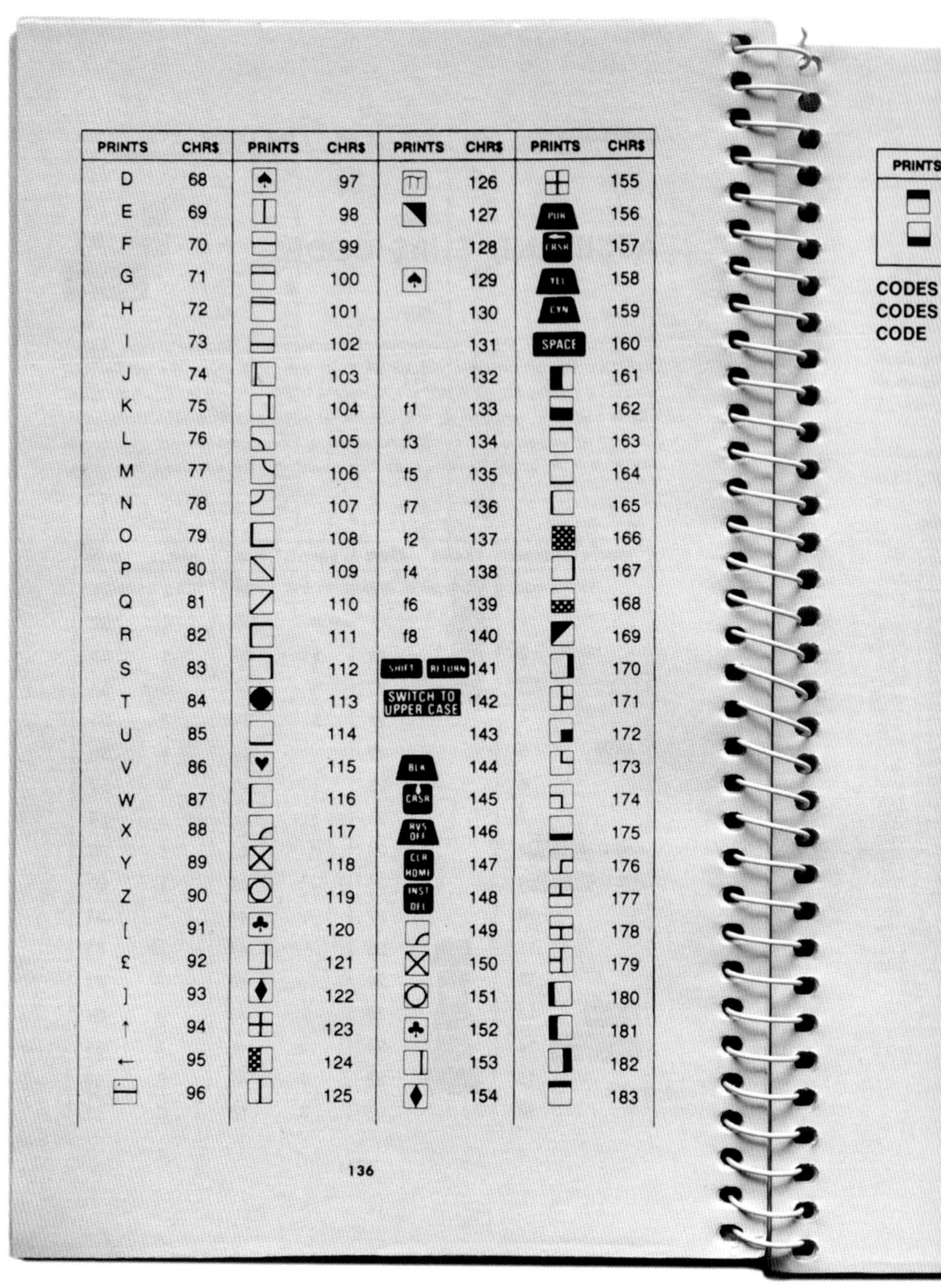

| PRINTS | CHR$ | PRINTS | CHR$ | PRINTS | CHR$ | PRINTS | CHR$ |
|---|---|---|---|---|---|---|---|
| D | 68 | ♠ | 97 |  | 126 |  | 155 |
| E | 69 |  | 98 |  | 127 | PUR | 156 |
| F | 70 |  | 99 |  | 128 | CRSR | 157 |
| G | 71 |  | 100 | ♠ | 129 | YEL | 158 |
| H | 72 |  | 101 |  | 130 | CYN | 159 |
| I | 73 |  | 102 |  | 131 | SPACE | 160 |
| J | 74 |  | 103 |  | 132 |  | 161 |
| K | 75 |  | 104 | f1 | 133 |  | 162 |
| L | 76 |  | 105 | f3 | 134 |  | 163 |
| M | 77 |  | 106 | f5 | 135 |  | 164 |
| N | 78 |  | 107 | f7 | 136 |  | 165 |
| O | 79 |  | 108 | f2 | 137 |  | 166 |
| P | 80 |  | 109 | f4 | 138 |  | 167 |
| Q | 81 |  | 110 | f6 | 139 |  | 168 |
| R | 82 |  | 111 | f8 | 140 |  | 169 |
| S | 83 |  | 112 | SHIFT RETURN | 141 |  | 170 |
| T | 84 | ● | 113 | SWITCH TO UPPER CASE | 142 |  | 171 |
| U | 85 |  | 114 |  | 143 |  | 172 |
| V | 86 | ♥ | 115 | BLK | 144 |  | 173 |
| W | 87 |  | 116 | CRSR | 145 |  | 174 |
| X | 88 |  | 117 | RVS OFF | 146 |  | 175 |
| Y | 89 | ╳ | 118 | CLR HOME | 147 |  | 176 |
| Z | 90 | ○ | 119 | INST DEL | 148 |  | 177 |
| [ | 91 | ♣ | 120 |  | 149 |  | 178 |
| £ | 92 |  | 121 | ╳ | 150 |  | 179 |
| ] | 93 | ♦ | 122 | ○ | 151 |  | 180 |
| ↑ | 94 |  | 123 | ♣ | 152 |  | 181 |
| ← | 95 |  | 124 |  | 153 |  | 182 |
|  | 96 |  | 125 | ♦ | 154 |  | 183 |

136

PRINTS

CODES
CODES
CODE

Figure 60.7

Appendix F of the 1982 *Commodore 64 User's Guide* lists the mapping between numerical values and graphical symbols in PETSCII.

set as ASCII; PETSCII was an informal name that came from the Commodore's users, not its engineers, that conflated PET and ASCII. The character set's creator, Leonard Tramiel, was not in favor of the name PETSCII, noting, "I never really liked that term since it was never much of a standard" (Bagnall 2010, 92).

## The Order of PETSCII

Another uncertainty about PETSCII is the order of the characters in the PETSCII table (figure 60.7). Very few related graphical characters are numerically adjacent to each other, neighbors according to character code. In fact, many related images (sets of corners, playing card suit symbols, and mirror images) appear to be scattered throughout the table. A spade is CHR$(97) while a heart is CHR$(115). The upper-right quarter of a circle is CHR$(105) while the upper-left quarter is CHR$(117). A filled-in circle is CHR$(113), the outline form CHR$(119).

Why is the order of graphical characters in the PETSCII table so seemingly haphazard? The answer is that arrangement was dictated by the PET keyboard design, a hardware-driven decision. The original PET 2001 keyboard is a variant of the QWERTY arrangement, featuring the graphical characters of PETSCII alongside the regular keyboard letters (figure 60.8). The grid of keys became a canvas for displaying logical groupings of related symbols. Thus the four corners of a square are grouped on the keys for O, P, L, and :. Similarly, the four arcs of a circle are found on the U, I, J, and K keys, and the four suits of a card deck on A, S, Z, and X.

There are times when the visual grouping on the keyboard and the numerical character codes logically coincide, namely with alphabetically adjacent keys on the QWERTY keyboard: F, G, and H; J, K, and L; N and M (though the letters are reversed here); and O and P. In these four instances, the CHR$ codes associated with each character *are* numerically adjacent, as is not the case with many of the other graphical characters, which, while adjacent on the physical keyboard, are effectively scrambled by the QWERTY layout before being placed in the alphabetized PETSCII index.

Not coincidentally, `10 PRINT` uses the NM pair—because it is visible on the interface, because it is elegant and concise in the code, and because the output is surprising, given the context of mazelike computer graphics at the time. There are other pairs of keys that share graphically

Figure 60.8

The PET 2001 keyboard had PETSCII graphics symbols printed on the front of the corresponding keys. The graphics were arranged spatially on the keyboard. For example, notice the arrangement ╱ and ╲, side by side on the N and M keys.

related characters (the right angles on the O and P keys, for example), but only NM will produce something more structural than textural, with pleasing large-scale variation.

Taking a closer look at the graphical characters on the N and M keys—CHR$(206) and CHR$(205), respectively—reveals more details about PETSCII. First, there are the numbers themselves. The ASCII chart included in appendix F of the *Commodore 64 User's Guide* lists the values of ╱ and ╲ as CHR$(110) and CHR$(109), yet the title of this book uses CHR$(205) as its touchstone, and the first two published versions of the program, in the very same *Commodore 64 User's Guide* and *Run* magazine, also use CHR$(205) as their base. The *Commodore 64 User's Guide* notes that "CODES 192-223 SAME AS 96-127" (Commodore 1982, 137), meaning that 109 and 110 are exactly the same as 205 and 206. But why? Why do early versions of the program use the upper character values (205 and 206), especially when the PETSCII chart that appears in the manual itself only lists the 109 and 110 values?

A likely explanation can be found in the way the Commodore 64 responds to `PRINT ASC("X")`, a technique used to determine the ASCII character code of any printable character. If a user were seeking the character code of a graphic symbol she saw on her keyboard, say, the heart on

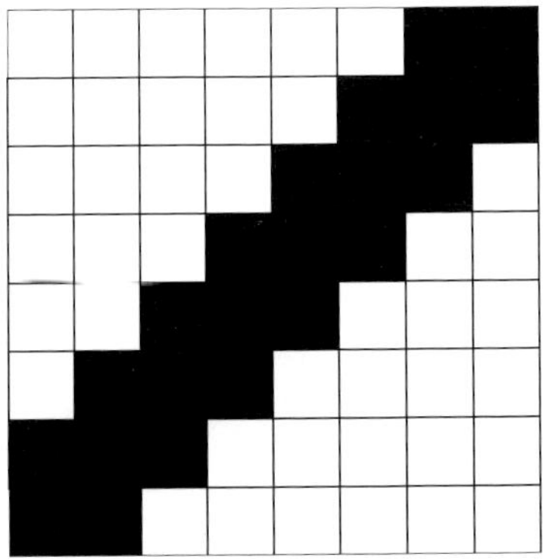

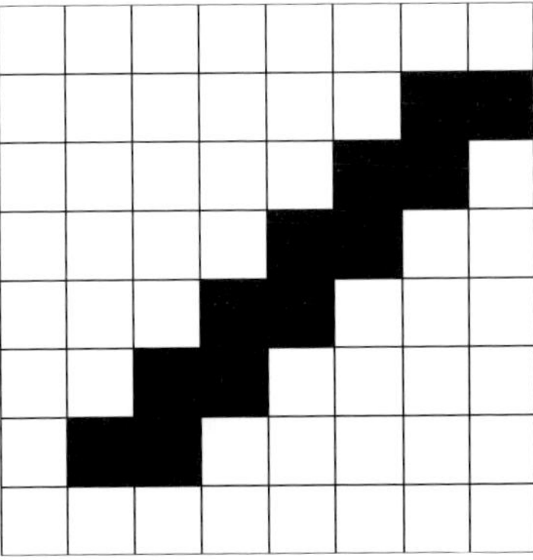

Figure 60.9
PETSCII character 206 (left) goes edge to edge within the grid, while character 47 (right), the forward slash, leaves space on the top and bottom for better spacing when used within a block of text.

the S key, or more to the point, the diagonal line on the N key, she could type `PRINT ASC("/")` and the computer would respond with "206." So, a possible implication of 205/206 being used in **10 PRINT** is that users were more likely to experiment with the keyboard in front of them than to look up codes in the back of the manual. Through the `ASC` function, BASIC became a self-contained pedagogical instrument itself, making outside manuals and guides less necessary.

### The Shape of PETSCII

There is yet more to discover about the two graphical characters that appear in **10 PRINT**. Like all PETSCII characters, the two characters are plotted out on an 8 × 8 matrix of pixels. Whereas regular alphanumerical characters are generally confined to a 7 × 7 portion of the matrix, leaving a single-pixel "border" between characters, many of the graphical characters extend to the edge of their 8 × 8 grid. Consider the close-up of `CHR$(206)` in figure 60.9. Its distinct features become apparent when compared to the typographical symbol that most closely resembles it, the forward slash, or `CHR$(47)`.

`CHR$(206)` is three pixels wide in its body and terminates on either end in a point, a thinning of the line that accounts for the divot that appears whenever two of the same characters are connected in the 10 PRINT maze. The CHR$(47) slash, meanwhile, is a uniform two pixels wide. The difference between the graphical character and the typographical symbol is a mere one pixel along some of the edges, but it is significant. The shape of CHR$(206)—as well as the shape of its mirror image, CHR$(205)—is essential to the texture of the maze.

## THE VIC-II CHIP

While the PETSCII character set remained the same from the PET to the VIC-20 and through to the Commodore 64, the means of displaying those characters—the chip controlling the graphics—changed dramatically over time. Despite its name, the 6567 (NTSC)/6569 (PAL) VIC-II graphics chip was not merely an improvement upon the VIC chip in the VIC-20. It was a complete redesign, led by Charpentier, the MOS engineer behind the first VIC. Home videogame systems, particularly Mattel's Intellivision, were the chief inspirations of the designers at MOS, who set out to create the most advanced graphics chip on the market (Bagnall 2010, 318).

The specifications of the final version of the chip were impressive for the time: three different forty-column text modes, two bitmap modes of 320 × 200 pixels each, eight hardware-driven sprites, hardware-supported screen scrolling, and a sixteen-color palette (Bauer 1996). The influence of videogames can clearly be seen in the VIC-II's built-in side and vertical scrolling (by seven pixels at a time) and the VIC-II's handling of sprites. Far more sophisticated than the sprites in the Atari 2600, the VIC-II sprites are 24 × 21 pixels and can be multicolored. The VIC-II chip can detect collisions between sprites; it can also detect when sprites have collided with other graphical data on the screen or individually specified raster lines (the horizontal scan lines on the CRT or television screen).

### Text on the VIC-II

Despite its advanced sprite handling, though, the text modes of the VIC-II chip are the most relevant to 10 PRINT. The text or character-based modes occupy one kilobyte of screen memory, and consist of forty columns and twenty-five rows of characters, namely 1,000 characters in total. As 10 PRINT writes the maze across the screen, row by row, it plots one of its two PETSCII characters in each space on the 40 × 25 grid, and just for a fraction of a second, 1,000 characters do fill the entire screen—in what might be considered an illusory consummation of the maze—before the text scrolls upward, leaving two more twenty-five-character rows to fill.

This point is key to understanding the dynamic between the aesthetic quality of the maze and the computer process by which it is plotted. While the code for 10 PRINT specifies one of two characters to display on the screen, it says nothing about where on the screen the chosen character should appear. That placement is defined by the VIC-II chip. More specifically, the placement of either CHR$(205) or CHR$(206) depends on the Commodore 64's screen memory map. To the user, the screen appears as a 40 × 25 grid, but to the VIC-II graphics chip, the screen is a series of memory slots, or locations. The first slot, 1024, is at grid location 0,0 and pixel location 0,0. Memory location 1025 maps to the space after this, to the right, and so on. Any character value that is stored in a memory slot will be displayed at the corresponding screen position. The large border that surrounds the maze is not addressable by the VIC-II; the thirty-two pixel borders on the left and right and thirty-five pixel borders on the top and bottom were created in consideration of the wide variation within cathode ray tube televisions of the era. The CRT screen of different televisions framed the pixels differently, making only a subset of pixels in the center reliable for display. Running 10 PRINT in a software emulator, of course, eliminates the need for such a border, though the Commodore 64's KERNAL nevertheless draws it.

The VIC-II also defines the way 10 PRINT scrolls upward across the screen. The maze is programmed to loop endlessly, so there must be a contingency available for when the cursor has filled the entire screen grid with characters and there is no next row. In addition to wrapping text automatically, the VIC-II also automatically scrolls the contents of the screen when the cursor is on the bottom row and attempts to move down. Though the screen appears to scroll up two lines after hitting the last character slot on the screen, from the Commodore 64's perspective only one line is advanced; the Commodore 64's physical screen is forty characters wide, but its logical screen width is eighty characters. While the continual scrolling might seem to be intuitive, it is not necessarily the only way it could have been done. A different environment could simply stop the program when the cursor reaches the last location on the screen, or return the cursor to the first row of the first column and begin again, overwriting the characters that had already appeared on the screen.

### Designing New Characters

An intriguing feature of the VIC-II is its ability to use RAM-programmable characters instead of the PETSCII characters permanently stored in the character generator ROM. The *Commodore 64 Programmer's Reference Guide* explains how the VIC-II can be pointed to a location in RAM to use as a new character set, giving users control over "an almost infinite set of symbols" (Commodore 1982, 104). It is possible, therefore, to modify **10 PRINT**, substituting alternate CHR$(205) and CHR$(206) characters for the default PETSCII ones. Recall that the stroke of both of these characters is three pixels wide. What might a single-pixel diagonal line look like as the fundamental building block of the maze?

With the VIC-II, that question can be answered. Using the POKE command, a program can create and store two new bitmaps into the locations of characters 205 and 206:

```
5 PRINT CHR$(142)
10 POKE 52,48:POKE 56,48:CLR
20 POKE 56334,PEEK(56334) AND 254
30 POKE 1, PEEK(1) AND 251
40 FOR I = 0 TO 511:POKE I+12288,PEEK(I+53248):NEXT
50 POKE 1, PEEK(1) OR 4
60 POKE 56334,PEEK(56334) OR 1
70 FOR I = 0 TO 7:POKE I+12904,2^I:NEXT
80 FOR I = 0 TO 7:POKE I+12912,2^(7-I):NEXT
90 POKE 53272,(PEEK(53272) AND 240) + 12
100 PRINT CHR$(205.5+RND(1)); : GOTO 100
```

This program causes diagonal lines a single pixel thick to be substituted for the standard PETSCII characters. (The two characters are written to memory in lines 70 and 80.) After this is done, **10 PRINT** (or in this new form, **100 PRINT**) produces a maze that is remarkably similar but that neverthe-

## THE SID CHIP

While the features of the Commodore 64 that made **10 PRINT** possible are chiefly BASIC, PETSCII, and the VIC-II graphics chip, it would be a disservice to the Commodore 64 to ignore another component that made the computer such a critical and popular success: the MOS Technology 6581 Sound Interface Device (SID) chip. Designed by Bob Yannes, the SID chip was a remarkable advance for its time. A three-voice synthesizer with variable pitch, amplitude, and harmonic tone controls, the SID made the Commodore a formidable music maker and game machine. With the SID, programmers could easily specify waveforms such as sawtooth or noise, as well as independently manage the attack, decay, sustain, and release times of the three oscillators (providing the three different voices) in the chip. Furthermore, the three voices could be used in conjunction with each other to create complex melodies, harmonies, and rhythms.

What is most interesting about the SID chip for the purposes of **10 PRINT** is that the third oscillator—the only of the three oscillators whose output can be fed back into the CPU—can be used for number generation. Poking SID memory location 54299 produces numbers from 0 to 255, while the waveform controls the sequence of those numbers. For example, a triangle waveform yields a cycling through every number from 0 to 255 and back down to 0, the rate controlled by the oscillator's frequency setting (Nelson 1987, 24). More relevant to **10 PRINT** is that the noise waveform produces random numbers, with the rate of the random number generation determined by the frequency of voice 3. Thus, even though the SID plays no part in **10 PRINT**, it could have a role in a similar program, and does, as evidenced by the assembly program "threadbare" that is discussed later.

less has a noticeably different appearance (see figure 60.10). The maze seems to have a sketched or stitched quality. The points on the ends of the original characters 205 and 206 are gone, so the computer screen's grid of characters is not accentuated by them. While the different lines can evoke drawing (as of a maze on paper) and craft, their more continuous nature and the greater difference between figure and ground makes the resulting output appear even more mazelike to many viewers.

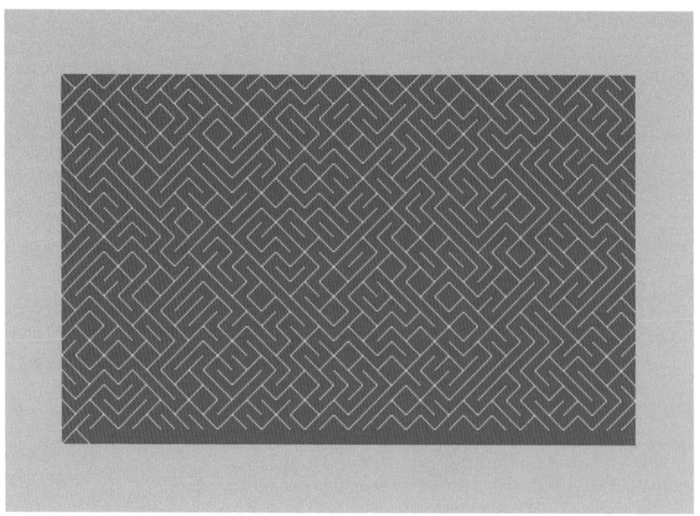

Figure 60.10
`10 PRINT` with the two standard characters replaced with custom-designed, single-pixel lines.

## THE KERNAL

The various components of the Commodore 64 discussed in this book—the **RND** function, BASIC, PETSCII, the VIC-II chip—are all held together by the machine's KERNAL, its underlying operating system. A misspelling of the word "kernel" that has stuck ever since it first appeared on draft documentation for the VIC-20 (Bagnall 2010, 330), the KERNAL controls all input, output, and memory management of the Commodore 64. Any keyboard input, any screen output, any interaction at all with the computer's RAM or ROM is governed by the rules of the KERNAL. It is the brainstem of the machine, its core, its always-present, unyielding, and unchangeable center. Residing in the last eight KB of the Commodore 64's ROM ($E000–$FFFF), the KERNAL is made up of a series of input and output routines, which can be found on the "Jump Table." Any command issued to the computer in BASIC (such as the `10 PRINT` program) is "translated" by the BASIC interpreter into a language that the CPU can understand, namely assembly language, which calls routines in the Jump Table.

The KERNAL is intended to make machine language coding easier, providing a stable set of instructions and registers a programmer can address. Yet as enabling as the KERNAL may be, it is also structuring and limiting, the basis of the Commodore 64.

### A View from Assembly Language

Writing a maze-generation program in BASIC leaves the programmer free from concerns about memory management, keyboard interrupts, screen outputs, and so on. All those things are provided. This is not the case when talking to the machine using a "low-level" language. In fact, Friedrich Kittler (1995) has famously argued that high-level languages essentially *obscure* the operations of the hardware. Skipping the BASIC interpreter or any other high-level language means the programmer must manipulate the microprocessor, memory, inputs, and outputs directly. Machine language itself exemplifies low-level programming, but since a machine language program is nothing but a series of numbers, it is not a very suitable language for humans. Low-level programming is typically done in assembly language instead. In assembly, the programmer provides instructions specific to the microprocessor, for example to load a value from a particular memory location into a particular processor register, or to perform a mathematical operation upon a memory location. In assembly, the programmer need not recall the numerical equivalents of such instructions, but only human-readable mnemonics for them—which are stored in the Commodore 64's KERNAL.

Recall that the microprocessor at the heart of the Commodore 64 is a modified 6502 chip. While it is not necessary to know everything about the 6502 to appreciate either the Commodore 64 or `10 PRINT`, it's worth noting that the chip essentially has three functions: it moves values between memory and one of three microprocessor registers (named X, Y, and Accumulator, abbreviated A); it executes mathematical operations on values in the accumulator; and it changes the address at which program execution takes place. The first type of operation is for loading or storing data (for example, the assignment `N = 1` in BASIC), the second type is a typical mathematical operation (say, + or − in BASIC), and the third corresponds to jumps and subroutine calls (analogous to `GOTO` and `GOSUB` in BASIC).

Like every BASIC program, `10 PRINT` is high-level. It relies on abstracted operations like `PRINT` and `RND` to perform complex tasks that would require considerably greater effort to accomplish at a low level. For this reason, it is useful to compare the BASIC version of `10 PRINT` on the Commodore 64 with its equivalent in 6502 assembly. Doing so will help clarify what features of the program are unique to its BASIC implementation.

`10 PRINT` seems to be a "native" BASIC program, meaning it was originally written in BASIC for the Commodore 64, not first rendered in assembly and then reimplemented in BASIC. No canonical assembly program is known to exist. As with literary translation or artistic adaptation, there are multiple ways to recast a computer program from one language into another, even on a relatively simple system like the Commodore 64, and even with a relatively simple program like `10 PRINT`. Along the way to developing a production for the demoscene party @party, in June 2010, an assembly port of `10 PRINT` called "threadbare" was created.

```
   *= $1000        ; starting memory location

   lda #$80        ; set this value in:
   sta $d40f       ; the noise speed hi SID register
   sta $d412       ; and the noise waveform SID register
loop               ; label for loop location
   lda $d41b       ; load a random value
   and #1          ; lose all but the low bit
   adc #$6d        ; value of "\" PETSCII
   jsr $ffd2       ; output character via KERNAL routine
   bne loop        ; repeat
```

This short program may look arcane, even to someone familiar with BASIC. Yet it can be explained without too much difficulty, step by step, by following each instruction in the order in which it is processed.

### `*= $1000`

This line tells the Commodore 64 where to put the program in memory, so that it can be run by the user. In this case, hexadecimal $1000 equals decimal 4,096, meaning the user can enter `SYS 4096` at the READY prompt to execute this program.

`lda #$80`

This instruction has two parts, not counting the comment: The opcode lda and the operand $80. All instructions have at least an opcode—an operation code that corresponds to something the 6502 processor can carry out. Not all opcodes need take an operand, although all the ones in this program do. Some of these operands are a single byte long, some are two bytes long.

`lda` is the opcode for *load into the accumulator,* and when used with # it loads the numeric value of the operand. In other cases in this program, `lda` and the corresponding opcode `sta` (*store from the accumulator*) use the operand as an address. Here, no lookup occurs; the immediate hexadecimal value $80 (decimal 128) is placed into the 6502's accumulator.

`sta $d40f`
`sta $d412`

These two instructions store the value held in the accumulator (`sta`) in two different memory locations. The operand is used as an address, to look up a location in memory. These memory locations are mapped to registers of the SID, the Commodore 64's sound chip.

`loop`

While all other lines of this program are indented, the "loop" line is flush left. This is not a mere typographical convention. The assembler treats lines that begin with whitespace as instructions and lines that do not as labels, which designate positions in the program. When the assembler encounters a label such as "loop," it turns the label into a memory address that corresponds with the current position in the program. Then, on another pass through the source code, the assembler replaces references to the label with the correct sixteen-bit address. This label does not appear directly as machine code in the assembled program; the address of this location is, instead, used later, at the very end of the program.

`lda $d41b`

Once the SID registers have been initialized, every time the program loads a value from the memory address $d41b, a new eight-bit random value will be provided. This instruction does one such load, bringing a random number into the accumulator.

**and #1**

The two diagonal-line characters are neighbors on the PETSCII chart, their values differing by one. Only one bit of randomness is needed to select one or the other. Generating a random number from the SID chip provides a much larger eight-bit number, which varies between 0 and 255. In order to change this number into a single bit—either a zero or a one—this instruction shears off all but the last bit by ANDing it with the decimal value 1. For example, here the binary number 10101011 (171 in decimal) is reduced to 00000001:

```
    %10101011
AND %00000001
=============
    %00000001
```

After this instruction, the accumulator will contain either the value 1 (as in the example above) or 0 (if the last bit of the original value was 0).

**adc #$6d**

The value obtained in the previous step (0 or 1) is added in this step to the hexadecimal value $6d (decimal 109), which corresponds to the PETSCII character used in the canonical BASIC `10 PRINT`. Note that though `adc` stands for *add with carry,* this instruction won't ever perform a carry. This addition will result in either 109 or 110. The value $cd (decimal 205) could have been used instead, as this character is the same as 109.

**jsr $ffd2**

All that's left is to output the character, either 109 or 110, to the screen. This instruction jumps to a subroutine (`jsr`) at memory location $ffd2. That routine, known as CHROUT and part of the KERNAL, takes care of putting the character on the screen at the current cursor location.

**bne loop**

Until this point is reached, the program will have output only a single character. The goal, of course, is a program that prints characters continuously until the user interrupts it. This instruction branches back to the label "loop" earlier in the program, from which point execution will continue by getting a new random value. The bne instruction is actually "branch if not equal," which will check to see if the processor's zero flag is set, and if not, it will complete the branch. In the case of the current program, the zero flag will never be set, so the branch will always be taken.

It would have been more straightforward to use the jump (jmp) instruction, assembly's equivalent of GOTO. However, bne was used because it results in a completed program that is one byte smaller. Because jmp can move the program counter to any location, it requires a sixteen-bit address as an operand. In contrast, bne can change the flow of the program to a location at most 128 bytes earlier or 128 bytes later; its operand is an eight-bit offset relative to the location of the instruction.

The completed assembly version of 10 PRINT elucidates several features of the program from the low-level perspective of the platform. Most crucially, the high-level abstractions of the BASIC program prove to be just as abstracted in the low-level assembly rendition. There are two such abstractions of note in the original, PRINT and RND, which constitute the majority of the program's computational work. Carrying out either one in assembly by coding them "from scratch" would be a more arduous task. Consider this common routine for generating a pseudorandom eight-bit number in 6502 assembly:

```
Rand8
   lda random            ; get seed
   asl                   ; shift byte
   bcc Rand8.no_eor      ; branch if flag not set
   eor #$CF              ; otherwise literal $CF
Rand8.no_eor
   sta random            ; save next seed
```

Each assembly instruction (lda, asl, etc.) uses a single byte in the program, and in this case those instructions that have operands (random, #$CF) have one-byte operands. This results in a routine nine bytes in size, or 25 percent of the space needed for the entire 10 PRINT program in BASIC (given that each character of BASIC takes up a byte).

While the MOS Technology 6502 processor requires this nine-byte subroutine to generate a random number, the Commodore 64 itself does not, due to a combination of seemingly unrelated affordances of its KER-

NAL and hardware. It's a simple matter with the Commodore 64 to use a random function, which although obviously used in BASIC, is found not in the BASIC ROM, but in the eight kilobytes of the Commodore 64 KERNAL, at address $e097. The assembly programmer can jump to that subroutine with `jsr $e097`, which will have the same effect as using `RND(1)` in BASIC.

A more unusual approach to random number generation—and the one that is taken in "threadbare"—involves the Commodore 64 sound chip, the SID (see sidebar). Apart from its sonic functions, the SID has the ability to generate random values. To do so, the programmer selects the noise waveform on the SID's third oscillator and sets that voice's frequency to a nonzero value. Setting a higher frequency value will cause the noise values to change more rapidly, yielding a greater variety of random numbers. The first three instructions of the preceding assembly program accomplish these settings:

```
lda #$80      ; set this value in:
sta $d40f     ; the noise speed hi SID register
sta $d412     ; and the noise waveform SID register
```

After this code has run, the program can get a new eight-bit random number by reading from memory location $d41b. While the code looks a little messier than does a simple call to `RND` in BASIC, the result is equally abstract from the programmer's perspective—it is simply abstracted to a different place, namely the SID chip instead of the KERNAL. This method of producing pseudorandom values is unusual, but certainly not unheard of. It is even documented in the *Commodore 64 Programmer's Reference Guide* (Commodore 1982, 202). Interestingly, this substitute for BASIC's `RND(1)` or the KERNAL's `jsr $e097` renders "threadbare" unusable on the VIC-20. That Commodore 64 predecessor did not include a SID chip, meaning it lacked this means of generating pseudorandom numbers. This incompatibility highlights the differences between a high-level language like BASIC, which will run `10 PRINT` on any of Commodore's computers, and a low-level language like assembly, which relies much more heavily on the specifics of the machine.

Drawing a character to the screen is an equally complex task that can prove challenging in 6502 assembly on the Commodore 64. `10 PRINT` places every character in the maze after the previous cursor position, making the maze appear to lay itself out column by column, row by row. To reproduce this behavior manually in 6502 assembly, the programmer would seem to have considerable work: determining the start of a screen, pausing, moving ahead one more position on the screen, repeating until the screen is filled, and then implementing a scrolling mechanism.

But as with the SID random number solution, the Commodore 64's KERNAL provides a much simpler solution. One subroutine of the KERNAL sends the PETSCII character value currently in the 6502 processor's accumulator to the current output device (the screen by default). That subroutine, CHROUT, lives at memory address $ffd2, and it can be executed in assembly by jumping to that address. This is precisely what "threadbare" does, after loading a random value and manipulating it to ensure that it will be one of the two slash characters that comprise the maze:

```
jsr $ffd2   ; output character via kernal routine
```

The output of the assembly program is essentially identical to that of `10 PRINT`, although the program runs a bit more quickly because the microprocessor is receiving machine instructions directly, rather than as translations of BASIC statements. "threadbare" is shorter than its BASIC cousin (twenty-two bytes for the assembly version, compared to thirty-six bytes, or characters, for the BASIC program). While "threadbare" is clearly more esoteric and less human-readable than its BASIC predecessor, its implementation reveals that the abstraction that makes the emergent elegance of `10 PRINT`'s output possible in such a small set of instructions is not entirely a feature of the BASIC interpreter, but also depends on the underlying hardware and operating system of the Commodore 64.

Though `10 PRINT` is an example of a robust one-liner that can be reimplemented in other languages and platforms, it is a program deeply tied to the material specifications of the Commodore 64, a bestselling personal computer that played a pivotal role in establishing a place for computers and programming in certain users' homes. While discussion in this book has so far focused on the code of `10 PRINT` and its effects, this chapter reveals the imbrication of code and platform and ways in which specific code can become a means of discussing the platform and its affordances.

## "THREAD," A TINY DEMOSCENE PRODUCTION

The demoscene is a programmer subculture centered on the design and manipulation of real-time audiovisual software. The origins of demoscene can be found in the cracking of eight-bit software for systems such as the Apple II, Commodore 64, and ZX Spectrum in order to remove copy protection. The individual or groups who cracked a particular piece of software would distribute the modified program with a signature of some sort (text-based or graphical) that displayed as the program loaded. Over time, these signatures began to include animated effects with sound. Eventually, productions growing from these additions were released apart from commercial software and called intros or (if they were more elaborate) demos. The hallmark of the demoscene is its emphasis on technical achievement and pushing the limits of earlier hardware systems. The demoscene also maintains interest in technically excellent systems from decades past, such as the Commodore 64: more than a hundred demos were programmed for the system in 2011 and music is continually being written for the system as well.

A demoscene production that was developed along with "threadbare" is a program called "thread"; it adds a progression through random colors to the drawing of the maze. This program, which is only thirty-one bytes long, shows some of the ways that a short assembly program can be extended. It takes advantage of some features of assembly, such as easy access to the zero page, which would have been much more difficult to incorporate in BASIC.

In "thread," the loop in the earlier program is elaborated in this way:

```
flourish
   tay
   lda ($f9),y      ; load color
   sta $0286        ; set char color
   lda $d41b        ; random
   and #1           ; lose all but low bit
   adc #$6d         ; value of one diag
   ; now either left or right diag
   jsr $ffd2        ; output character
   inx
```

```
bne flourish     ; do 256 times...
inc $f9          ; shift to new region
```

10 PRINT was not intended to be a demo; it was not created within the demoscene, or with competition of any kind in mind. Nevertheless, the program's abstract, full-screen graphics bear similarity to the animated effects that characterize demoscene productions. While those features could be attributed to the canonical, BASIC version of 10 PRINT, "thread" adds a simple form of color-cycling. The method by which this small alteration in the program's visual output is accomplished likewise embraces the spirit of the demoscene. While the color shift appears dramatic (at least in the context of a simple thirty-one-byte program like this one), it is created by two assembly instructions totaling five bytes:

```
lda ($f9),y        ; load color
sta $0286          ; set char color
```

This portion of the program loads an arbitrary value from memory and stores it in the memory location that sets the character color. While far simpler than some of the feats of demoscene programs, this small act is suggestive of the competitive nature of the subculture: an attempt to produce impressive results with limited resources.

Another feature of "thread" distinguishes it from the BASIC rendition of 10 PRINT: it was written in a different social context. BASIC programming on home computers like the Commodore 64 almost always involved sharing, often through magazines and face-to-face computer club meetings. But demos are often written in the context of demoparties, events that hundreds of people may attend and that typically last several days. Participants program, socialize, share tricks, collaborate on programs, and watch and vote on the output of productions. "thread" was produced at a small-scale party of this sort.

Within the demoscene, it is a typical pastime to try to compress similar programs into less and space. Indeed, "thread" was created in the hopes of reducing the program to thirty-two bytes or below—bit-boundaries or powers of two offer popular ways to set goals for demos. There is a whole category for thirty-two byte demos on the demoscene community website pouet.net. The version of "thread" above just makes the cut: it is thirty-one bytes—small by any reasonable measure. But subsequent to the appearance of "thread" and "threadbare," other members of the C64 demoscene community went on to fashion even smaller versions that produce the same output as **10 PRINT** in an impressive eighteen bytes. This was accomplished in the program "Thread Up," written in February 2012 by 4-Mat of the demoscene groups Ate Bit and Orb: <http://noname.c64.org/csdb/release/?id=106005>. A follow-up a few days later, in March, by Wisdom of Crescent is called "Thread Down" and squeezed the same essential effect into sixteen bytes, half our original limit: <http://noname.c64.org/csdb/release/?id=106044>. The obvious question: can you make a smaller version?

# 65
# REM MAZE WALKER IN BASIC

FIXING THE MAZE
WALKING THE MAZE
TOUCHING THE MAZE
TESTING THE MAZE

10 PRINT can be appreciated purely for its visual qualities—its regular asymmetry, its determined ranging over and across the screen, and even its colors, two shades of blue that can be pleasing. But 10 PRINT can also be interpreted as a maze, a labyrinth with routes and potentially with a solution. One might even wander through the maze, tracing a path with one's eyes, a finger, or some computational procedure.

What would such a computational procedure, and a program that supports its use, look like?

To see the answer, this section uses a software studies approach, writing programs to interpret other programs. It takes this approach to the extreme and builds a large program, using 10 PRINT as the starting point. Just as literary scholars study a text by generating more texts, it is productive to study software by coding new software. In this particular case, it's possible to develop a series of hermeneutic probes in Commodore BASIC—probes of increasing complexity, programs that transform 10 PRINT's output into a stable, navigable, and testable maze.

## FIXING THE MAZE

The first step in this process is to freeze the pattern so that it can be contemplated as a fixed maze. 10 PRINT, of course, produces an endlessly scrolling sequence of two symbols, an animated effect lost in the static images shown in this book. For at most an instant—after the screen has filled and the lower-right character has been drawn, but before the pattern has scrolled up to make room for the next line—is there ever a rectangular maze pattern filling the entire screen within the border.

To draw a stable rectangular maze pattern, 10 PRINT must be modified to draw a finite number of symbols, rather than an infinite sequence. As described in the chapter Regularity, the program must use a bounded rather than unbounded loop, placing characters on the screen a set number of times. To fill the forty columns and twenty-five rows, 1,000 characters must be drawn (40 × 25 = 1000).

This task can be accomplished using the FOR . . . NEXT construct discussed in the Regularity chapter. Here is a program that uses PRINT to output exactly 1,000 characters:

```
10 FOR I=1 to 1000
20 PRINT CHR$(205.5 + RND(1));
30 NEXT I
```

As might be expected from observation of 10 PRINT, the screen scrolls up when the last character is printed; in this case, there are four lines at the bottom that lack the maze pattern. Furthermore, once the program ends, the "READY." prompt appears with a blinking cursor stationed after it.

Trying to avoid this nonmaze text, one could add 40 GOTO 40 at the end of the program. This would create a continuous loop that did nothing but keep the program from terminating. This valiant attempt fails; "READY." and the blinking cursor are avoided, but a two-line gap still appears at the bottom of the screen. Changing "1000" in line 10 to "999" moves the program closer to the goal; everything but the lower-right character is drawn, and there are no blank lines at the bottom. But the program is still one character away from completely filling the screen with the maze.

As discussed in the chapter The Commodore 64, PRINT invokes the operating system's CHROUT routine with its automatic scrolling and eighty-character logical lines. When the one-thousandth character is printed (at the eightieth character of the last logical line on the display), the screen scrolls up by two physical (forty-character) lines to make room for the next eighty-character logical line. To generate a complete screen of a stable maze, it is necessary to use a mechanism other than the virtual Teletype provided by PRINT and the CHROUT routine it invokes.

To create a fixed screen-sized maze, a program can directly place PETSCII character codes into the computer's video memory. Rather than iterating from one to 1,000, the FOR loop must iterate though the 1,000 characters as locations in video memory, which begin at memory location 1024 and end 1,000 characters later at 2023. Because these invocations of POKE rely on memory locations rather than character codes, this modified program must also refer the correct screen codes for the diagonal-line characters (77 and 78), rather than the 205 and 206 values that are the PETSCII codes used in the CHR$ statement. This same use of 77 and 78 was seen in the POKE variation near the end of the Variations in BASIC remark.

```
10 FOR I=1024 TO 2023
20 POKE I,77.5+RND(1)
```

```
30 NEXT I
40 GOTO 40
```

One final nicety can be added: a standard statement at the beginning to clear the screen, PRINT CHR$(147);. This is not strictly necessary for this program, since the full screen will be overwritten one way or the other with a maze, but it makes the initial unfolding of the maze look a bit neater. It actually helps in the next step and in future programs, because this statement also restores color memory, cleaning up the traces of previous walks of the maze.

## WALKING THE MAZE

Now that code has been developed to draw a stable full-screen maze pattern, work can begin on a program that treats this pattern as a maze and "walks" it, moving through it with respect for the "walls" set up by the two characters. The first step is to determine a location within the maze. Viewers will often interpret the lighter slanting characters as thin walls and the dark blue background as the floor, although the opposite interpretation is possible. The program discussed here considers the light, thinner lines to be walls.

The first step in operationalizing this view of the maze—that is, in creating a computational system that functions in a way that is consistent with this interpretation—involves defining what it means to occupy a location within the maze. How can a "walker" be placed at a particular point in the maze?

The challenge is that the visual distinction between walls and floor is not explicitly represented in the program. A close-up of the maze pattern, with black outlines around the individual characters, each of which is plotted out on an 8 × 8 matrix, shows these distinctions. The dark blue is the background of characters, but positions within the dark blue "corridor" have no unique character locations. Dark-blue and light-blue areas of the screen are distinguished at the level of individual pixels, but in the graphics mode used, it is only possible to manipulate the larger 8 × 8 pixel characters:

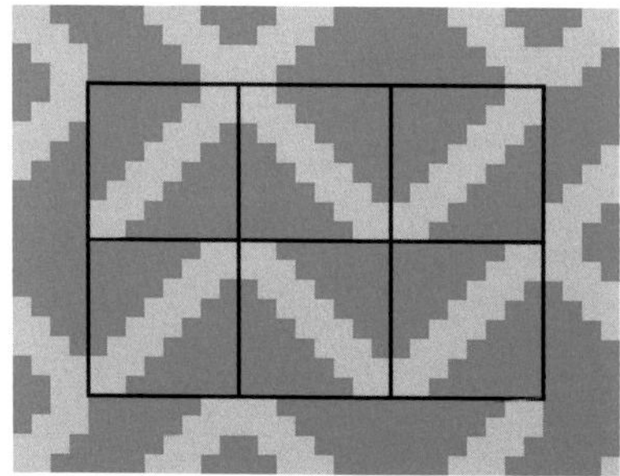

Designating a particular screen location (such as the highlighted location in maze below) would identify one of the slanting characters (a wall segment), but would not identify which side of the wall is currently occupied:

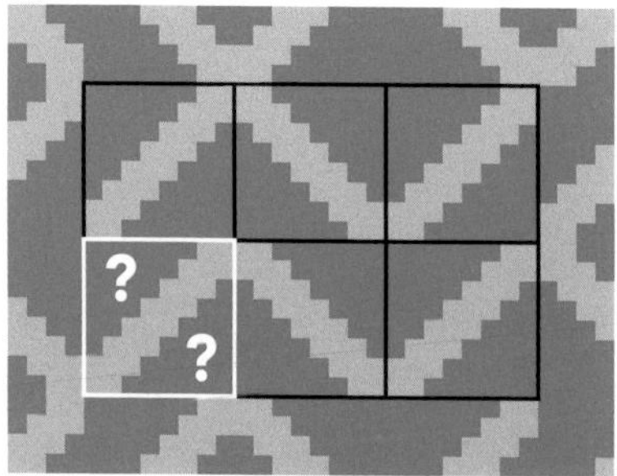


Given a diagonal wall location, it's possible to imagine someone approaching that wall from above, below, left, or right—that is, along a particular course or heading. The walker, in this view, would ricochet off the wall along particular headings. Approaching a right-leaning diagonal from above or from the left implicitly indicates that the walker is in the corridor segment above the wall, while approaching from below or from the right suggests the walker is in the corridor segment below the wall. These relationships are reversed for the left-leaning diagonals. In this view, in addition to a particular X, Y location, a third piece of information—a heading, or particular direction of movement—can be used to uniquely identify the maze location and where the walker will go next:

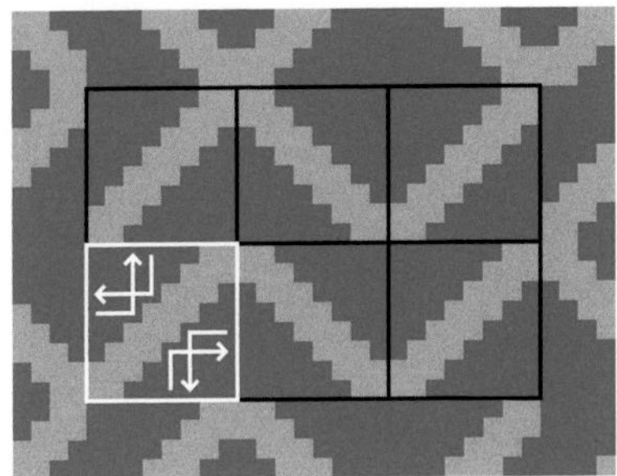

Given an initial location and a heading, the walker moves through the maze in a sort of drunken (or very determined) walk, not unlike the first run of Claude Shannon's Theseus mouse through its maze of relays and switches. In the case of the "Maze Walker" program here, the walker encounters and bounces off the walls in the manner depicted:

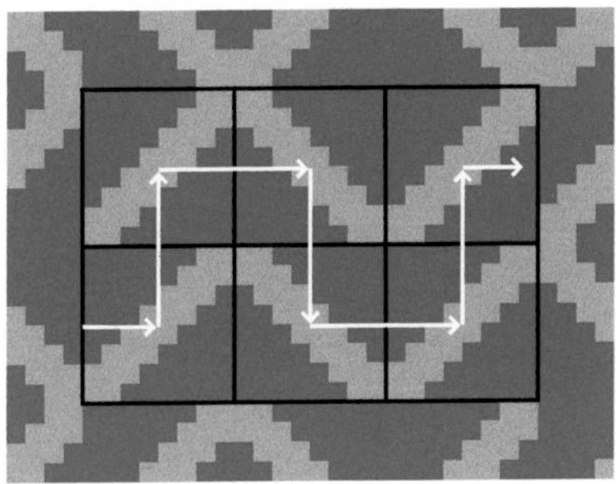

The BASIC code for "Maze Walker" is as follows:

```
10 REM PRODUCE A STABLE MAZE
20 PRINT CHR$(147)
30 FOR I=1024 TO 2023
40 POKE I,77.5+RND(1)
50 NEXT I

100 REM SET INITIAL X AND Y WALKER LOCATION AND DIRECTION
110 REM DIRECTION IS EITHER 0 LEFT, 1 RIGHT, 2 UP, 3 DOWN
120 X=INT(RND(0) * 39) : XOLD=-1
130 Y=INT(RND(0) * 24) : YOLD=-1
140 DIR=INT(RND(0) * 3)
```

```
150 WOLD=-1
160 GOSUB 500

200 REM START WALKING MAZE USING RULES FOR BOUNCING OFF WALLS
210 REM COMPUTE NEW LOCATION BASED ON INITIAL DIRECTION
220 IF DIR=0 THEN X=X - 1 : GOTO 270
230 IF DIR=1 THEN X=X + 1 : GOTO 270
240 IF DIR=2 THEN Y=Y - 1 : GOTO 270
250 IF DIR=3 THEN Y=Y + 1

260 REM DETERMINE IF THE WALKER IS OFF THE SCREEN
270 IF X >= 0 AND X <= 39 AND Y >= 0 AND Y <= 24 THEN GOTO 300
280 GOSUB 600 : GOSUB 650
290 GOTO 10

300 REM BOUNCE OFF WALL AS FUNCTION OF DIRECTION
310 REM 77 IS \, 78 IS /
320 WALL=PEEK(1024 + X + (Y * 40))
330 IF WALL=78 THEN GOTO 380
340 IF DIR=0 THEN DIR=2 : GOTO 420
350 IF DIR=1 THEN DIR=3 : GOTO 420
360 IF DIR=2 THEN DIR=0 : GOTO 420
370 IF DIR=3 THEN DIR=1 : GOTO 420
380 IF DIR=0 THEN DIR=3 : GOTO 420
390 IF DIR=1 THEN DIR=2 : GOTO 420
400 IF DIR=2 THEN DIR=1 : GOTO 420
410 IF DIR=3 THEN DIR=0
420 GOTO 160

500 REM DRAW WALKER, RESTORING PREVIOUS WALL CHARACTER
510 GOSUB 600
520 XOLD=X : YOLD=Y
530 M=1024 + X + (Y * 40)
540 WOLD=PEEK(M)
550 C=55296 + X + (Y * 40)
560 POKE C, 1 : POKE M, 87
570 GOSUB 650
```

```
580 RETURN

600 REM RESTORE WALL AT PREVIOUS WALKER LOCATION
610 IF XOLD=-1 THEN GOTO 630
620 POKE 1024 + XOLD + (YOLD * 40), WOLD
630 RETURN

650 REM PAUSE FOR 500 LOOPS
660 FOR I=1 TO 500 : NEXT I
670 RETURN
```

Because it is written in BASIC, the code to "Maze Walker" is fairly legible, even if it is significantly longer than BASIC programs discussed so far. A line-by-line explication will highlight the process by which "Maze Walker" walks the maze. The program begins with lines 20 through 50, filling the screen with a random maze as described in the last section.

Line 120 initializes a random horizontal (X) location between 0 and 39, representing the forty columns across the screen. The range 0 to 39 is used instead of 1 to 40 because this X value indexes a location in video memory; counting from 0 more directly corresponds to memory locations.

The variable `OLDX` holds the previous X coordinate of the walker. Initially, since a new X coordinate has just been initialized, there is no old value—so the X coordinate is set to an invalid value, −1. A common technique when dealing with a variable that can take a range of values, this method allows the variable to be easily tested to determine whether it has a valid value yet. Similarly, line 130 initializes a random Y coordinate between 0 and 24 (for the twenty-five rows on the screen), and initializes `OLDY`, the previous Y location, to −1, since there is no previous Y coordinate.

Line 140 sets the initial heading to a number between 0 and 3; the program will interpret 0 as left, 1 as right, 2 as up, and 3 as down. `WOLD`, initialized in line 150, stores the value of the screen code at the given location. The program "remembers" the location, so that the maze wall can be redrawn after the walker has passed.

Line 160 jumps to a subroutine at line 500. This program has three subroutines: one to draw the current location of the walker, changing the color of walls that have been bumped into; one to redraw the wall after the walker has passed; and one that simply pauses (using a loop that does nothing) so that the walker's movement is not too fast. The GOSUB at line 160 jumps to the first draw subroutine, pinpointing the initial location of the walker.

Lines 220 through 250 determine the next position of the walker (as an X, Y coordinate) by referring to the walker's heading. Leftward movements decrease the X value, rightward movements increase it; upward movements decrease the Y value, downward movements increase it. For the Y values, this change is the opposite of the standard Cartesian grid, in which the 0,0 coordinates rest in the lower left-hand corner. Screen coordinates commonly begin in the upper left-hand corner, just as CRT monitors scan the screen from left to right and top to bottom.

Lines 270 through 290 define what happens if the walker runs off the edge of the screen. Line 270 uses an conditional statement, an IF . . . THEN statement, to test whether the walker has a legal position on the screen; if it does, the program jumps to line 300, where a new heading for the walker is determined. Otherwise, two subroutines are called. These restore the wall at the walker's last location and wait for a short span of time. Line 290 then jumps back to the beginning of the program, drawing a new maze and re-initializing the walker at a random location.

Lines 320 through 410 determine the new heading of the walker using the current location's wall segment and the current heading. Line 320 uses the PEEK command to see what is in video memory—what character is stored at the current location. In this line, the 2D grid of the screen is rolled up into one-dimensional video memory. Screen location 0,0 in the upper left-hand corner corresponds to the first location in video memory, 1024. Each line of forty characters corresponds to a range of forty memory locations, with each group of forty following each other successively in memory. So multiplying the vertical Y coordinate by forty, and adding the horizontal X coordinate, yields the appropriate location in video memory.

Each of the four headings resolves into one of four new headings for a right-leaning diagonal character and one of four new headings for a left-leaning diagonal character. The eight IF . . . THEN statements at lines 340 to 410 handle each of these eight cases. The IF . . . THEN at line 330 jumps to the second group of four IF . . . THEN statements for a right-leaning diagonal character, allowing program execution to fall through to the first group of IF . . . THEN statements for the other character. The GOTO statements at the end of each line jump over the rest of the IF . . .

THEN statements once the correct new heading has been set.

Line 420 is the last line of the main loop. It loops back to start the process of drawing the walker at its current location, and updating location and heading, all over again.

The subroutine at line 500 draws the walker at its current location and redraws the wall in the location that it just left. At the beginning, in line 510, there is a call to the subroutine at line 600, placing the correct wall character in the old position of the walker. Then, the subroutine saves the current X, Y to the old location XOLD, YOLD. Line 540 computes the location in video memory (M) for the current X, Y location. This memory location is used twice: on line 530 to save the current character at this location, and in the second POKE on line 560 to change this character to a new character representing the walker. It would be ideal to use a character that shows the walker standing next to the wall, but there is no character in the standard character set that combines a diagonal line with a shape next to it. It is possible to define custom characters for the four combinations of walls with walkers, but this program uses the built-in character with screen code 87 to represent the walker. This has the disadvantage that from a static screen shot that walker's exact maze location is visually ambiguous. While watching the walker move as the program executes, however, the location is discernible from the pattern of movement.

Line 550 computes the memory location in color memory given the X, Y screen location. There are 1,000 bytes of color memory, as with video memory. The effect of values in color memory on the display depends on the graphics mode. In character mode (used in 10 PRINT and in this program), each location in color memory stores a color code that tells the system what color should be used to draw the character indicated by the screen code in the corresponding location in video memory. The first POKE on line 560 stores a color code of 1, which draws the corresponding screen code using the foreground color white. Finally, line 570 makes a nested call to the subroutine at 650, which adds a delay to the maze walker, making it easier to observe the details of the walker's movement.

The subroutine at line 600 redraws the wall character from the maze walker's previous location. Without this subroutine, the walker would leave a trail behind it, slowly replacing the walls of the maze. The IF . . . THEN at line 610 tests whether the previous location is a valid location, which it is not on the first call, when XOLD is initialized to −1. Although the wall is restored as the walker passes by, the color code in color memory is not restored. This means that the redrawn wall will appear in white, leaving a trail of white walls to mark the walker's passage.

Finally, the subroutine at line 650 adds a delay between each step through the maze. The `FOR` loop contains no statements before the `NEXT`; it simply counts to 500. To increase or decrease the delay time, this value can be increased or decreased.

There are a number of observations to make about the **10 PRINT** maze, the representational properties of BASIC, and the Commodore 64 environment based on the development of "Maze Walker." First, it takes considerable effort to transform the visual perception of a maze with walls and a floor into a practical functioning model of this perception. Decisions must be made about what it means to hold a location in the maze and to move through it. This program sharpens the somewhat vague visual perception of "mazeness" into a highly detailed understanding of the local structure of the maze.

Second, the representation of movement requires repeatedly drawing and erasing a shape (the representation of the walker), with the need to remember what lies "under" the shape so that the occluded object can be correctly redrawn. This basic principle of continuously drawing and erasing static snapshots to produce the illusion of movement is a fundamental feature of modern media, seen in everything from the latest Pixar movie to the latest blockbuster Xbox game. The related principle of collision with virtual objects, when combined with the representation of movement, defines graphical logic, a representational trope that underlies the computer's ability to represent virtual spaces. In the compressed form of "Maze Walker," there are specific lines that encode the concept of collision with walls: lines 320 through 410.

Finally, the ability to observe walks through the maze brings clarity to the structure of the **10 PRINT** maze. A typical (stabilized) **10 PRINT** maze consists of loops of various lengths that are interspersed with runs connecting two locations on the edge of the maze. The pattern therefore consists of multiple, intertwined unicursal mazes; once embarked on a particular path from edge to edge, there are no choices to make. A **10 PRINT** maze might be considered multicursal if there is a choice of where to enter the maze from one of the outside "openings," but once such a choice is made, the path will lead irrevocably to its paired entrance or exit.

## TOUCHING THE MAZE

While "Maze Walker" allows the user to watch a computer "other" navigate the maze, a program can turn this spectacle into an interactive environment. Here, computation acts as a prosthesis, or extension of the user's sense of touch, presenting the user with solid walls that constrain navigation.

```
10 REM PRODUCE A STABLE MAZE
20 PRINT CHR$(147)
30 FOR I=1024 TO 2023
40 POKE I,77.5+RND(1)
50 NEXT I

100 REM SET INITIAL X AND Y WALKER LOCATION AND DIRECTION
110 REM DIRECTION IS EITHER 0 LEFT, 1 RIGHT, 2 UP, 3 DOWN
120 X=INT(RND(0) * 39) : XOLD=-1
130 Y=INT(RND(0) * 24) : YOLD=-1
140 DIR=INT(RND(0) * 3)
150 WALL=-1
160 GOSUB 500

200 REM WAIT FOR LEGAL MOVE GIVEN LOCATION AND DIRECTION
210 GET A$ : IF A$="" GOTO 210
220 IF A$=" " THEN GOSUB 600 : GOTO 120 : REM HYPERSPACE
230 REM 77=\, 78=/ 0 LEFT, 1 RIGHT, 2 UP, 3 DOWN
240 IF WALL=78 THEN GOTO 310
245 REM UP
250 IF (DIR=0 OR DIR=3) AND ASC(A$)=145 THEN DIR=2 : GOTO 400
255 REM RIGHT
260 IF (DIR=0 OR DIR=3) AND ASC(A$)=29 THEN DIR=1 : GOTO 400
265 REM DOWN
270 IF (DIR=1 OR DIR=2) AND ASC(A$)=17 THEN DIR=3 : GOTO 400
285 REM LEFT
290 IF (DIR=1 OR DIR=2) AND ASC(A$)=157 THEN DIR=0 : GOTO 400
300 GOTO 200

310 REM DOWN
```

```
320 IF (DIR=0 OR DIR=2) AND ASC(A$)=17 THEN DIR=3 : GOTO 400
330 REM RIGHT
340 IF (DIR=0 OR DIR=2) AND ASC(A$)=29 THEN DIR=1 : GOTO 400
350 REM UP
360 IF (DIR=1 OR DIR=3) AND ASC(A$)=145 THEN DIR=2 : GOTO 400
370 REM LEFT
380 IF (DIR=1 OR DIR=3) AND ASC(A$)=157 THEN DIR=0 : GOTO 400
390 GOTO 200

400 IF DIR=0 THEN X=X - 1 : GOTO 450
410 IF DIR=1 THEN X=X + 1 : GOTO 450
420 IF DIR=2 THEN Y=Y - 1 : GOTO 450
430 IF DIR=3 THEN Y=Y + 1

450 REM DETERMINE IF THE WALKER IS OFF THE SCREEN
460 IF X >= 0 AND X <= 39 AND Y >= 0 AND Y <= 24 THEN GOTO 160
470 GOSUB 600
480 GOTO 10

500 REM DRAW WALKER, RESTORING PREVIOUS WALL CHARACTER
510 GOSUB 600
520 XOLD=X : YOLD=Y
530 M=1024 + X + (Y * 40)
540 WALL=PEEK(M)
550 C=55296 + X + (Y * 40)
560 POKE C, 1 : POKE M, 87
570 RETURN

600 REM RESTORE WALL AT PREVIOUS WALKER LOCATION
610 IF XOLD=-1 THEN GOTO 630
620 POKE 1024 + XOLD + (YOLD * 40), WALL
630 RETURN
```

The change between this and the previous walker is found in lines 200 through 390. These lines replace the code that changed the walker's heading given the current heading and the wall type. Now the program reads the keyboard, looking for arrow keys. The user can use the arrow keys to move backward and forward along the current path as allowed by the wall at the current location and the current heading. Line 210 uses the `GET` statement to read a character from the keyboard. If no key has been pressed, `GET` returns the empty string. The `IF . . . GOTO` in the second statement on line 210 loops continuously until a key has been pressed.

Line 220 tests whether the spacebar has been pressed. If so, the subroutine at line 600 that redraws the wall at the current walker location is called, and the program jumps to 120, initializing the current location and heading to new random values. This allows the user to jump to a new location after exploring the current path to the edge of the screen, or after completing a loop.

Line 240 selects between the four different cases for ╲ and ╱. Consider the cases for ╲, when `WALL` is 77. If the current heading is left or down, the walker is on the left side of the slash. The valid headings to move are right and up. If the current heading is right or up, the walker is on the right side of the slash. The valid headings to move are left or down. Now consider the cases for ╱, when `WALL` is 78. If the current heading is left or up, then the walker is on the right side of the slash. The valid headings to move are down or right. If the current heading is right or down, the walker is on the left side of the slash. The valid headings to move are up or left.

The eight `IF . . . THEN` statements from 250 through 380 handle these eight cases, checking whether the user has hit an arrow key corresponding to a valid heading given the current heading. If a key other than space or an arrow key is hit, or if the arrow key is not valid given the current wall and heading, control will fall through to 300 or 390, and the program will loop back to 200 to continue scanning the keyboard. Thus, the walker only moves when the user pushes an arrow key in a valid heading, enforcing the "solidity" of the walls and responding only to valid input.

The interactive maze walker allows the user to trace a finger along the maze pattern, kinesthetically experiencing the ricocheting movement employed by the maze walker. The ability to jump randomly about the maze allows the user to explore many paths in the same maze, observing how the various loops and trails intertwine.

## TESTING THE MAZE

What would it mean for the 10 PRINT maze to have a solution? Given that the only choice to be made is outside the maze, in choosing an entry point, one definition of a solution would be a path that leads all the way from one side of the maze to the other. Solving the maze would, in this case, consist of choosing the right entry point to make it all the way to the other side.

This question of solutions is just one example of the more general question of determining maze properties. One could as easily be interested in mazes that have really long loops, or as many loops as possible, or as many side-to-side paths as possible, or lots of really short paths, and so forth. Is it possible to computationally recognize such properties, so that the design space of 10 PRINT mazes can be explored and mazes can be generated with specific properties?

The perhaps-surprising answer is yes. Computer science offers a general approach to such problems called generate and test. It is based on the observation that, while directly generating a solution to a problem is generally difficult, recognizing whether a proposed solution is in fact a solution is easy. Therefore, to solve problems, or to generate artifacts with desired properties, one approach is to use a relatively simple generator to generate candidates and then test them to see if they have the desired property. For 10 PRINT, this means generating random maze patterns (as explored throughout this book), and then testing them to see if they have the desired property. In the explorations that led to this book, the authors wrote programs as a method for better understanding 10 PRINT. The generate and test paradigm provides a framework for extending this practice by writing programs to analyze the output of 10 PRINT.

To illustrate this approach, here is a program that looks for mazes with solutions, that is, with a path from one side to the other. While searching for a path, the program systematically tries every left-hand and upper entrance into the maze, testing whether this passage goes through to the other side. As paths are searched, walls are changed to white. If a solution is found, the maze is redrawn in its original color with just the solution path redrawn in white, to allow the user to behold the maze with a solution in its purity, before randomly generating a new maze to test. If every path is explored with no solution found, a new maze is generated and the search begins anew.

```
10 DIM B1(3),B2(3) : REM 'BOUNCE' ARRAYS
20 B1(0)=2 : B1(1)=3 : B1(2)=0 : B1(3)=1
30 B2(0)=3 : B2(1)=2 : B2(2)=1 : B2(3)=0

40 REM PRODUCE A STABLE MAZE
50 PRINT CHR$(147)
60 FOR I=1024 TO 2023
70 POKE I,77.5+RND(1)
80 NEXT I

90 REM TEST: SOLUTIONS MUST BE PATHS ACROSS WIDTH OR HEIGHT
100 FOR S=0 TO 24
110 X=-1 : Y=S : DIR=1 : XOLD=-1 : YOLD=-1 : WOLD=-1
120 SX=X : SY=Y: SD=DIR
130 GOSUB 410 : GOSUB 520
140 IF X > 39 THEN GOTO 290 : REM FOUND A SOLUTION
150 IF X < 0 OR Y < 0 OR Y > 24 THEN GOTO 180
160 GOSUB 610
170 GOTO 130
180 GOSUB 710 : NEXT S
190 FOR S=0 TO 39
200 X=S : Y=-1 : DIR=3 : XOLD=-1 : YOLD=-1 : WOLD=-1
210 SX=X : SY=Y : SD=DIR
220 GOSUB 410 : GOSUB 520
230 IF Y > 24 THEN GOTO 290 : REM FOUND A SOLUTION
240 IF X < 0 OR Y < 0 OR X > 39 THEN GOTO 270
250 GOSUB 610
260 GOTO 220
270 GOSUB 710 : NEXT S
280 GOTO 50
290 FOR I=55296 TO 56295 : POKE I,14 : NEXT I
300 X=SX : Y=SY : XOLD=-1 : YOLD=-1 : WOLD=-1 : DIR=SD
310 GOSUB 410 : GOSUB 520 : GOSUB 610
320 REM DETERMINE IF WE'RE OFF THE SCREEN
330 IF X >= 0 AND X <= 39 AND Y >= 0 AND Y <= 24 THEN GOTO 360
340 GOSUB 710 : GOSUB 800
350 GOTO 50
```

```
360 GOTO 310

400 REM COMPUTE NEW LOCATION BASED ON INITIAL DIRECTION
410 IF DIR=0 THEN X=X - 1 : GOTO 450
420 IF DIR=1 THEN X=X + 1 : GOTO 450
430 IF DIR=2 THEN Y-Y - 1 : GOTO 450
440 IF DIR=3 THEN Y=Y + 1
450 RETURN

500 REM BOUNCE OFF CURRENT WALL AS FUNCTION OF DIRECTION
510 REM 77=\, 78=/
520 WALL=PEEK(1024 + X + (Y * 40))
530 IF WALL=77 THEN DIR=B1(DIR) : GOTO 550
540 IF WALL=78 THEN DIR=B2(DIR)
550 RETURN

600 REM DRAW WALKER, RESTORING PREVIOUS WALL CHARACTER
610 GOSUB 710
620 XOLD=X : YOLD=Y : I=X + (Y * 40)
630 M=1024 + I
640 WOLD=PEEK(M)
650 C=55296 + I
660 POKE C, 1 : POKE M, 87
670 RETURN

700 REM RESTORE WALL AT PREVIOUS WALKER LOCATION
710 IF XOLD=-1 THEN GOTO 730
720 POKE 1024 + XOLD + (YOLD * 40), WOLD
730 RETURN

800 FOR I=1 TO 2000 : NEXT I
810 RETURN
```

The two biggest differences from the initial "Maze Walker" are the line blocks 100–180 and 190–270. Lines 100–180 systematically set the initial position to a character on the left-most side of the maze, and the heading to right. A solution is detected if the walker runs out the right-hand side of

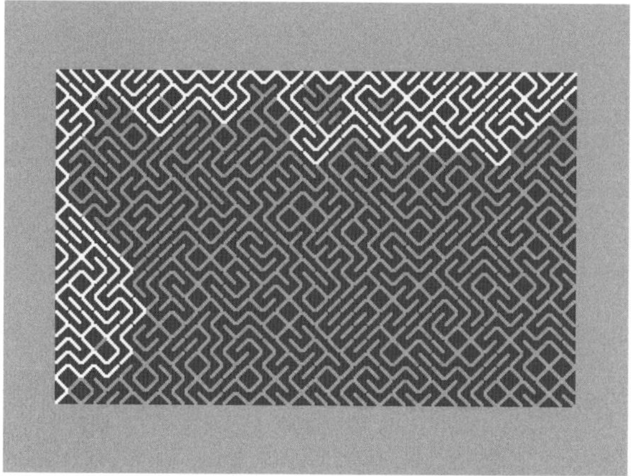

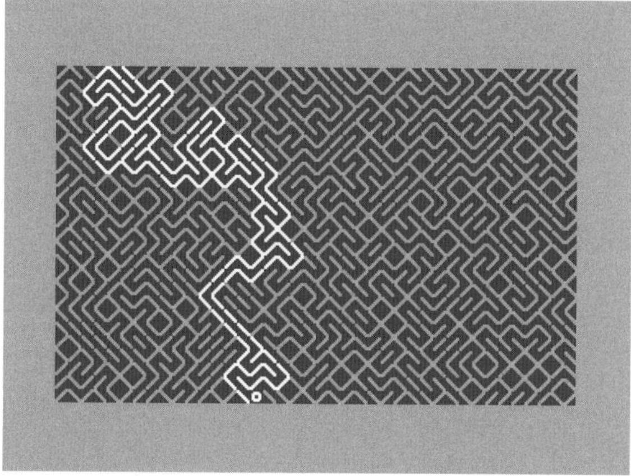

Figure 65.1

"Maze Walker" can determine whether a maze has solution (top) or not (bottom).

the maze. Lines 190–270 systematically set the initial position to a character on the top of the maze, and the heading to down (entering the maze). A solution is detected if the walker runs out the bottom of the maze. Figure 65.1 provides an example of a maze with no solutions and an example of a maze that has a solution.

# 70
# CONCLUSION

10 PRINT has generated far more than a pattern that resembles an unending scrolling maze. It has generated talks, posts, papers, online conversation, demoscene productions, and now this book. But its most important product may be the countless programmers inspired by its concision, enticed by its output, and intrigued by its clever manipulation of two very simple symbols.

While 10 PRINT is a very particular, historically located object of study, it is not completely unique, precious, or rare. Whether or not new Commodore 64 owners realized it, a version of the program was included with every new computer, making it one of the most commonplace pieces of code of the era. There is no evidence to suggest that it was considered the best BASIC program, or even the best one-line BASIC program, for the Commodore 64. Rather, 10 PRINT is emblematic of the creative deluge of BASIC programming in and around the early 1980s. Many programmers at this time were home computer users who, in the years when the personal computer was just emerging as a household technology, seized on programming as a means of play, learning, and expression.

Yet, as this book has indicated, 10 PRINT *resonates*. It is more compelling than many similar Commodore 64 programs, works better than random-maze-generating programs on other platforms did, and can be varied and expanded in interesting and powerful ways. Still, it is only one example of how computers are used to explore computation and to create beautiful artifacts. 10 PRINT was selected as the focus of this book not because the program sits at the summit of all possible one-liners in any language and for any platform, but because the program can lead the way to appreciating code and the contexts in which it emerges, circulates, and operates.

Reading this one-liner also demonstrates that programming is culturally situated just as *computers* are culturally situated, which means that the study of code should be no more ahistorical than the study of any cultural text. When computer programs are written, they are written using keywords that bear remnants of the history of textual and other technologies, and they are written in programming languages with complex pasts and cultural dimensions, and they lie in the intersection of dozens of other social and material practices. Behind the ordinary features of a program—a call to produce random numbers, a printing mechanism, a repeating loop—lie ghostly associations with distant and forgotten forms of cultural activity and production whose voices echo from somewhere inside the labyrinth of material history accumulated in a particular technology.

Code is not only a conventional semiotic system. At its essence, code also functions. Code runs. Code does something. Code executes on the computer and has operational semantics. But code means things to people as well, both implicitly and explicitly. What this book has done for a single line of code can be done for much larger programs as well, for programs of many other sorts. While other programs and other categories of program have been discussed in this book, the focus on a single short program has been productive rather than restricting. We hope this will encourage the detailed analysis of other short programs and suggest that it is worthwhile to focus on important subroutines, functions, and procedures within larger systems of code.

Looking at each token, each character, of a program is a helpful start, but only a foundation for the understanding of how code works for individuals and in society. It can show not only why a particular program functions the way it does but also what lies behind the computers and programs that are essential to the current world. In considering the `PRINT` keyword and the way it is used in `10 PRINT`, it is possible to see that `PRINT` invokes the CHROUT routine in the Commodore 64's KERNAL, that it provides the ability to append text at the current position (using ";") and to automatically scroll the screen upward when necessary. This particular behavior is a convenience in many cases and contributes to the visual effect of `10 PRINT`. At the same time, `10 PRINT` is a reminder of the history of computer output devices and of BASIC itself being developed on upward-scrolling Teletypes that literally printed.

To understand `10 PRINT`, it helps to identify the program as a one-liner and to note that it produces a seemingly random maze. Yet, a study of the code itself shows much more about BASIC, the Commodore 64, and the program itself than does a high-level categorization and description of function. This is true even though this code does not contain the easiest hooks for traditional interpretation, such as comments or variable names. `10 PRINT` shows that much can be learned about a program without knowing much of anything about its conditions of creation or intended purpose—or indeed, without it even having an intended purpose.

Today, some people who do not mainly identify as "programmers" nevertheless do program computers; they harness the ability of these machines to do provocative work. This is the case with designers who use

Processing, for instance, and with some who work in HTML, CSS, and JavaScript to create interesting programs on the Web. But the widespread access to programming that was provided by early microcomputers does not exist in the same form today as it did in the 1970s and 1980s. When people turn on today's computers, they do not see a "READY" prompt that allows the user to immediately enter a BASIC program.

The science fiction author David Brin wrote a few years ago on Salon.com about the difficulty of getting any form of BASIC running. He reported that he and his son "searched for a simple and straightforward way to get the introductory programming language BASIC to run on either my Mac or my PC," but could find none (Brin 2006). There are BASICs available now, including Microsoft Small Basic, explicitly intended to embrace the spirit of the original language. But in the early twenty-first century, such tools are still somewhat esoteric specialty items, not standard features of every home computer that make themselves available upon startup.

For popular programming, the early 1980s were certainly a special time. Computers were more difficult to use in some ways. The Commodore 64 required its users to issue complex commands to read a disk and run a program from it. But programming was easier. Over the past two decades, academic and industrial research labs have attempted to invent or apply simple programming tools for educational purposes, to teach anyone how to program at a rudimentary level. On the one hand, this book reminds us that a straightforward way for people to program their computers—either in BASIC or another simple language—is indeed possible, since it has already been achieved. But on the other hand, it also accentuates the many significant differences in the way computers are designed and used today compared to the heyday of the Commodore 64, differences that help explain why researchers can't simply recommend that interested parties buy an inexpensive home computer, turn it on, and experiment with it.

Computer programs can be representational; they can depict worldly things and ideas, and they can resonate with related figures, images, and designs. In the case of `10 PRINT`, the program's mazelike output is not a neutral pattern, but one wrapped up in numerous contradictory Western ideas about the notion of a maze. Whether a program's representations are incidental or very deliberate, they have a meaning within culture. The cultural history of the maze demonstrates that there are more and less obvious associations with this type of structure, some wrapped up with the history of science in the twentieth century and others emerging from computing itself. Although a program's output is only one of its aspects, a reading of code should certainly take into account what a program does and what texts, images, and sounds it produces.

While 10 PRINT is a text, it exists in the material context of computing. It was printed (in different versions) first in a spiral-bound manual and later in a glossy magazine. It ran on a particular taupe unit, the Commodore 64, the components of which were influenced by economic circumstance and the physical possibilities of chip design and selection. The BASIC programming language in which 10 PRINT is written was shaped by the sharing of programs in print and in human memory, and by the specific technical aspects of the Altair 8800 and the Dartmouth Time-Sharing System. Our discussion of 10 PRINT has tried to account for these relevant material qualities while also attending to the formal, computational nature of the code—what it does—and how that interacts with material, historical, and other cultural aspects of the program.

All programs are written in particular settings (a corporate office, a computer clubhouse, a university, a coffeehouse) and are influenced by the means by which they are written. Whenever code is considered, it is worthwhile to investigate how it was written and what material factors came into play as it was transmitted, shared, and elaborated. As with the Teletypes that preceded computers like the Commodore 64 and the laptops that eventually replaced them, the physical makeup, cost, contexts of use, and physical form of computers have significant effects on how they are put to use.

People tend to imagine computer programs as largely static, frozen masses of code. To the extent that this view is valid at all, it makes sense only within a small slice of computing history. It is true, for instance, that the retail market for shrink-wrapped software and the sale of videogames on cartridges tend to support the view that a program is a particular, stable sequence of code and nothing else.

Of course, this era has passed. Software of all sorts, including videogames, is distributed on systems that can and frequently do patch and update programs. Download a mobile phone app or even a Playstation 3 game that is initially free of advertisements and, after running an update, the program can start downloading and displaying ads while it runs. People now think little of modifications of their software, even those that are intrusive and annoying. At the same time, today's operating systems are easily patched online to prevent security problems and to add new features, bringing benefits to users.

The view of programs as static is even less tenable when one considers the writing, running, and distribution of programs throughout the history of computing. Custom software written for businesses has long been maintained and updated—for half a century. The BASIC programs people keyed in from magazines invited users to modify them. In educational and software development settings programs have typically been converted to other programs by elaboration and modification.

`10 PRINT` is not just a line of code; it defines a space of possible variations (some of which were explored in the remark Variations in BASIC), possible ports (see the remark Ports to Other Platforms and other ports throughout the book), and possible elaborations (such as the one described in the remark Maze Walker in BASIC). `10 PRINT` can simply be run, but it can also be considered as an instant in the process of programming, a process that can lead to a better understanding of and relationship with computation, in addition to leading to other aesthetically interesting and differently functioning programs. This book has tried to establish `10 PRINT` not just as a program, but also as part of the process of learning about and developing programs—something that can be said about almost any code.

Since programs are dynamic, and some of them explicitly invite modification, and since modifying programs is a way to better understand them, the platform, and computing generally, why not modify a program as part of a scholarly investigation of the program? This is one approach taken in this book. The variations, ports, and elaborations in this volume set some of the qualities of the canonical `10 PRINT` into relief in an interesting and informative way.

To see what is special about different platforms, and how platforms differ from one another, we have produced ports of `10 PRINT` during our investigation of it and the writing of this book. Porting a specific program makes for a very different and more revealing comparison than does simply lining up the technical specs of the two systems for side-by-side comparison. It shows what specific qualities of a platform are important for particular effects and for the functioning of particular programs. Similarly, developing variations allows programmers to explore the space of possibility within a platform. In all of these cases, programming is not a dry technical exercise but an exploration of aesthetic, material, and formal qualities.

Whether one is studying a videogame, some other aesthetic object, or code that runs a voting machine or defines a climate change model, writing programs can help us comprehend the code and its cultural relevance. In the case of large systems, it could be unwieldy to re-implement and modify the entire program. This approach, however, is being tried with the story generator MINSTREL (Tearse, Mateas, and Wardrip-Fruin 2010), explicitly for the purpose of better understanding that influential system and how it tells stories. It is possible to reimplement and modify important routines, functions, and procedures, to grasp more firmly what a program does as opposed to what it could have been written to do. Analyzing the code by interacting with it, revising it, and porting it is one of the main critical activities this book contributes to critical code studies and related fields in digital media.

Early on, a variant of `10 PRINT` was presented to novice readers to hint at the tremendous potential of the computer using a simple but elegant technique. This book is meant to serve a similar function. Through its many approaches to a one-line program, the book is meant to unlock the potential for analyzing digital objects and culture through code.

75
END

# 80 THANKS

We wish to thank those at the MIT Press who supported this radical and challenging project—particularly Doug Sery, who saw the potential of the project from the beginning and worked with the team of authors to help them complete it. We also thank Katie Helke Dokshina, the anonymous reviewers who offered their consideration and advice, and Noah Wardrip-Fruin, who worked with us as an editor of the Software Studies series. Finally, thanks go to Kathy Caruso for seeing the book through into print.

Many programs are considered in this book. Some of these we found, some we wrote ourselves. A few programs are in a different category: they were prompted by this book project, but programmers who were not authors of the book worked on them. Our thanks to Ben Fry for the second Processing port that was discussed, to Stéphane Hockenhull for collaborating with two of the authors on "threadbare" and "thread," and to Warren Sack for his Perl and Javascript ports, the first ports discussed in the book and the ones that introduced us to the idea of porting `10 PRINT` as a way of better understanding it.

# 85 WORKS CITED

Ahl, David. 1973. *101 BASIC Computer Games*. Maynard, MA: Digital Equipment Corporation.

Ahl, David. 1978. *BASIC Computer Games: Microcomputer Edition*. Morristown, NJ: Creative Computing Press.

*Altair BASIC Reference Manual*. 1975. Albuquerque, NM: MITS.

*Atari Inc. v. North American Philips Consumer Electronics Corp.*, 672 F.2d 607 (7th Cir.) (full-text), cert. denied, 459 U.S. 880 (1982).

Bagnall, Brian. 2010. *Commodore: A Company on the Edge*. Winnipeg, Canada: Variant Press.

Barthes, Roland. 1977. "From Work to Text." *Image, Music, Text*. Trans. Stephen Heath. London: Fontana. http://evans-experientialism.freewebspace.com/barthes05.htm

Bauer, Christian. 1996. "The MOS 6567/6569 Video Controller (VIC-II) and Its Application in the Commodore 64." *cebix.net*. August 28. http://www.cebix.net/VIC-Article.txt

Benjamin, Walter. 1999. *The Arcades Project*. Ed. Rolf Tiedemann. Trans. Howard Eiland and Kevin McLaughlin. Cambridge, MA: Belknap-Harvard University Press.

Bennett, Deborah. 1998. *Randomness*. Cambridge, MA: Harvard University Press.

Bergin, Thomas J., ed. 2000. *Fifty Years of Army Computing*. Aberdeen, MD: U.S. Army Research Laboratory.

"Better Mouse: A Robot Rodent Masters Mazes." 1952. *Life* 32, no. 4 (July 28): 45–46.

Bogost, Ian. 2010. Comment on "Program Your Apple II! Why Not Program Today?" *Computing Education Blog*. February 20. http://computinged.wordpress.com/2010/02/20/program-your-apple-ii-why-not-program-today/

Brandon, Ruth. 1999. *Surreal Lives: The Surrealists 1917–1945*. London: Macmillan.

Brecht, George. 1966. *Chance Imagery*. A Great Bear Pamphlet. New York: Something Else Press.

Brett, Guy, and Marc Nash. 2000. *Force Fields: An Essay on the Kinetic*. Barcelona: Actar.

Brin, David. 2006. "Why Johnny Can't Code." *Salon.com*. September 14. http://www.salon.com/2006/09/14/basic_2/

Brooks, Ruven. 1983. "Towards a Theory of the Comprehension of Computer Programs." *International Journal of Man-Machine Studies* 18: 543–554.

Buckley, Kerry W. 1989. *Mechanical Man: John Broadus Watson and the*

*Beginnings of Behaviorism*. New York: Guilford Press.

Burroughs, William S. 2003. "The Cut-Up Method of Brion Gysin." In *The New Media Reader*, ed. Noah Wardrip-Fruin and Nick Montfort, 90–91. Cambridge, MA: MIT Press.

Cabanne, Pierre. 1971. *Dialogues with Marcel Duchamp*. New York: Viking.

Cage, John. 1966. *Silence*. Cambridge, MA: MIT Press.

Caillois, Roger. 2003. *Man, Play, and Games*. Trans. Meyer Barash. New York: The Free Press.

Campbell-Kelly, Martin, and William Aspray. 1996. *Computer: A History of The Information Machine*. New York: Basic Books.

Chun, Wendy. 2011. *Programmed Visions: Software and Memory*. Cambridge, MA: MIT Press.

Commodore. 1982. *Commodore 64 Programmer's Reference Guide*. Wayne, PA; Indianapolis, IN: Commodore Business Machines. Distributed by Howard W. Sams & Co.

Commodore. 1982. *Commodore 64 User's Guide*. Wayne, PA; Indianapolis, IN: Commodore Business Machines. Distributed by Howard W. Sams & Co.

Commodore Computer Club. 2010. "Video: Commodore VIC-20 Ad with William Shatner." November 17. http://www.commodorecomputerclub.com/video-commodore-vic-20-ad-with-william-shatner/

da Cruz, Frank. 2011. "Programming the ENIAC." *Columbia University Computing History*. January 25, updated April 2, 2012. http://www.columbia.edu/acis/history/eniac.html

Dartmouth College Computation Center. 1964. *BASIC*. October 1. http://www.bitsavers.org/pdf/dartmouth/BASIC_Oct64.pdf.

Davenport, Nancy. 2002. "Artist Questionnaire: 21 Responses." *October* 100: 65–67.

Doctorow, Cory. 2002. "0wnz0red." Salon.com. August 28. http://www.salon.com/2002/08/28/0wnz0red/

Doob, Penelope Reed. 1990. *The Idea of the Labyrinth: from Classical Antiquity through the Middle Ages*. Ithaca and London: Cornell University Press.

Doüat, Dominique. 1722. *Methode pour faire une infinité de desseins differens avec des carreaux mi-partis de deux couleurs par une ligne diagonale: ou observations du Père Dominique Doüat Religieux Carmes de la Province de Toulouse sur un memoire inséré dans l'Histoire de l'Académie Royale des Sciences de Paris l'année 1704, présenté par le Reverend Sebastien Truchet, religieux du même ordre, Académicien honoraire*. Paris: Chez

Florentin de Laulne . . . Claude Jombert . . . [et] André Cailleau.

Dreiser, Theodore. 1981. *Sister Carrie*. New York: Penguin.

Driscoll, Kevin. 2010. "Critical Code Studies 2010." Driscollwiki. July 23. http://kevindriscoll.org/wiki/Critical_code_studies_2010

Driscoll, Kevin. 2011. "Revisiting Bill Gates' 'Open Letter to Hobbyists.'" Media in Transition 7, MIT, Cambridge, MA, May 14.

Duchamp, Marcel. 1975 *Salt Seller: The Essential Writings of Marcel Duchamp*. Ed. Michel Sanouillet and Elmer Peterson. London: Thames and Hudson.

Dyson, George. 1997. *Darwin among the Machines: The Evolution of Global Intelligence*. Reading, MA: Addison-Wesley.

Essinger, James. 2004. *Jacquard's Web: How a Hand-Loom Led to the Birth of the Information Age*. Oxford: Oxford University Press.

Evans, Davis S., Andrei Hagiu, and Richard Schmalensee. 2006. *Invisible Engines: How Software Platforms Drive Innovation and Transform Industries.* Cambridge, MA: MIT Press.

Fabre, Gladys, and Doris Wintgens Hotte, eds. 2009.*Constructing a New World, Van Doesburg & The International Avant-Garde*. London: Tate Publishing.

Faison, Seth. 1992. "John Kemeny, 66, Computer Pioneer and Educator." *The New York Times*. December 27. http://www.nytimes.com/1992/12/27/us/john-kemeny-66-computer-pioneer-and-educator.html

Foltin, Martin. 2011. "Automated Maze Generation and Human Interactions." Master's thesis. http://is.muni.cz/th/143508/fi_m/thesis.pdf

Freiberger, Paul. 1982. "Commodore Founder Tramiel: PETs for World Market." *InfoWorld* 4, no. 16 (April 26): 13.

Fuchs, Martin. 2011. *Written Images*. Rendered February 9. Book number 182/230, page 161.

Fuegi, John, and Jo Francis. 2003. "Lovelace & Babbage and the Creation of the 1843 'Notes.'" *IEEE Annals of the History of Computing* 25, no. 4 (October–December): 16–26.

Gates, Bill. 1976a. "An Open Letter To Hobbyists." *Homebrew Computer Club Newsletter* 2, no. 1 (January): 2.

Gates, Bill. 1976b. "A Second and Final Letter." *Computer Notes* 1, no. 11 (April): 5.

Gerdes, Paul. 1998. *Women, Art and Geometry in Southern Africa*. Trenton, NJ: Africa World Press.

Gere, Charlie. 2006. "Genealogy of the Computer Screen." *Visual Communication* 5, no. 2 (June): 141–152.

Gerstner, Karl. 1964/2009. "Designing Programmes." *Graphic Design Theory: Readings from the Field*, ed. Helen Armstrong, 58–61. Princeton, NJ: Princeton Architectural Press.

Gilbert, Sandra, and Susan Gubar. 2000. *The Madwoman In the Attic: The Woman Writer and the Nineteenth-Century Literary Imagination*. 2nd ed. New Haven, CT: Yale University Press.

Gombrich, E. H. 1994. *The Sense of Order: A Study in the Psychology of Decorative Art*. 2nd ed. Oxford: Phaidon Press.

Green Jr., Bert F., J. E. Keith Smith, and Laura Klem. 1959. "Empirical Tests of an Additive Random Number Generator." *Journal of the ACM (JACM)* 6, no. 4: 527–537.

Hayles, N. Katherine. 2005. "Speech, Writing, Code: Three Worldviews." In *My Mother Was a Computer: Digital Subjects and Literary Texts*, 39–61. Chicago: University of Chicago Press.

Heim, Kristi. 2008. "Seattle Man Who Helped Launch Microsoft Left $65M for Gay Rights." *Seattle Times*. February 24. http://seattletimes.nwsource.com/html/localnews/2004197961_weiland24.html

Holmes3000. 2006. "Commodore 64 Commercial (1985)." *YouTube*. May 31. http://www.youtube.com/watch?v=D_f3ulzElxo

Huang, Xiu Wu, Cheryl Kolak Dudek, Lydia Sharman, and Fred E Szabo. 2005. "From Form to Content: Using Shape Grammars for Image Visualization." *Proceedings of the Ninth International Conference on Information Visualisation*, London, July 6–8.

Hubbard, Paul L. 1987. "$3B2 Checking Monitor Resolution." "Magic" section, *RUN* 39 (March): 10, 12.

Inacio da Silva, Cicero. 2008. "Software Arte," slide 17. SlideShare. November 18. http://www.slideshare.net/cicerosilva/software-arte-presentation

Kemeny, John G. 1972. *Man and the Computer*. New York: Simon & Schuster.

Kemeny, John G., and Thomas E. Kurtz. 1985. *Back to BASIC: The History, Corruption, and Future of the Language*. Boston: Addison-Wesley.

Kern, Hermann. 2000. *Through the Labyrinth: Designs and Meanings over 5,000 Years*. Trans. [from German] Abigail H. Clay with Sandra Burns Thomson and Kathrin A. Velder. Munich and New York: Prestel.

Kidd, David. 2011. Backstrip.net. April 8. http://backstrip.net/post/4432566244/ive-been-tooling-around-with-street-making

Kidware Software, LLC. 2011. "Small Basic Computer Games: New 2010 Small Basic Edition." http://computerscienceforkids.com/SmallBasicComputer

Games.aspx

Kittler, Friedrich. 1995. "There Is No Software." *CTheory.* http://www.ctheory.net/articles.aspx?id=74

Knuth, Donald E. 1969. *The Art of Computer Programming*, vol. 2. Reading, MA: Addison-Wesley.

Kominski, Robert. 1991. "Computer Use in the United States: 1989." U.S. Bureau of the Census Current Population Reports, Series P-23, No. 171. U.S. Government Printing Office, Washington, DC.

Kominski, Robert, and Eric Newburger. 1999. "Access Denied: Changes in Computer Ownership and Use: 1984–1997." American Sociological Association, Chicago, Illinois, August 6–10.

Krauss, Rosalind. 1979. "Grids." *October* 9 (Summer): 50–64.

Krueger, Dan A. 1984. "Trick $93." "Magic" section, *RUN* 7 (July): 13–14.

Krumins, Peteris. 2009–2011. "Perl One-Liners Explained." http://www.catonmat.net/series/perl-one-liners-explained

Kurtz, Thomas E. 2009. "'BASIC' [Interview]." In *Masterminds of Programming: Conversations with the Creators of Major Programming Languages*, ed. Federico Biancuzzi and Shane Warden, 79–100. Sebastopol, CA: O'Reilly Media.

Langway, Lynn. 1981. "Invasion of the Video Creatures." *Newsweek*, November 16.

Latham, Aaron. 1981. "Video Games Star War." *The New York Times*, October 25, Late City Final edition, sec. 6.

Lemov, Rebecca. 2005. *World as Laboratory: Experiments with Mice, Mazes, and Men.* New York: Hill and Wang.

Levy, Steven. 1984. *Hackers: Heroes of the Computer Revolution.* New York: Dell.

Lipton, Richard J., and Lawrence Snyder. 1977. "On the Power of Applicative Languages." Research Report 94, Department of Computer Science, Yale University.

Lord Ronin. 2008. "In the Beginning Part 8." *Commodore Free Magazine*. September. http://commodorecomputerclub.co.uk/view.php?art=commodore_free_23&loc=magazine

Lutz, Theo. 1959/2005. "Stochastic Texts." Trans. Helen MacCormac, "Stochastische Texte." *Augenblick* 4, no. 1: 3–9. http://www.stuttgarter-schule.de/lutz_schule_en.htm

Mac Low, Jackson. 2009. *Thing of Beauty: New and Selected Works.* Ed. Anne Tardos. Berkeley: University of California Press.

Malaby, Thomas M. 2003. *Gambling Life: Dealing in Contingency in a Greek City.*

Urbana: University of Illinois Press.

Malone, Meredith. 2009. *Chance Aesthetics*. St. Louis, MO: Mildred Lane Kemper Art Museum.

Manovich, Lev. 2009. "Cultural Analytics." Software Studies Initiative. June 20, updated September 2011. http://lab.softwarestudies.com/2008/09/cultural-analytics.html

Marino, Mark C. 2006. "Critical Code Studies." Electronic book review. December 4. http://www.electronicbookreview.com/thread/electropoetics/codology

Marino, Mark C. 2010. "The ppg256 Perl Primer: The Poetry of Techneculture." *Emerging Language Practices*, no. 1. (Fall). http://epc.buffalo.edu/ezines/elp/issue-1/ppg256.php

Mateas, Michael, and Nick Montfort. 2005. "A Box, Darkly: Obfuscation, Weird Languages, and Code Aesthetics." In *Proceedings of the 2005 Digital Arts and Culture Conference,* 144–153. Denmark: IT University of Copenhagen.

Matthews, William Henry. 1922. *Mazes and Labyrinths: A General Account of Their History and Developments.* New York: Longmans, Green.

McDonnell, Eugene E. 1988. "Life: Nasty, Brutish, and Short." *APL'88 Conference Proceedings*, 242–247. Sydney, Australia, February 15.

Menabrea, L. F. 1842. "Sketch of the Analytical Engine Invented by Charles Babbage." Trans. and notes by Ada Augusta, Countess of Lovelace. From *Bibliothèque Universelle de Genève* 82 (October 1842). Web edition, 2006. http://www.fourmilab.ch/babbage/sketch.html

Michel, Jean-Baptiste, et al. 2010. "Quantitative Analysis of Culture Using Millions of Digitized Books." *Science* 331, no. 6014: 176–182. Published online December 16. doi: 10.1126/science.1199644. http://www.sciencemag.org/content/early/2010/12/15/science.1199644.abstract

Miller, George A. 1956. "The Magical Number Seven, Plus or Minus Two." *Psychological Review* 63 (2): 81–97. doi:10.1037/h0043158.

Mohr, Manfred. 2007. *Manfred Mohr: Broken Symmetry.* Ed. Wulf Herzogenrath, Barbara Nierhoff, and Ingmar Lähnemann. Bremen: Kunsthalle Bremen.

Montfort, Nick. 2004. "Continuous Paper: The Early Materiality and Workings of Electronic Literature." Modern Language Association (MLA) Convention, Philadelphia, December 28.

Montfort, Nick. 2008. "Obfuscated Code." In *Software Studies: A Lexicon*, ed. Matthew Fuller, 193–199. Cambridge, MA: MIT Press.

Montfort, Nick. 2009. "The ppg256 Series of Minimal Poetry Generators." *Proceedings of the Digital Arts and Culture Conference, 2009.*

UC Irvine, December 14. http://escholarship.org/uc/item/4v2465kn

Montfort, Nick. 2010. "Random Mazes." Code Critiques. Critical Code Studies Working Group. February 5. Unpublished online discussion.

Montfort, Nick. 2010. "@party: Weaving thread." *Post Position*. June 20. http://nickm.com/post/2010/06/party-weaving-thread/

Montfort, Nick. 2010. "Colloquium Past, Conference to Come in Mexico." *Post Position*. November 17. http://nickm.com/post/2010/11/colloquium-past-conference-to-come-in-mexico/

Montfort, Nick. 2011. "10 PRINT Talks Galore." *Post Position*. January 26. http://nickm.com/post/2011/01/10-print-talks-galore/

Montfort, Nick, and Ian Bogost. 2009. *Racing the Beam: The Atari Video Computer System*. Cambridge, MA: MIT Press.

Montfort, Nick, Patsy Baudoin, John Bell, Ian Bogost, Jeremy Douglass, Mary Flanagan, Mark Marino, Michael Mateas, Casey Reas, Warren Sack, Mark Sample, and Noah Vawter. 2010. "Studying Software by Porting and Reimplementation: A BASIC Case." Presented by Nick Montfort, Jeremy Douglass, and Casey Reas. Critical Code Studies Conference, University of Southern California. July 23. http://thoughtmesh.net/publish/382.php

Moretti, Franco. 2007. *Graphs, Maps, Trees: Abstract Models for Literary History*. New York: Verso.

Motherwell, Robert, and Jack D. Flam. 1989. *The Dada Painters and Poets: An Anthology*. Cambridge, MA: Harvard University Press.

"Mouse with a Memory." 1952. *Time* 59, no. 20 (May 19).

Mullish, Henry. 1976. *A Basic Approach to BASIC*. New York: John Wiley & Sons.

MuppetMan et al. 2010. "Maze Code" discussion thread, Commodore 64 (C64) Forum, Lemon64.com. August 12–16. http://www.lemon64.com/forum/viewtopic.php?t=34879&sid=9526087188346ea3450fe0568566466b

Nake, Frieder. 2008. Personal communication, via email, with Casey Reas. August 18.

Nelson, Philip I. 1987. "Exploring the SID Chip." *Compute! Gazette* (August): 22–24.

noknojon. 2011. Bleepingcomputer.com. February 17, 8:01 p.m. http://www.bleepingcomputer.com/forums/topic380106.html/page__p__2138153#entry2138153

Noll, Michael A. 1962. "Patterns by 7090." Bell Telephone Laboratories Technical Memorandum, MM-1234-14, August 28.

Noll, Michael A. 1970. "Art Ex Machina." *IEEE Student Journal* 8, no. 4: 10–14.

Olivarez-Giles, Nathan. 2011. "Commodore 64 Is Back, With the Same Ol' Look But Modern Insides." *Los Angeles Times*. April 7. http://latimesblogs.latimes.com/technology/2011/04/commodore-64-is-back-with-hdmi-out-intel-atom-chip blu-ray.html

Orlowski, Andrew. 2001. "Microsoft Altair BASIC Legend Talks about Linux, CPRM and That Very Frightening Photo: A Very Rare Interview with Monte David off." *The Register.* May 11. http://www.theregister.co.uk/2001/05/11/microsoft_altair_basic_legend_talks/

"Out of the Woods." 1962. *Time* 80, no. 21 (November 23) http://www.time.com/time/magazine/article/0,9171,829487-1,00.html

Pearson, Lisa. 2011. *It Is Almost That: A Collection of Image+Text Work by Women Artists & Writers.* Los Angeles: Siglio Press.

Pfeiffer, John E. 1962. *The Thinking Machine*. Philadelphia, PA: Lippincott.

Raley, Rita. 2006. "Code.surface || Code.depth." *Dichtung-Digital* 36. http://www.dichtung-digital.org/2006/1-Raley.htm

RAND Corporation. 1955. *A Million Random Digits with 100,000 Normal Deviates.* http://www.rand.org/pubs/monograph_reports/MR1418/index2.html

"random, n., adv., and adj." 2011. *OED Online*. June. Oxford University Press. [Subscription-only electronic resource.]

Rapp, Larson. 1985. "$1C1 April Fool's Program." "Magic" section, *RUN* 16 (April): 8.

Reas, Casey. 2010. 10 PRINT CHR$(205.5+RND(1)); : GOTO 10. Twitter. July 25. https://twitter.com/ - !/REAS/status/19475597776

Reinfurt, David. 2009. "Six Prototypes for a Screensaver: A Retroactive History." *Thinking for a Living*, http//www.thinkingforaliving.org/archives/5465 (part 1) http://www.thinkingforaliving.org/archives/5466 (part 2).

Resnick, Mitchel, Brian Silverman, Yasmin Kafai, John Maloney, Andrés Monroy-Hernández, Natalie Rusk, Evelyn Eastmond, Karen Brennan, Amon Millner, Eric Rosenbaum, and Jay Silver. 2009. "Scratch: Programming for All." *Communications of the ACM* 52, no. 11: 60–67. Scratch Documentation Site, MIT, Cambridge, MA. http://web.media.mit.edu/~mres/papers/Scratch-CACM-final.pdf

Rettberg, Jill Walker. 2011. "10 PRINT CHR$(205.5+RND(1)); : GOTO 10." Flickr. February 9. http://www.flickr.com/photos/lij/5431033237/

Roberts, H. Edward, and William Yates. 1975. "Altair 8800 Minicomputer." *Popular Electronics* 7, no. 1 (January): 33–38.

Rose, Barbara. 1991. *Art-as-Art, The Selected Writings of Ad Reinhardt.* Berkeley: University of California Press.

Rotenberg, A. 1960. "A New Pseudorandom Number Generator." *Journal of the ACM (JACM)* 7, no. 1: 75–77.

Rotman, Brian. 1987. *Signifying Nothing: The Semiotics of Zero.* Palo Alto, CA: Stanford University Press.

Salen, Katie, and Eric Zimmerman. 2004. *Rules of Play: Game Design Fundamentals.* Cambridge, MA: MIT Press.

Selfridge, R. G. 1977. "Fun and Games, Good and Bad, with APL." In *ACM-SE 15 Proceedings of the 15th Annual Southeast Regional Conference*, 238–244. New York: ACM.

Shneiderman, Ben. 1976. "Exploratory Experiments in Programmer Behavior." *International Journal of Computer and Information Sciences* 5, no. 2: 123–143.

Singer, Susanna, ed. 1984. *Sol LeWitt Wall Drawings 1968–1984.* Amsterdam: Stedelijk Museum.

Smith, Adam. 2010. "the infamous c64 maze generator." Flickr. October 6. http://www.flickr.com/photos/rndmcnlly/5058442151/

Smith, Cyril Stanley, and Pauline Boucher. 1987. "The Tiling Patterns of Sebastien Truchet and the Topology of Structural Hierarchy." *Leonardo* 20, no. 4: 373–385.

Steil, Michael. 2011. "How Many Commodore 64 Computers Were Really Sold?" *pagetable.com.* February 1. http://www.pagetable.com/?p=547

Strachey, Christopher. 1954. "The 'Thinking' Machine." *Encounter* 3, no. 4 (October): 25–31.

Swaine, Michael. 2006. "Dr. Dobb's Journal @ 30." *Dr. Dobb's: The World of Software Development.* January 1. http://drdobbs.com/architecture-and-design/184406378

Tearse, Brandon, Michael Mateas, and Noah Wardrip-Fruin. 2010. "MINSTREL Remixed: A Rational Reconstruction." In *INT3 '10: Proceedings of the Intelligent Narrative Technologies III Workshop*, 1–7. New York: ACM.

th0ma5w. 2011. "10 PRINT CHR$(205.5+RND(1)); : GOTO 10." YouTube. July 23. "As demonstrated by Casey Reas at the Eyeo Festival, June 2011, Minneapolis, Minnesota, a random maze generation program in one line of Commodore 64 Basic." http://www.youtube.com/watch?v=m9joBLOZVEo

Thomas, Douglas. 2002. *Hacker Culture.* Minneapolis: University of

Minnesota Press.

TIOBE Software BV. 2012. "TIOBE Programming Community Index for January 2012." *TIOBE Software*. January 8. http://www.tiobe.com/index.php/content/paperinfo/tpci/index.html

Tribble, David. 2005. "Go To Statement Considered Harmful: A Retrospective." *david.tribble.com*. Revision 1.1, November 27. http://david.tribble.com/text/goto.html

U.S. Bureau of the Census. 1988. "Who Uses a Computer?" Statistical Brief SB-2-88. U.S. Government Printing Office, Washington, DC.

von Neumann, John. 1961. "Various Techniques Used in Connection with Random Digits." In *Collected Works: Design of Computers, Theory of Automata and Numerical Analysis*, vol. 5, ed. A. H. Taub, 768–769. Oxford: Pergamon Press.

Waldrop, M. Mitchell. 2001. *The Dream Machine: J.C.R. Licklider and the Revolution That Made Computing Personal.* New York: Viking.

Wallace, James, and Jim Erickson. 1992. *Hard Drive: Bill Gates and the Making of the Microsoft Empire.* New York: Wiley.

Wardrip-Fruin, Noah. 2005. "Christopher Strachey: The First Digital Artist?" *Grand Text Auto* blog. August 1. http://grandtextauto.org/2005/08/01/christopher-strachey-first-digital-artist/

Weinberger, Eliot, and Octavio Paz. 1987. *Nineteen Ways of Looking at Wang Wei: How a Chinese Poem Is Translated.* Mount Kisco, NY: Moyer Bell.

Widenbeck, Susan. 1986. "Beacons in Computer Program Comprehension." *International Journal of Man–Machine Studies* 25: 697–709.

Wright, Craig M. 2001. *The Maze and the Warrior: Symbols in Architecture, Theology and Music.* Cambridge, MA: Harvard University Press.

Zelevansky, Lynn. 2004. *Beyond Geometry: Experiments in Form, 1940s–1970s.* Cambridge, MA: MIT Press.

Zemanek, H. 1976. "Computer Prehistory and History in Central Europe." In *AFIPS'76 Proceedings of the June 7–10, 1976, National Computer Conference and Exposition*, 15–20. New York: ACM.

Zlokower, Roberta. 2005. "Martha Graham Dance Company: Errand into the Maze, El Penitente, Sueno, Sketches from Chronicle." *Roberta on the Arts*. April 17. http://www.robertaonthearts.com/dance/Martha%20Graham%20Dance%20Company%20Errand%20into%20the%20Maze,%20El%20Penitente,%20Sueno,%20Sketches%20from%20Chronicle.html

# 90
# VARIANTS OF 10 PRINT

While the specific line of code `10 PRINT CHR$(205.5+RND(1)); : GOTO 10` is the focus of this book, and has been treated as canonical, this program is not a simple transcription of some authoritative version. The authors of this book developed this variant of the program in an attempt to represent many of the common features of a BASIC one-liner and to embody aspects of the earliest two variants that we found. Variants of this maze-generating code have appeared in print and other contexts over the course of the Commodore 64's commercial lifetime and beyond. Some of these variants are addressed in the chapters and remarks; others are listed only here. The following variants of `10 PRINT` may differ in length, line numbering, and character codes used, but they are all meant to produce the same output. These are all the variants the authors are aware of as of May 2012, with full bibliographic information for each known appearance of each of them.

## VARIANT 1982

```
10 PRINT "[CLR/HOME]"
20 PRINT CHR$(205.5 + RND(1));
40 GOTO 20
```

Commodore, Inc. 1982. *Commodore 64 User's Guide.* Wayne, PA and Indianapolis, IN: Commodore Business Machines. Distributed by Howard W. Sams & Co. p. 53.

## VARIANT 1984

```
8 PRINT CHR$(205.5 + RND(8)); : GOTO 8
```

Krueger, Dan A. 1984. "Trick $93." "Magic" section, *RUN* 7 (July): 13–14.

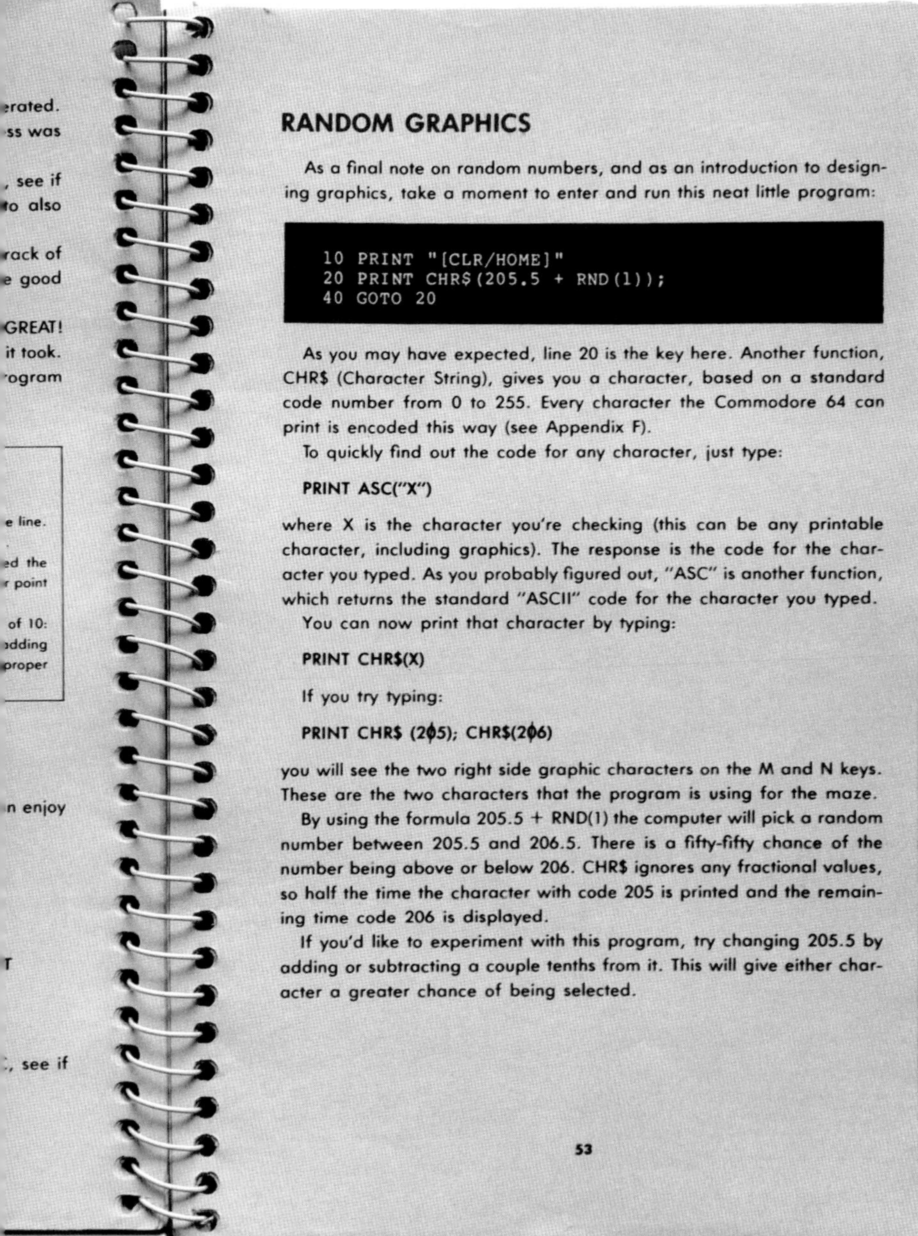

## RANDOM GRAPHICS

As a final note on random numbers, and as an introduction to designing graphics, take a moment to enter and run this neat little program:

```
10 PRINT "[CLR/HOME]"
20 PRINT CHR$(205.5 + RND(1));
40 GOTO 20
```

As you may have expected, line 20 is the key here. Another function, CHR$ (Character String), gives you a character, based on a standard code number from 0 to 255. Every character the Commodore 64 can print is encoded this way (see Appendix F).

To quickly find out the code for any character, just type:

**PRINT ASC("X")**

where X is the character you're checking (this can be any printable character, including graphics). The response is the code for the character you typed. As you probably figured out, "ASC" is another function, which returns the standard "ASCII" code for the character you typed.

You can now print that character by typing:

**PRINT CHR$(X)**

If you try typing:

**PRINT CHR$ (2Ø5); CHR$(2Ø6)**

you will see the two right side graphic characters on the M and N keys. These are the two characters that the program is using for the maze.

By using the formula 205.5 + RND(1) the computer will pick a random number between 205.5 and 206.5. There is a fifty-fifty chance of the number being above or below 206. CHR$ ignores any fractional values, so half the time the character with code 205 is printed and the remaining time code 206 is displayed.

If you'd like to experiment with this program, try changing 205.5 by adding or subtracting a couple tenths from it. This will give either character a greater chance of being selected.

53

Figure 90.1

A three-line variant of `10 PRINT` in the *Commodore 64 User's Guide*, 1982.

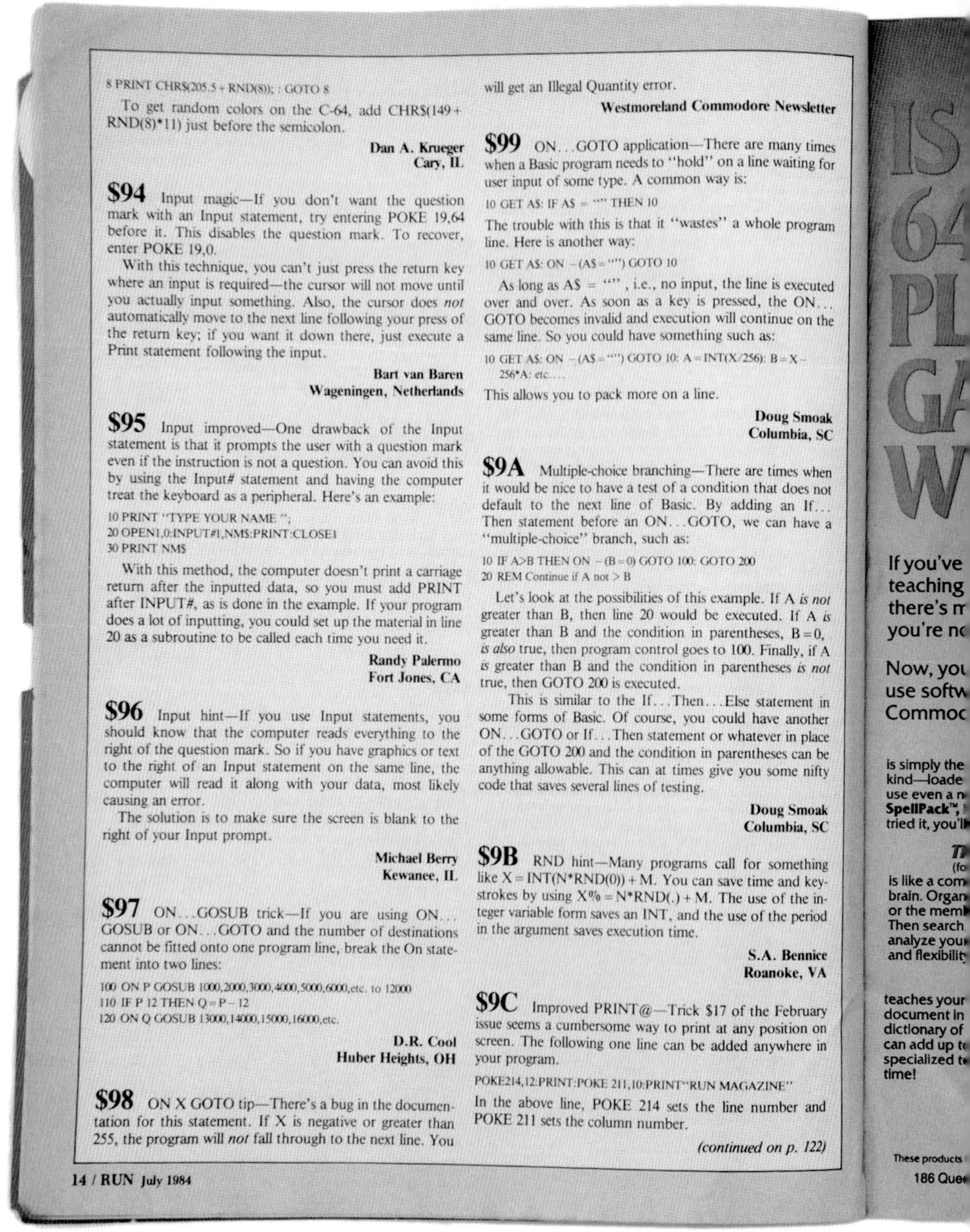

```
8 PRINT CHR$(205.5+RND(8)); : GOTO 8
```

To get random colors on the C-64, add CHR$(149+RND(8)*11) just before the semicolon.

**Dan A. Krueger**
**Cary, IL**

**$94** Input magic—If you don't want the question mark with an Input statement, try entering POKE 19,64 before it. This disables the question mark. To recover, enter POKE 19,0.

With this technique, you can't just press the return key where an input is required—the cursor will not move until you actually input something. Also, the cursor does *not* automatically move to the next line following your press of the return key; if you want it down there, just execute a Print statement following the input.

**Bart van Baren**
**Wageningen, Netherlands**

**$95** Input improved—One drawback of the Input statement is that it prompts the user with a question mark even if the instruction is not a question. You can avoid this by using the Input# statement and having the computer treat the keyboard as a peripheral. Here's an example:

```
10 PRINT "TYPE YOUR NAME ";
20 OPEN1,0:INPUT#1,NM$:PRINT:CLOSE1
30 PRINT NM$
```

With this method, the computer doesn't print a carriage return after the inputted data, so you must add PRINT after INPUT#, as is done in the example. If your program does a lot of inputting, you could set up the material in line 20 as a subroutine to be called each time you need it.

**Randy Palermo**
**Fort Jones, CA**

**$96** Input hint—If you use Input statements, you should know that the computer reads everything to the right of the question mark. So if you have graphics or text to the right of an Input statement on the same line, the computer will read it along with your data, most likely causing an error.

The solution is to make sure the screen is blank to the right of your Input prompt.

**Michael Berry**
**Kewanee, IL**

**$97** ON...GOSUB trick—If you are using ON... GOSUB or ON...GOTO and the number of destinations cannot be fitted onto one program line, break the On statement into two lines:

```
100 ON P GOSUB 1000,2000,3000,4000,5000,6000,etc. to 12000
110 IF P 12 THEN Q=P-12
120 ON Q GOSUB 13000,14000,15000,16000,etc.
```

**D.R. Cool**
**Huber Heights, OH**

**$98** ON X GOTO tip—There's a bug in the documentation for this statement. If X is negative or greater than 255, the program will *not* fall through to the next line. You will get an Illegal Quantity error.

**Westmoreland Commodore Newsletter**

**$99** ON...GOTO application—There are many times when a Basic program needs to "hold" on a line waiting for user input of some type. A common way is:

```
10 GET A$: IF A$ = "" THEN 10
```

The trouble with this is that it "wastes" a whole program line. Here is another way:

```
10 GET A$: ON -(A$="") GOTO 10
```

As long as A$ = "", i.e., no input, the line is executed over and over. As soon as a key is pressed, the ON... GOTO becomes invalid and execution will continue on the same line. So you could have something such as:

```
10 GET A$: ON -(A$="") GOTO 10: A=INT(X/256): B=X-
   256*A: etc....
```

This allows you to pack more on a line.

**Doug Smoak**
**Columbia, SC**

**$9A** Multiple-choice branching—There are times when it would be nice to have a test of a condition that does not default to the next line of Basic. By adding an If... Then statement before an ON...GOTO, we can have a "multiple-choice" branch, such as:

```
10 IF A>B THEN ON -(B=0) GOTO 100: GOTO 200
20 REM Continue if A not > B
```

Let's look at the possibilities of this example. If A *is not* greater than B, then line 20 would be executed. If A *is* greater than B and the condition in parentheses, B=0, *is also* true, then program control goes to 100. Finally, if A *is* greater than B and the condition in parentheses *is not* true, then GOTO 200 is executed.

This is similar to the If...Then...Else statement in some forms of Basic. Of course, you could have another ON...GOTO or If...Then statement or whatever in place of the GOTO 200 and the condition in parentheses can be anything allowable. This can at times give you some nifty code that saves several lines of testing.

**Doug Smoak**
**Columbia, SC**

**$9B** RND hint—Many programs call for something like X=INT(N*RND(0))+M. You can save time and keystrokes by using X%=N*RND(.)+M. The use of the integer variable form saves an INT, and the use of the period in the argument saves execution time.

**S.A. Bennice**
**Roanoke, VA**

**$9C** Improved PRINT@—Trick $17 of the February issue seems a cumbersome way to print at any position on screen. The following one line can be added anywhere in your program.

```
POKE214,12:PRINT:POKE 211,10:PRINT"RUN MAGAZINE"
```

In the above line, POKE 214 sets the line number and POKE 211 sets the column number.

*(continued on p. 122)*

14 / RUN July 1984

Figure 90.2

A one-line variant of 10 PRINT (upper left) in the "Magic" section of *RUN* 7, July 1984.

## VARIANT 2008A

```
10 PRINT CHR$(109+RND(1)*2); : GOTO 10
```

Montfort, Nick. 2008. "Obfuscated Code." In *Software Studies: A Lexicon*, ed. Matthew Fuller. 193–199. Cambridge, MA: MIT Press.

Inacio da Silva, Cicero. 2008. "Software Arte," slide 17. SlideShare. November 18. http://www.slideshare.net/cicerosilva/software-arte-presentation

Marino, Mark C. 2010. "The ppg256 Perl Primer: The Poetry of Techne culture." *Emerging Language Practices*, no. 1 (Fall). http://epc.buffalo.edu/ezines/elp/issue-1/ppg256.php

## VARIANT 2008B

```
10 ?"<CLEAR/HOME>"
20 ? CHR$(205.5)+RND(1))
40 GOTO20
```

Lord Ronin. 2008. "In the Beginning Part 8." *Commodore Free Magazine*, September. http://commodorecomputerclub.co.uk/view.php?art=commodore_free_23&loc=magazine

Entering and running this program as it appears above will cause it to terminate abnormally with the message "?TYPE MISMATCH ERROR IN 20." The immediate culprit is the extra right parenthesis that appears after "205.5." However, even if this superfluous character is removed, the program will not work as intended, because the semicolon that should appear at the end of line 20 is missing. The intention for this program to function like the others listed here is clear from the discussion in the surrounding article, however.

**VARIANT 2010A**

```
10 PRINT CHR$(109+RND(0)*2);:GOTO 10
```

Bogost, Ian. 2010. Comment on "Program Your Apple II! Why Not Program Today?" *Computing Education Blog*. February 20. http://computinged.wordpress.com/2010/02/20/program-your-apple-ii-why-not-program-today/

**VARIANT 2010B**

```
10 PRINT CHR$(205.5+RND(1)); : GOTO 10
```

Montfort, Nick. 2010. "@party: Weaving thread." *Post Position*. June 20. http://nickm.com/post/2010/06/party-weaving-thread/

Montfort, Nick, Patsy Baudoin, John Bell, Ian Bogost, Jeremy Douglass, Mary Flanagan, Mark Marino, Michael Mateas, Casey Reas, Warren Sack, Mark Sample, and Noah Vawter. 2010. "Studying Software by Porting and Reimplementation: A BASIC Case." Presented by Nick Montfort, Jeremy Douglass, and Casey Reas. Critical Code Studies Conference, University of Southern California. July 23. http://thoughtmesh.net/publish/382.php

Driscoll, Kevin. 2010. "Critical Code Studies 2010." Driscollwiki. July 23. http://kevindriscoll.org/wiki/Critical_code_studies_2010

Reas, Casey. 2010. 10 PRINT CHR$(205.5+RND(1)); : GOTO 10. Twitter. July 25. https://twitter.com/ - !/REAS/status/19475597776

Montfort, Nick. 2010. "Colloquium Past, Conference to Come in Mexico." *Post Position*. November 17. http://nickm.com/post/2010/11/colloquium-past-conference-to-come-in-mexico/

Montfort, Nick. 2011. "10 PRINT Talks Galore." *Post Position*. January 26. http://nickm.com/post/2011/01/10-print-talks-galore/

Rettberg, Jill Walker. 2011. "10 PRINT CHR$(205.5+RND(1)); : GOTO 10." Flickr, February 9. http://www.flickr.com/photos/lij/5431033237/

Kidd, David. 2011. Backstrip.net. April 8. http://backstrip.net/post/4432566244/ive-been-tooling-around-with-street-making

th0ma5w. 2011. "10 PRINT CHR$(205.5+RND(1)); : GOTO 10." YouTube.

July 23. "As demonstrated by Casey Reas at the Eyeo Festival, June 2011, Minneapolis, Minnesota, a random maze generation program in one line of Commodore 64 Basic." http://www.youtube.com/watch?v=m9joBLOZVEo

### VARIANTS 2010C–F

```
1 printchr$(205.5+rnd(1));:goto1
```

```
1 ?chr$(205.5+rnd(1));:run
```

```
1?chr$(205.5+rnd(1));:rU
```

```
0?cH(205.5+rN(1));:gO
```

MuppetMan et al. 2010. "Maze Code" discussion thread, Commodore 64 (C64) Forum, Lemon64.com. August 12–16. http://www.lemon64.com/forum/viewtopic.php?t=34879&sid=9526087188346ea3450fe0568566466b

### VARIANT 2010G

```
10 print chr$(205.5 + Rnd(1));
20 goto 10
```

Smith, Adam. 2010. "the infamous c64 maze generator." Flickr. October 6. http://www.flickr.com/photos/rndmcnlly/5058442151/

### VARIANT 2011A

```
10 PRINT CHR$(205.5+RND(1)) GOTO 10
```

Fuchs, Martin. 2011. *Written Images*. Rendered February 9. Book number 182/230, page 161.

This is printed as the title of Casey Reas's contribution to this volume, seven pages of white, blue, and black images generated with a Processing program that is inspired by **10 PRINT**. The semicolon and colon, which are necessary for the program's proper functioning and its validity as BASIC, were removed in error during editing in this limited-edition book. This title is also presented this way on page 1 of *Written Images*, in the table of contents.

### VARIANT 2011B

```
10 PRINT "(It indicates that here you press Shift and
CLR/Home Keys" I found my 7 key has Home on it -)" note
the " marks at start and end
20 PRINT CHR$(205.5+RND(1))
30 PRINT GOTO 20
```

noknojon. 2011. Bleepingcomputer.com. February 17, 8:01 p.m. http://www.bleepingcomputer.com/forums/topic380106.html/page__p__2138153#entry2138153

Entering and running this program as it appears above will cause it to terminate abnormally with the message "? SYNTAX ERROR IN 30." Two changes need to be made for this code to function as intended: a semicolon should be added at the end of line 20 and "PRINT" should be removed from line 30.

In addition, this text indicates that one should hold SHIFT and then press the CLR/HOME key. This causes the screen to be cleared when the program is run and it moves printing of characters to the upper left. If CLR/HOME is pressed without holding SHIFT, as the 1982 and 2008b variants seem to suggest one should do, the printing of characters will move to the upper left but the display will not be cleared, so the maze will move downward to cover whatever is already on the screen.

# 95
# ABOUT THE AUTHORS

Nick Montfort is associate professor of digital media at MIT. He co-edited *The New Media Reader*, co-authored *Racing the Beam*, and wrote *Twisty Little Passages* and the book of poems *Riddle & Bind*.

Patsy Baudoin is the MIT Libraries liaison to the MIT Media Lab and the visual arts, film studies, and foreign languages and literatures librarian at MIT.

John Bell is assistant professor of Innovative Communication Design at the University of Maine and senior researcher at Still Water for Network Art and Culture.

Ian Bogost is associate professor in the School of Literature, Communication, and Culture at the Georgia Institute of Technology and founding partner, Persuasive Games LLC. He is an author of *Unit Operations*, *Persuasive Games*, *Newsgames*, *How to Do Things with Video Games*, and *Alien Phenomenology*.

Jeremy Douglass is assistant professor of English at the University of California, Santa Barbara.

Michael Mateas is an associate professor of computer science at the University of California, Santa Cruz whose research focus is AI-based art and entertainment.

Mark C. Marino is an associate professor (teaching) of writing at the University of Southern California where he directs the Humanities and Critical Code Studies Lab. In 2010 he hosted the online Critical Code Studies Working Group, where the first extensive discussion of the `10 PRINT` program occurred.

Casey Reas is an artist and professor of Design Media Arts at the University of California, Los Angeles; with Ben Fry, he initiated the open source programming platform Processing. He is an author of *Processing: A Programming Handbook for Visual Designers and Artists*; *Form+Code in Design, Art, and Architecture*; and *Process Compendium 2004–2010.*

Mark L. Sample is associate professor of English at George Mason University, where he teaches and researches contemporary literature and new media.

Noah Vawter earned his PhD at the MIT Media Lab. He is a sound artist and invented Ambient Addition, 1-bit groovebox, and other musical instruments.

# 100
# INDEX

*Note: The appearance of "f" after a page number (e.g. 48f) indicates that the reference is to a figure on the specified page.*